ESCAPE

ESCAPE

A LOVE LETTER TO A CULT FOOTBALL CLASSIC

JOHN SMITH

First published by Pitch Publishing, 2025
1

Pitch Publishing
9 Donnington Park,
85 Birdham Road,
Chichester, West Sussex,
PO20 7AJ
www.pitchpublishing.co.uk
info@pitchpublishing.co.uk

© 2025, John Smith

Every effort has been made to trace the copyright. Any oversight will be rectified in future editions at the earliest opportunity by the publisher.

All rights reserved. No part of this book may be reproduced, sold or utilised in any form or transmitted in any form or by any means, electronic or mechanical, including photocopying, recording or by any information storage and retrieval system, without prior permission in writing from the publisher.

A CIP catalogue record is available for this book from the British Library.

ISBN 978 1 80150 967 1

Typesetting and origination by Pitch Publishing

Printed and bound on FSC® certified paper in line with our continuing commitment to ethical business practices, sustainability and the environment.

Printed and bound in India by Replika Press Pvt. Ltd.

CONTENTS

Acknowledgements 7

1. Blue Tickets 11
2. The Film Part I 15
3. How We Got Here 24
4. Putting the Band Together 42
5. The Players 72
6. The Film Part II 112
7. The Book of the Film 131
8. Between the Sticks 152
9. The Film Part III 171
10. On Set 192
11. Off Set 221
12. The Match 231
13. Football on Film 256
14. Victoire 273
15. Release 290
16. Legacy 303

Bibliography 313

ACKNOWLEDGEMENTS

FIRSTLY, MY thanks go to Jane Camillin, Alex Daley, Ian Passingham, Dean Rockett, Graham Hales and everyone at Pitch Publishing for having me again and for all that they do. And to Duncan Olner for his design.

I would like to say a special thank you to everyone who agreed to be interviewed for this book; for their time, insight and enthusiasm. These people are Russell Osman, John Wark, Kevin O'Callaghan, Paul Cooper, Laurie Sivell, Ossie Ardiles, Mike Summerbee, Clive Merrison, Harvey Harrison, Wendy Banks and Werner Roth. Without them, the book would be nothing – so, thank you. I'd also like to add my thanks to Russell Osman and to Tom Davis for their kind words in the cover quotes.

I would also like to thank Matt McNally for his help with editing and transcribing and for his encouragement, Matt Holland and Simon Milton at Ipswich Town for their help with contacting their former players and anyone else who gave me a lead or a number as I tried to contact interviewees. There are many people and there was a lot of scrounging. A thank you, also, to author Jonathan Melville for some advice early in the process and the staff at the exceptional BFI Library, where there is fun to be had among the archives.

Special thanks to my wife, Jo, for some important transcribing work, for her support and for generally being my favourite person. And to my wonderful kids, Archie, Evie and Martha, for their patience, understanding, occasional welcome distractions and very occasional cups of tea.

And, finally, my heartfelt thanks to whoever made the anti-piracy advert that appeared on DVDs in the early 2000s, which I sat through many, many times as I navigated the menu to put *Escape to Victory* on for research. I have a new-found appreciation for it and, thanks to their guidance, I promise that, no, I truly wouldn't steal a car, a handbag, a television or a DVD.

AUTHOR'S NOTE

IF THIS book has found its way into your hands, then thank you very much. There are a lot of books to choose from and I very much appreciate you spending time with mine. And if you are reading this, I am going to go ahead and assume that you probably like the film *Escape to Victory* or, at the very least, have seen it.

If you have never watched it, then seriously, what have you been doing with your life? I actively encourage you to temporarily put down the book and watch the film first, because you will certainly get a lot more out of the book. If the book was a gift for Christmas or, perhaps, for a birthday near a Bank Holiday weekend, then there's a good chance that it's on TV right now. In which case, just flick it on.

What I'm getting at here is that, inevitably and, hopefully, understandably – HERE BE SPOILERS.

Don't say that you haven't been warned.

Enjoy.

1.
BLUE TICKETS
An Introduction

I CAN'T tell you exactly how many times I've watched *Escape to Victory* but I imagine that, like many of you, it is more than once or twice. Nor can I tell you exactly when I first saw it but I can remember the circumstances as if it were yesterday.

Our telly came from a shop called Radio Rentals, which always confused me a bit, because I'm pretty sure we owned our radio. Renting our telly brought two huge benefits as far as the childhood me could tell, neither of which was about the cost. After all, as a kid, that was never my department and you wouldn't expect it to be. The first benefit was that if the telly ever needed fixing, they would send 'The Man' round to take the back off and fix it. This was fascinating to me, as a youngster, and I can still see the different colours of the circuit board and smell the soldering iron now. I always found something incredibly reassuring about being in the presence of an expert and probably still do. I also just really liked the telly and, on a much shallower psychological level, when 'The Man' came, it would mean that the telly went from not working to working again. Yeah, it's probably that. Maybe this is what Lou Reed was singing about in 'I'm Waiting for the Man'.

These sorcerers of the circuit board might have wondered to themselves why this weird little kid was watching them do their job but I remain forever grateful for their work – even if my mum still insists that one of them stole her Phil Collins 'No Jacket Required' cassette tape on one visit. We'll never know for sure but, either way, I'd chalk that up as a small price worth paying.

The second benefit was that we seemed to change our telly from time to time, possibly because they kept breaking. Eventually, one fateful day, a TV arrived with a VHS recorder attached to it – and my world changed. Of course, the machine is only as good as what you put into it and that brings us to Videotheque. We all remember Blockbuster Video but before their rise and fall, there was so much joy to be had in your local independent version. Our one was called Videotheque and I loved it, unconditionally.

The shop had a simple system whereby if a tape had a blue ticket sticking out of it, then a VHS was available. If there was a pink ticket, then it was available in Betamax. And if it had no ticket at all sticking out of it, then you'd better find something else to watch.

Our very first selection was the Oscar-laden, if slightly pedestrian, *On Golden Pond*, most notable in our house for the fact that we rewound it once it had finished by taking it in turns to keep our finger firmly on the rewind button on the machine, muttering 'this can't be right' throughout the process. Stop and rewind was a technique that we hadn't yet quite grasped. Can you imagine the unconfined joy when we did?

In those early, magical days, I remember *Blade Runner* being a big deal and *Raiders of the Lost Ark* being an even bigger deal. I seem to remember that, early on, we used our membership to watch those Clint Eastwood films with Clyde the orangutan and I can vividly recall a very exciting Sunday afternoon when we watched both *Rocky* and *Rocky II*, back-to-back. Imagine that. How cool were my parents? See what I mean about a whole new world? What a time to be alive.

Given that you're currently holding this book, it won't surprise you to learn that among those films that first caught my eye on the shelves was *Escape to Victory*. There it sat, quite high up as I recall – in my mind's eye, it was next to *Escape from Alcatraz* and sat below *Mad Max* – but I couldn't swear to it. The picture on the front was that now familiar but curious image of Sylvester Stallone, Pelé and Michael Caine seemingly emerging out of one conjoined red mass, each with an arm raised and open-mouthed in defiance.

I knew that the guy on the left was Rocky and I knew the guy on the right from, probably at that time, *The Italian Job*, *The Eagle Has Landed* and perennial Sunday afternoon favourite *Zulu* but what was Pelé doing in between them? He was very definitely a footballer rather than an actor. This warranted further investigation. My parents and my older brother and sister were probably already aware of the film but this was very much my introduction to it. I don't think anyone needed too much persuasion for us to give it a go, so, when the sweet, sweet day arrived that it had a blue ticket sticking out of the box, we took our opportunity.

Here was a war film that bore more than a passing resemblance to *The Great Escape* but with football – and what sort of monster doesn't want that? Add Bobby Moore to the mix – royalty to our West Ham-supporting family – and, at the age I was, you could not have made a film more up my street if you had precision-tooled it into existence with me in mind. I must have sat there spellbound and my love for the film lives strong to this day, as you can no doubt already tell.

I can only hope that this book maintains some of the wide-eyed wonder I felt as we made the short walk back home from Videotheque and that I've held ever since. Everything in this book comes from a profound love of this film. It's not post-modern and ironic, because who has the time to research and write a post-modern and ironic book about a film that they only enjoy ironically? Not me.

Escape to Victory is a film with flaws, for sure, and there will be a time to discuss those but, overwhelmingly, this book comes from affection. I've enjoyed every minute of contacting as many of the players and actors as I could and listening to the stories they shared with me. I've learned a lot along the way – and not just where to stand for a corner kick.

In talking through the film itself, how it came into being, how the stars came to be the stars and what the film means to people, I hope to do justice to those who were kind enough to speak to me about this unique and special film.

2.

THE FILM – PART I

PUTTING FOOTBALL front and centre of *Escape to Victory* may make it stand apart among prison movies but at the very beginning of the film, we are on very familiar territory, with an image we can recognise from any number of other prison dramas – searchlights cutting through the dark. Here we see them being dutifully swept along the camp perimeter by a couple of 'goons' while a hero silently darts, rolls and crawls in between the beams in search of a way out. This is clearly not a heat-of-the-moment dash for the wire but, rather, the culmination of weeks or even months of planning. From the hut to the fence, from the fence to the woods, then on to who knows where in the German countryside before finding a way out of the country, into friendly hands and across the sea back to good old Blighty.

After a promising start, the prisoner makes it as far as the wire, pulls out the clippers – that no doubt took an age to either scrounge from a malleable guard or fashion from a metal bed frame – and cuts himself a hole just big enough to drag himself and his desperation through. It's at this point that things go awry, as an Alsatian catches him in the act. Some people will have you believe that a dog is man's best friend but this one isn't – this one is a rotten grass. If it could talk, it would probably say it was only doing its job and following orders but we've all heard that one before. The Alsatian barks loud and long in German, the alarm is raised, the siren wails and guards quickly arrive on the scene. Other prisoners get to the windows of their huts just in time to see their comrade, hands raised in surrender, dying in a hail of machine gun bullets, his riddled body falling into the tangle of barbed wire beyond the fence which confines them all.

It's a hard-hitting opening, which certainly grabs the attention of anyone who has tuned in simply to watch Pelé and Bobby Moore kick a ball around. We're left in no doubt that, whatever else is to follow, we are grounded, at this point, more in a traditional war movie than in the stuff that soccer dreams are made of.

We cut immediately to the opening credits, which are accompanied by the stirring strains of Bill Conti's score – and a terrific one it is, too. Conti frequently scored the films of Sylvester Stallone and while this one may not reach the heights of the music in *Rocky*, not much does. His work on this film runs the gamut from gritty military through jaunty football training sequences to the stirring stuff of the finale and, right now, it's the military end of things that sets the mood.

'A Freddie Fields Production' is the first credit we see on screen, white against a blood red background, and, as we'll come to see, Fields earned that top billing. As the credits continue, we see the name of John Huston, Hollywood royalty and esteemed director of classics like *The African Queen*, *The Maltese Falcon* and *The Man Who Would Be King*. He's followed by Sylvester Stallone of *Rocky* fame, British acting legend Michael Caine and Max von Sydow, Ingmar Bergman's favourite actor in all those Swedish films we pretend we've watched. Big names. We're in safe hands. Then, things get curious. As the camera pulls out slightly to pique our interest by revealing that the red backdrop is a Red Cross flag on the roof of a moving vehicle, the next name that appears on screen is Pelé. And now we know we're in for something a little bit different.

Of course, sports stars had appeared in the movies before. Jim Brown's memorable turn in *The Dirty Dozen* springs to mind, OJ Simpson was already making his way as an actor in the 70s, before all the awful business that followed and, long before both, Johnny Weismuller had climbed out of the Olympic swimming pool, set aside his gold medals and not bothered to get dressed before swinging his way through the jungle many times in a series of Tarzan movies. There were other actors who had at least a background in sports, such as Carl Weathers, so memorable as Rocky's nemesis and best friend (it's complicated), Apollo Creed, who had played American football for the Oakland Raiders before becoming the 'Master of Disaster' on screen. But Pelé? This feels different. The undisputed biggest name in the biggest global sport. In a film with Stallone and Caine. All bets are off.

The Red Cross car and an army staff car continue to wind along roads flanked by the German military, through towns and out into rural lanes, until they arrive at Gensdorf Prison Camp, where the bulk of our story will take place. As the cars approach the compound, we get a lovely big wide shot from up above, showing us the full scale of the camp, built to order for the production company Lorimar at riding stables outside Budapest in Hungary, substituting here for Germany. At the bottom of the picture, we can see prisoners playing football and, suddenly, the presence of Pelé in the credits list doesn't seem quite so incongruous. Welcome to Stalag Hackney Marshes. We can also see prisoners playing volleyball but who among us, hand on heart, can say that they would want the volleyball film? It would be a few years yet before *Top Gun* would give volleyball – or, at least, its beach-bound cousin – an oiled-up, testosterone-drenched moment in the sun on film.

Once inside Gensdorf, we discover that the travelling party has arrived to inspect conditions at the camp in the wake of the death of the attempted escapee from the pre-credits sequence. We learn that he was an officer by the name of Williams. We learn nothing further about him, such as a first name, rank, unit, the family he left behind or who inherited his tobacco after the unfortunate incident. Perhaps more importantly, given what will follow, we are left to ponder whether he might have been a useful holding midfielder or tricky winger who could have been a difference-maker in the footballing finale to come.

Among the visitors is Max von Sydow in the role of Major von Steiner. We can see from our first meeting with him that this is no ruthless Nazi, because he's clearly far more interested in the game of football he can spy in the distance than he is with whatever it is he's won his medals for or whatever official business he is on today. When the whistle is blown and the teams move away, a ball runs loose off a poor touch from the lad Stallone, showing an early

THE FILM – PART I

glimpse of his character Hatch's shortcomings as a player. In that overly keen way that you or I might react when a ball heads towards us from a park kickabout while out on a walk with a loved one, Von Steiner pounces on it, keen to be involved and to give it back. Ignoring Hatch's sarcastic 'Please sir, can I have my ball back?', Von Steiner looks him dead in the eye, flicks up the ball, executes the couple of modest keepy-uppies that his fine leather boots will allow him and delivers the ball, not to Hatch but, instead, into the arms of a waiting and watching Michael Caine.

Such is my obsession with this film that I have long wondered who it really was inside the boots for the close-up showing such a deft touch. I did ask one or two of the players that I was lucky enough to speak to but nobody seemed to know or remember. If it was Von Sydow himself, then he is robbed of the glory by the close-up of the boots rather than a full-length shot that would have given him his moment but I suspect there was somebody better qualified standing by to don the bottom half of the uniform and get the shot.

The German asks Caine if he is the 'Sportfuhrer', which is not a role or word I'm familiar with but one I might start trying to use with the Sunday team I coach. And then comes possibly my favourite moment of the film. Michael Caine introduces himself as Colby and, after some good-natured banter between the two about the footballing set-up they have going on at the camp, Von Steiner deduces that Colby is in fact John Colby, of West Ham United and England.

I want you to imagine, for one moment, the glee that would have been etched on my little face watching this at home on video when I heard this. Not only were my beloved West Ham getting a mention in what was already shaping up to be a very watchable war film but they were being mentioned because Michael Caine was playing somebody who had turned out for them. Yes, there was also England but never mind all that. Here were West Ham, front and centre of our story. It remains thrilling to me that this script would have been doing the rounds in Hollywood and beyond with various prospective stars, directors and crew, all of them reading the West Ham reference. They never get mentioned again, of course, but no matter, it's already out there. Nor did it hurt that his name was John. This film was really spoiling me. Thrilled though I was, there is a point where Colby claims that the war has merely interrupted his career rather than ended it and I have to say that this seems an ambitious statement. Although the condition that Michael Caine was in for this film is often cruelly overstated by some critics ('paunchy', said the *Sunday Times*), he is 47 at the time of filming and if he is still getting a game for West Ham after the war, then we are bang in trouble. Having said that, I feel like I've seen players in worse condition turning out in the claret and blue over the years and some nearly as old.

Later that night, we see Hatch making notes while he watches the movements of the guards, which lets us know that he's, ahem, hatching an escape plan of some sort. This surely stood him in good stead for the three films he later made called *Escape Plan*, *Escape Plan 2* and, you guessed it, *Escape Plan 3*, although he had Arnold Schwarzenegger to help him in at least one of those.

Then we see the altogether more relaxed surroundings of the officers' hut, where Hatch plays cards with Shurlock and Rose, played by Julian Curry and Tim Pigott-Smith, two of the leading lights of the escape committee, while Colby reads on a nearby bunk. Rose asks Colby what he was chatting to Von Steiner about and, despite a brusque 'none of your business', Colby coyly gives up that Von Steiner recognised him as the West Ham legend that he is. We learn here that Von Steiner was a player himself, playing for Germany in 1938, which makes them equals in footballing stature, if not in their current life situation.

The next day, the two like-minded men, divided by war but united by a love of football, chat once more. After agreeing that World War Two is a 'regrettable mistake', Von Steiner dangles the carrot of a football match, as friendly as it could be, between the best of Colby's prisoners and a team of German soldiers from a local barracks. Colby is, naturally, intrigued by the prospect, so long as it's not an order, but wavers slightly, citing his men's clothes, boots and spectacular lack of talent as reasons why they would be humiliated in any match of the sort. As he says this, most players are, indeed, running around in heavy army gear and boots behind him but there is one lad in the background, bare-chested and barefoot, just wearing a pair of white shorts like he's kicking around outside his caravan in Cromer. Unfazed by this, Von Steiner says that the right gear could be supplied and he can tell that he almost has Colby hooked, despite the Englishman's protestations and initial refusal to sign up. Whatever it was that earned Von Steiner his Knight's Cross, he's now far from the battlefield, fulfilling a cushy desk job in the propaganda business, and he clearly knows how to sell an idea. The German apologises and feigns to walk away, offer withdrawn, only for Colby to finally take the bait. The British officer demands kit, living quarters, meat, fresh veg, eggs and beer – the latter seems a bit of a liberty – for his hypothetical team and insists that, whether his commanding officer, Colonel Waldron, likes it or not, Von Steiner has a game if he can guarantee all of that. So, we are on.

The German major cites boredom in the camp as an issue but, I'll be honest, with all the football going on, it looks kind of all right to me, apart from the ever-present threat of being machine-gunned to death if you go near the wire. If prison is like this or like it is in *Porridge*, I might even be able to cope. It's only when it gets a bit *Scum*, *McVicar* or *Bronson* that I really don't fancy it so much.

This scene is a cracker and played well by two fine actors. Not only does it sow the seed for the epic game which this casual arrangement grows into, it also establishes Colby's character in a couple of ways. With his line, 'If it's officers only, I'm not bloody playing! I want a decent team. I want the lads,' Michael Caine introduces a class element to the proceedings. Here, he's an officer himself, albeit one a million miles away from the upper-class general's son and military man of several generations with which he announced himself to the world in *Zulu*. Colby is a soldier and an officer by circumstance, not by choice or family tradition like Gonville Bromhead, and it's clear that he hasn't forgotten his roots. It's an interesting note in the film and possibly unnecessary, other than to portray Colby as strong-willed and class-conscious.

THE FILM – PART I

Alternatively, he may not be striking a class blow, he may just think he's got a better chance of winning the game of football if he's not limited to officers. Either way, we now have a game on our hands between some local German soldiers and the best of what Colby can pull together from his 'bloody useless' lads.

3.

HOW WE GOT HERE

WITH THE game within the film already starting to come together, it's time to zoom out and look at the bigger picture of how this project came into being. It's hard to imagine a time when *Escape to Victory* didn't exist but, incredibly, there was; and it's important that we spend time in that barren cultural desert, to see how it sprang into life.

It's my contention that the window for getting this film green-lit would have been a small one. I can't imagine that, prior to this film being made, Hollywood was tripping over itself to make a film about football but, in that moment, the perfect conditions existed for it to grow. Pelé was a huge star who transcended the sport and he had, by that stage, played for a few years in the North American Soccer League for the impossibly exotic New York Cosmos. Although the standard of football was an obvious step down from its European and South American counterparts at the time, the NASL was, undeniably, very sexy. Within this very sexy league, the Cosmos were by far the sexiest team, with their showbiz links to Warner Bros, their iconic kits and just by virtue of being from New York in the 70s, with all the images of Studio 54 and disco that came with that. And in a league stocked full of bright, albeit faded and past their best, football gems like Johan Cruyff, Franz Beckenbauer and Bobby Moore, Pelé shone like the brightest diamond. His turn at the glitzy Cosmos is a major factor in making American finance for a film about football a possibility at that time. As his team-mate Shep Messing, the goalkeeper turned broadcaster, put it: 'In simple terms, Pelé made soccer cool.' Add into the mix the tantalising prospect of Sylvester Stallone in another sports movie, after two incredibly successful *Rocky* films, and it becomes easier to see why a previously reluctant Hollywood might have found some enthusiasm for the project.

Let's not get ahead of ourselves, though. Before there is a movie, you need a script and, before that, an idea. So where did these come from?

Is *Escape to Victory* based on a true story? Not as such, no. It's a flight of fancy, with big Hollywood names, big football names and smashing kits. One of the reasons I decided to call this book *Escape*, apart from the obvious, is that the film is an enjoyable piece of escapism. It is a loveable bit of fantasy, for sure, but, beyond the overhead kicks, the big stadium and the international Allies dream team, there are, inevitably, some elements that are grounded in reality. The script did take some inspiration from certain real-life events.

We know that there was some football being played in prisoner of war camps during World War Two. Of course there was. So long as you can get access to a football, which alongside food and water seems to form a triumvirate of the most basic of all human rights, there will be a kickabout. How formalised this football was would surely have varied from camp to camp but we are, at the very least, aware that Allied prisoners were playing football in German camps and Germans were playing football in British camps.

One such German to make the most of playing behind bars was Bert Trautmann. He was a paratrooper during the war, fighting in Russia, France and the Ardennes, as well as at Arnhem, before being captured in 1945 and imprisoned, initially, at the Marbury Hall camp in Cheshire. There, the prisoners were allowed access to balls and spent time playing football and handball amongst themselves. Trautmann, of course, went on to become a goalkeeper of some repute, famously winning the FA Cup with Manchester City in 1956, despite breaking his neck in the final against Birmingham. That same year, he was voted the Football Writers' Association Footballer of the Year and, by then, was a hero to tens of thousands of people. But, back in the camp at the start of that football journey, he played as a centre-half and he competed exclusively against fellow PoWs. That was until a Scottish major, at Trautmann's second camp at Ashton-in-Makerfield, took the football activities under his wing and realised that his best team might be able to do a little better than the intramural games they had been playing.

According to Catrine Clay's excellent book, *Trautmann's Journey: From Hitler Youth to FA Cup Legend*, the major asked his commanding officer for permission to contact 'a few of the local teams for his first XI to play against? Good for morale, good for community relations, that kind of thing.' That was his big sell. Permission was granted and, soon, the first local team tentatively arrived at the camp for an understandably ill-tempered match, in which Bert was sufficiently injured that he was forced to drop out of defence and go in goal.

A football match of prisoners against local players, with a stand-in goalkeeper who goes on to be a hero. Even with the sides swapped around, already *Escape to Victory* doesn't seem so much of a stretch, does it?

It seems that this initial foray into local competition did a little bit of healing, with the visitors heartily congratulating Trautmann and his team-mates after the German PoWs won the game. The success of this trial run made other matches easier to arrange and the prisoners were soon playing every Sunday against teams from the likes of Haydock, Wigan and Skelmersdale.

Across 1946, conditions relaxed sufficiently for prisoners to be allowed out at times, with football-mad Bert using his privileges to watch Everton matches and, in particular, goalkeeper Ted Sagar. When the repatriation of prisoners began the same year, Bert, along with thousands of his countrymen, decided to stay in England. In many cases, this might have been because they would have faced an uncertain future at home in post-war Germany. In Trautmann's case, it was partly because a young local woman was pregnant with his child and partly because he began playing in goal for St Helens Town. He made enough of a name for himself that scouts came calling and, in 1949, the German goalkeeper signed for Manchester City. Inevitably, there were protests, both at Maine Road and across the letters page of the *Manchester Evening News*, but it was in that letters page that he received the support of Dr Altmann, a Manchester rabbi who preached forgiveness, despite the way those Germans had carried on during the war. He wrote that: 'We would not try to punish an individual German, who is unconnected with these crimes, out of hatred. If this footballer is a decent fellow, I would say there is no harm in it.' Many others disagreed and the taunts at his first game were plentiful but, as we all know, there are none so fickle as football fans and a crowd can be moved to forgive, or at least overlook, any number of past misdemeanours in a player soon enough, so long as they are doing the business on the pitch. This is a truism we see in action at any number of clubs in the present day and precious few among us are immune to it. Bert Trautmann was soon accepted and became a darling of the Manchester City fans long before his brave, or very silly, decision to play on with a broken neck at Wembley in 1956. And his journey to professional football began with his kickabouts as a prisoner of war.

In the publicity around the making of *Escape to Victory*, director John Huston told *The Guardian*: 'A match of the sort we're depicting did happen in World War Two, in Holland. It wasn't on this scale, though, and, of course, no one escaped.' But despite the namecheck for the possible Holland match, of which little is known, few would dispute that the biggest inspiration for the film was the so-called 'Death Match' – an infamous game which took place in German-occupied Ukraine in August 1942.

The match is understandably shrouded in mystery and myth, as it has been filtered through Soviet propaganda, and has been, at times, reduced to the straightforward scenario that, having convincingly beaten their German occupiers, a team of Kiev bakers were gunned down on the pitch as punishment for their defiance. Though this is not quite what happened, the truth is in there somewhere. What we do know is that, under German occupation, sports teams including the famous Dynamo Kiev were suspended but that, in 1942, allowances began to be made for some sport to take place and clubs to form. Around a Kiev bread factory, a team named Start were formed, and the players included several who had been with Dynamo Kiev. Start were invited to play against a team from the Luftwaffe, called Flakelf. A debate took place among the Start players about whether taking part in the game would represent resistance or collaboration – not dissimilar to the argument put forward by Colby's superiors in our film – but, ultimately, the game did take place on 6 August 1942, with Start running out 5-1 winners. I wanted to use the phrase 'comfortable winners' there but I suspect that there wasn't very much about it all that was comfortable.

There were no immediate reprisals from the Germans, despite the defeat, but they recognised the boost the match could have given local morale so they ordered a rematch to take place three days later. It seems that, at the very least, Flakelf returned for the second game with a stronger team packed with better players co-opted from further afield and it is alleged that they had a German referee to look after them when decisions needed to be made. There is also a suggestion that the Germans insisted that the Ukrainians gave the Nazi salute before the game, which was played in front of a crowd of 2,000 people, who were presumably under heavy guard. Instead, the crowd placed a hand on their heart and shouted 'FitzcultHura!', as Soviet footballers were known to do. However, this may be another detail that we need to consider as, at best, shaky.

What we do know is that Start also won the rematch, this time 5-3, and that nobody was murdered on the pitch as a result. Indeed, Start went on to play another match the following Sunday, beating fellow Ukrainian side Rukh 8-0.

However, in the days that followed, the Gestapo questioned and arrested the Start players in the hope that, under interrogation, they would confess to being a part of the resistance. In his excellent book, *The Outsider*, Jonathan Wilson takes up the sorry tale: 'None broke and, with the exception of the winger, Mykola Korotkykh, the players were moved to the Siretz prison camp near Baba Yar, the ravine where thousands of Jews had been massacred in 1941. Korotkykh had been an active officer in the NKVD, the forerunner to the KGB, ten years earlier and when that was discovered, he was subjected to far harsher treatment than the others, dying after 20 days of torture.' Furthermore, three of the players – Nikolai Trusevich, Olexi Klimenko and Ivan Kuzmenko – were subsequently executed some months later at the camp. The reason for their execution is disputed. Reported reasons for their horrific demise include punishment for other prisoners escaping, reprisals following a local partisan attack and the killing of the camp commandant's dog – but the match itself does not appear to have been a direct reason in their case.

The whole story is shrouded in a certain amount of mystery, because it took place under German occupation and was subsequently subject to Soviet interpretations of the tale, which seemed to waver between praise for the team who defeated their Nazi oppressors and condemnation for them as supposed collaborators. In 1992, around the 50th anniversary of the 'Death Match' and in the post-Soviet era, some eyewitness accounts did begin to appear, which at least confirmed that the games took place.

Obviously, the true circumstances of those games are far removed from the *Boy's Own* adventure that *Escape to Victory* emerged as but the core story of captors meeting prisoners – or oppressors meeting the oppressed – on a sports field clearly remains and it isn't the only film to take inspiration from a similar source.

The 1961 Hungarian film *Two Half-Times in Hell* was directed by Zoltan Fabri and tells the story of prisoners of war playing a football match against their Nazi captors to mark Adolf Hitler's birthday. In an obvious parallel with *Escape to Victory*, the Hungarian team is led by a former player who demands special conditions for his team and time to train for the match. In a second parallel, when the game kicks off, the German team race into a healthy lead by half-time, in this case 3-1. In a third parallel, the team of prisoners come roaring back in the second half and score three times. Unfortunately, that's where the films certainly do differ, because just after the comeback is completed from the penalty spot, the entire Hungarian team is executed, mid-match, right there on the pitch. It's a bit downbeat, to say the least, and it's entirely fitting that the writers of *Escape to Victory* eschewed it and added a Hollywood ending when creating their own version. You can't very well gun down Bobby Moore on screen now, can you? Although anyone who has seen the fever dream that is Dave Bautista action movie *Final Score* will know that, in that film, terrorists occupy Upton Park and that both Tony Cottee and Rufus Brevett are shot and killed, each acting their hearts out as they fling themselves backwards – proving that West Ham legends don't have total immunity in the movies.

Hollywood's first stab at the prisoners versus guards genre was *The Longest Yard*, in 1974. The film, released as *The Mean Machine* in the UK, stars Burt Reynolds as a former NFL star who, while behind bars, puts together a team of inmates to take on the wardens in an American football match. It also featured some genuine NFL stars in supporting roles, setting something of a template in that regard. Not only is the fun film another clear influence on *Victory* but it has been remade a few times. In 2005, Adam Sandler starred in a remake, with Burt Reynolds also appearing; but in 2015 in Egypt and in 2001 in the UK, the sport was changed to proper football or, if you prefer, soccer. The UK version was released as *Mean Machine* and is enjoyable enough, featuring turns from any number of much-loved British actors from David Hemmings to Robbie Gee. It is a cast that is, of course, led by Vinnie Jones, who has surely turned himself into the most successful footballer-turned-actor of them all since swapping Wimbledon (the football team, not the movie) for *Lock, Stock and Two Smoking Barrels* (the movie) back in the late 90s.

From true stories of prisoners of war taking on the Germans to the movies that had already been inspired by such tales, all these elements fed into the script for what became *Escape to Victory* – which was a first-time effort by screenwriter Yabo Yablonsky. Yablonsky, a writer with a Russian background, has very few other credits in the industry, though, if IMDB is to be believed, he did direct

Willie Nelson's 4th July Celebration. Can that be right? Being called John Smith, I have a natural suspicion of people with the same name having their credits mixed up on that website but surely that wouldn't be a problem for Yabo?

Regardless of whatever else he did or didn't do, Yablonsky is unquestionably the father of the film. He was inspired by the 'Death Match' story and his first draft had the Gestapo offering a deal, of sorts. 'If they lost the match, they would all be taken to Switzerland and released; if they won, they would be killed. What happens then is that the prisoners say "Fuck 'em. Victory!" Hence the title,' he helpfully explained.

The wheels really started to roll on the film, however, when Yablonsky crossed paths with a producer called Tom Stern. This was still the late 60s and, as Stern tells it, 'nobody even had soccer in their brain' in America but he was confident it would hit the country sooner or later, given its worldwide popularity. He was interested enough to read the speculative script and option it for three years to see if he could get the movie made. The closest he got during this time to securing the finance was when he took the movie to Warner Bros, which owned the nascent New York Cosmos. Warner offered him $15,000 for a standard development deal, with the promise that it would get someone 'better' to rewrite it. Stern did not take the deal. His decision wasn't made from a sense of loyalty to Yablonsky's artistic vision but rather through his own misjudgement. 'I don't know what the fuck was in my brain but I said "no". You never say "no". Somebody offers you something, you say "yes". But I didn't think I was making the wrong decision.'

What the bullish Stern did learn about the script was that it needed a second look. However, he clearly didn't feel that it was Yablonsky's inexperience that was any sort of problem, because the person he hired to do a draft was Djordje Milicevic, a friend of Stern's from back in New Jersey. Milicevic would go on to write the 80s action movie *Runaway Train*, starring Jon Voight and Eric Roberts, which features a prison break and, you guessed it, a runaway train. But at this earlier point in his career, he had even less experience and fewer credits than Yablonsky. Irrespective of this, Stern felt that the new script, although way too long, was more to his taste, being more 'anti-German' than he felt the original draft had been. At this point, the script began to receive a little more attention and attracted the interest of hot new producers Andy Vajna and Mario Kassar, as well as the man *Variety* described as a 'powerful and charming talent manager and agent', Freddie Fields.

Tom Stern also alleges that around this time, the script was stolen and adapted into the aforementioned *The Longest Yard*. However, given that the script for that film also appears to have been around since the late 60s, it seems a baseless claim. As discussed, it's clear that the inspiration for both films shared a source but I suspect that is often the case in the film-making business. In an effort to get some momentum behind the screenplay, Stern then did something very interesting. He visited Jack Nicholson in Florida and showed it to him. Stern insists that Nicholson 'read it and he loved it', agreed with him that the screenplay was way too long and told him: 'I'm not committing to it but I like it.' This is an intriguing proposition. Nicholson is one of the greats and the prospect of him being involved is interesting. In truth, by the time the film was made, he may have been a little old to play Hatch but it's quite something to imagine him in the film – and he is not the only near miss we'll hear about.

Stern's account of what came next for the film must be tempered by his assertion that: 'Everybody always said that Freddie Fields was a prick and I can vouch for that.' It's fair to say that he may not be giving the most balanced account. In his version, Fields waded in at this point and wanted to deal with Vajna and Kassar to get his hands on the film. The three existing producers debated the insubstantial deal that was on offer, with Stern thinking it wasn't enough and Kassar suggesting that they take the deal, reasoning that they had held the film too long and it was unlikely to get made as things stood. Stern certainly feels that the $25,000 he received in the deal, along with a co-producer credit, was insufficient compensation for the work he had already put in, which he claims included being 'in touch with Pelé long ago'. On top of this, he also felt that he was completely sidelined by Fields, with Stern maintaining that he 'didn't want anyone else on set'. However, Fields did continue to work with Vajna and Kassar on the project, so it perhaps wasn't the case that he didn't want to work with anybody at all that had previously had hands on the movie but, instead, may have had a particular issue with Stern. Stern says that he was never invited to the set and that his name was 'so far down in the credits that IMDB didn't believe me'. So, his place in the making of the film has been somewhat lost. Certainly, there seems to have been a personality clash between the two men. This Tom

Stern version of events comes from a very entertaining interview he did with *Retrofiend Radio*, which you can find on YouTube and is well worth a listen, but sadly he leaves our story at this point.

For Mario Kassar's part, he says that the biggest stumbling block in getting the film made was their idea of casting some real footballers, saying: 'We hit a wall, because every time we talked to a studio, nobody knew what we were talking about. The audience, they're not into soccer here. Now they are but in those days, they weren't.' That change had, of course, been initiated by the presence of Pelé and his New York Cosmos team. By the time he retired amid great fanfare in 1977, aged 36, with a 70,000 crowd at Giants Stadium watching him play a final half for each team as the Cosmos took on his old team Santos, it's fair to say that the Brazilian had won some people over in the States to the game. His profile was sufficiently high for audiences to be interested in what he did next.

Add to that the aforementioned selling point of Sylvester Stallone in a sports movie and suddenly everything seems possible. As Kassar says: 'Once you get Sly, then you get Michael Caine. Once you get Michael Caine, then you get Pelé and you get everybody.' The tipping point in getting more people interested in a football-based project appears to have been the influence of a French woman who worked with Freddie Fields. Kassar says that: 'When she heard about it, because she was French, she knew about soccer and she thought this project was great.' Her enthusiasm seemingly convinced Fields to become involved himself and, once he was on board, his influence with the studios made getting finance and distribution for the film significantly easier. Suddenly, from Yablonsky's original script some years earlier, a film was finally emerging. And while it wasn't yet quite the movie we have come to know and love, the ball was certainly rolling.

Before dipping his toe directly into film production, Freddie Fields had been known as something of a 'super agent' whose clients included Paul Newman, Steve McQueen, Robert Redford, Barbra Streisand, Sidney Poitier, Roberto De Niro, Al Pacino, Gene Hackman and Dustin Hoffman, with some of whom he founded the independent production company First Artists, so it's fair to say he was probably doing all right for a dollar or two. The *Journal du Show Business* – which sounds made up but, I promise, isn't – referred to him as 'the biggest middleman in US showbiz'. He had been in the business practically his whole life, as his father ran a resort in the Catskills (think Kellerman's in *Dirty Dancing*) and his brother, Shep, was a band leader. He started working as a New York booking agent in the 1940s and by 1960 had set up Creative Management Associates (or CMA). In his role as an agent, he is credited as being something of a pioneer of the 'back-end' deal for his clients, whereby they took a smaller upfront fee for appearing in a movie in return for a cut of any profits that came rolling in. He also had a reputation for the kind of stunt in negotiations that could be written off as eccentricity if it paid off but could get you in trouble if it didn't land. Like the time he wooed James Coburn away from a rival agency by arriving at a meeting and taking off his jacket to reveal a holstered gun. *Daily Variety* reported that 'the tactic was a joke but it got the job done' and Coburn signed.

In his role at CMA, Fields worked on packaging several movies that starred one – and often more than one – of his stable of superstars, such as *Butch Cassidy and The Sundance Kid*, *Papillon*, *Dog Day Afternoon*, *The Sting* and *The Towering Inferno*, all of which makes him all right by me. *The Towering Inferno* is probably the biggest and the best of the popular genre of star-studded, overblown disaster movies which bestrode the 70s. Famously, the on-screen billing for the film placed Steve McQueen's name to the left of the picture, with Paul Newman slightly higher up but to the right, in an effort to establish equal status and ensure that everyone's ego was sufficiently massaged. This stroke of genius is credited to Freddie Fields and it's a trick that is still used today to convey the equal billing of two stars. This aptitude for compromise and negotiation would certainly have stood Fields in good stead for his threshold-crossing step into full production on *Escape to Victory*. A publicity quote from Fields at the time stated that: 'Becoming a producer was a natural outgrowth of my work with CMA. I felt I had reached my peak as an agent and that I would never have the creative involvement that makes this business so exciting.'

The three years that Fields spent getting *Victory* over the line certainly earned him the praise of his film's three biggest stars, with Stallone talking of his admiration for him, Pelé saying that he made his Hollywood introduction a pleasure and Michael Caine being even more effusive, calling him 'absolutely fantastic' and saying: 'I have quite sincerely never seen a producer work harder in my life, on what was a very difficult film to do. The location, Budapest, was difficult, of course. I couldn't wish success more for anyone than for Freddie Fields. He really worked hard to make this film a success; bloody hard, right down to where we were doing the football matches with a crowd of 38,000 people. I saw Freddie out there doing second assistant jobs, directing extras, holding people back, doing everything.' And you can tell it's a genuine Michael Caine quote because it's got a 'bloody' in there.

Fields did clash with Yabo Yablonsky, however, over what you might call artistic differences. Fields's entertainment-inclined sensibilities naturally made the film a lighter adventure in the same way that *The Great Escape* retains elements of knockabout fun, despite its ultimately tragic denouement. Obviously, it is hard to tell who is responsible for which aspects when a project has multiple writers but, certainly, Fields hired screenwriters Evan Jones and Jeff Maguire to give everything a pass and perhaps they took it further away from Yablonsky's original concept, too. Maguire was just starting out in the business but would go on to write *In the Line of Fire*, while Evan Jones had dabbled in movies before working on one of Michael Caine's Harry Palmer movies, *Funeral in Berlin*. Whoever was ultimately responsible, an exasperated Yablonsky knew where he wanted to direct his anger and he was moved to refer to Fields as a 'fucking moron' and say some pretty rum things about the finished film.

Whatever else it was that Fields felt the film needed – more laughs, more heroism, the development of the Hatch character – one thing he knew for sure was that he wanted Pelé. He felt, quite rightly, that the involvement of the Brazilian would vastly improve the chances of the movie succeeding internationally, citing in the production notes 'the worldwide popularity of this man', writing: 'He attracts crowds everywhere he goes – fanatic, adoring crowds that just want to touch him. You have to see it to believe it.' Fields was clearly a convert to the beautiful game, even if it had required that nudge by his French colleague to help him see the light. He even told the *Daily Express* that: 'Soccer is now such a worldwide phenomenon that America can no longer lock it out. We even have our own league back in the States.' They certainly did and, by the end of the decade, Pelé radically transformed American attitudes to the sport and won some hearts and minds.

Pelé had arrived in the US in 1975, coming out of semi-retirement to do so and made an instant impact. As he starred for Cosmos, their games were attended by such luminaries as Mick Jagger, Elton John and Robert Redford. At that spectacular 1977 retirement match, Muhammad Ali was there on the field to see him and, as Shep Messing quite rightly says: 'At that time, the two most recognisable people on the planet were the two of them.' Just prior to that final staged match, Pelé signed off his career in fairy-tale fashion by leading the Cosmos to Soccer Bowl victory. A year later, he was still the star attraction as a pre-match guest, even if, at that stage, he was just there to ceremoniously kick a game off.

In 1979, the BBC's *Brass Tacks* current affairs strand released a film called *A Whole New Ball Game*, which looked at the burgeoning football scene in the United States, with its tailgate parties and family game vibe. The programme comes across as if it is looking elsewhere for something to be cheerful about, given the parlous state of the game in the UK at the time. Riddled as the English game was with hooliganism and financial problems, it's understandable that they were casting an admiring eye at the US: 'Nobody could deny that American soccer has arrived in a big way. And nobody could deny that that success is down to one man, Pelé.' NASL marketing director Steve Caspers is quoted on the show as saying that 'we're selling sizzle and romance' and, indeed, they were. Sizzle and romance were not two words you would have used to describe football in England in the 70s, with its defining image being Franny Lee and Norman Hunter swinging punches at each other on a muddy Baseball Ground. But sizzle and romance were what American soccer was all about and it's what Hollywood has always been about, so it was not unreasonable that given his successful spell in the former, Pelé would soon be co-opted into the latter.

When I spoke to actor Clive Merrison, who plays the memorable role of the forger in *Escape to Victory*, he agreed with me that Stallone in a sports film and Pelé in a film at all were the vital components in getting it made when it got made. 'I imagine Pelé would have been paid a lot of money', he told me, 'and Freddie Fields didn't like spending money.' Money well spent, I say.

4.
PUTTING THE BAND TOGETHER

WITH FREDDIE Fields now firmly at the helm of the production, he and his colleagues set about the task of securing the right talent to put the vision on to the screen – both in front of the camera and behind it. As a result of their activity, the Hollywood press began to take notice of the project and started to run stories about the potential cast and crew.

In July 1979, *Daily Variety* reported that the film was to be directed by Brian Hutton and who among us can say that it would have been a bad fit if he had taken the job? Although he is perhaps not the household name that John Huston is, Hutton is the director of possibly the second-most repeated film on UK television, *Where Eagles Dare*, as well as *Kelly's Heroes* – so, it's clear that he knew his way around a good war film. He feels like a perfect fit for *Escape to Victory* and its fanbase. My guess would be that those familiar enough with Colby, Hatch and the rest to want to read this book are, like me, probably equally excited by the merest mention of 'Broadsword calling Danny Boy'.

Although, ultimately, Hutton did not direct the film, the rumours of his involvement were sufficiently strong for speculation to grow that Clint Eastwood, who starred as Schaffer in *Where Eagles Dare* and, well, Kelly in *Kelly's Heroes*, might join him and take a starring role. *Daily Variety* then also went on to confidently report that French star Alain Delon was cast in the film, while elsewhere Lloyd Bridges's name was mentioned, though who knows for which part. Ultimately, however, their involvement went the same way as that of Jack Nicholson and Clint Eastwood, with none of them appearing in the finished film.

In his posthumously published memoir *A bientot*, James Bond star Roger Moore stated that he was approached by Hutton to take on the role of Colby but that he had grave concerns about his own ability to keep the British end up in any football scenes in which he might have been called upon to take part. He states: 'The thing is, I can't run and to be on a field of professional football players and look convincing was something I had terrible apprehensions about.' Based on these comments, it's possible that the subject of a potential body double to do the football work while Roger sat in a chair nearby sipping a shaken-not-stirred vodka Martini was never raised. But if Kevin Beattie was selected as Michael Caine's body double because of a passing resemblance, I wonder which Ipswich player might have got the nod to step in as Roger Moore's Colby if things had come to pass. Each of these potential casting choices is an intriguing one but, even if you squint really hard, it's difficult to imagine any of them taking the places of either Sylvester Stallone or Michael Caine here.

Perhaps most unusual of all casting suggestions is the claim in his autobiography by singer Rod Stewart that he was asked to be in the film and that only his touring schedule prevented him from doing so. 'How different the history of cinema could have been,' he says but I think John Wark speaks for all of us when he reacted to the suggestion with a startled 'Oh my God!' when I broke the news to him. Rod can play a bit by all accounts but who on earth would he have been in the film? My best guess would be one of the players, with not too much reliance on any acting skills, but, surely, he would not have even contemplated getting his hair cut like a prisoner of war back when he was in his coiffured pomp.

Outside of the casting rumours, the trade papers also reported that filming locations were being scouted in Ireland, England, Austria, Germany and Canada but, ultimately, of course, Hungary was settled upon. Producer Andy Vajna may have influenced the decision for filming to take place in his home country but, overwhelmingly, the reasons were financial. Freddie Fields told *Daily Variety* that shooting in communist Hungary cost 'less than half the estimated budgets given by four other countries' and that it came in at $12m. Clive Merrison suggested to me that the main reason for this was 'the price of wood. To make it anywhere else would have cost a fortune.' Budapest was also chosen because of its resemblance to wartime Paris and the availability of the MTK Stadium, which was a decent stand-in for the Stade de Colombes, for which it doubles in the film – not least because, in 1980, it still had no floodlights, which maintained the required 1940s feel.

The impressive Gensdorf prison camp set was to be constructed over a three-month period in the grounds of the Allag Riding Stables, 18km outside of Budapest. The

Hungarian government assisted with the building of the camp as part of the deal that brought the production to the country and there was an agreement that the set would not be used again by anybody until the film was finished and released, although there is no evidence that it was ever used in another film, which feels like a shame. But if it wasn't going to be Clint Eastwood, Roger Moore or Rod the Mod who got to strut their stuff on the newly built set, who would it be?

Sylvester Stallone coming on board as Hatch was a real coup for the production and it happened because of what Freddie Fields described as 'an interesting accident'. Any sentence that starts with 'he came to look at one of the beach houses that I own in Malibu' fancies itself a bit but, apparently, it was only this chance meeting that led to Stallone doing the film. Fields was on hand at the house, presumably having baked some biscuits and been on his hands and knees all morning with the Flash to make the place look more appealing, and, while he was there, he asked the actor what his next project was likely to be. Stallone said that he had nothing lined up and asked Fields if he had a script in mind. Fields told him 'I've got a perfect script for you' and handed over *Escape to Victory*. You can see why the part of Hatch would appeal to Stallone. He is described in the publicity for the film as 'a chronic escaper' who has made several attempts at getting out. This immediately gives the character some of the cool of Steve McQueen as Hilts in *The Great Escape* – even the names are a little similar.

In a *Times* piece from May 1980 about the making of the movie, it is reported that Stallone was, initially, not so keen on the project but was talked into accepting the part by his manager, Herb Nanas, who convinced him of the worldwide popularity of football. If I'm being totally honest, I've only included this slight element of doubt from Stallone so that I could mention Herb Nanas, because I think it's a great name. I like to think that Herb Nanas is a shortened version of his full name, which may or may not be Herbie Goes Bananas. Regardless of this nonsense, Stallone called him three days later and said that he wanted to do the movie and a deal was swiftly done to have him on board.

Stallone was at an interesting moment in his career when he committed to the script Fields gave him. He had the box office hit and the critical acclaim of *Rocky* under his belt and he was a big star but it seemed that audiences were struggling to accept him as anything other than Rocky Balboa. In the few years since his Oscar win, both *F.I.S.T.* and *Paradise Alley* had somewhat flopped and police thriller *Nighthawks* wouldn't do much better, with only *Rocky II*, in the middle of those, giving him more success. As a kid, I would have watched all three of these non-*Rocky* films on video, purely on the strength of Stallone being in them, but it is fair to say that they are underwhelming in comparison to the *Rocky* films. Even *Nighthawks*, which throws Lando Calrissian (Billy Dee Williams) from *The Empire Strikes Back* and Roy Batty (Rutger Hauer, as the baddie) from *Blade Runner* into the mix and adds a surprise ending involving a wig, can't quite make up for the lack of boxing action. Stallone needed a hit and, perhaps, saw parallels between *Victory* and his more successful work. Indeed, he was quoted as saying:

'The last 20 minutes of the film are like *Rocky*, with the underdog going for the big fella.'

In many ways, Stallone had always been an underdog himself when it came to being a movie star. His mother, Jackie, of unforgettable *Celebrity Big Brother* fame, endured a particularly difficult labour, which left baby Sylvester with nerve damage on one side of his face and gave him his distinctive slightly droopy look. He endured a difficult childhood, about which he has opened up in recent years, talking about his rotten relationship with his father and saying that his mum told him more than once that he was an unwanted child. He spent his earliest years in care at a boarding house and the time he did spend with his family was in New York's tough Hell's Kitchen district. One silver lining was that he dodged the bullet of being called Tyrone Stallone, which his mother had considered because she liked the movie star, Tyrone Power. Although, if anybody could have pulled off being called Tyrone Stallone, it was him. On top of his early problems, his voice is, at best, unconventional for a matinee idol. He says of his own distinctive drawl that: 'I have the voice of a Mafia pallbearer.' So, perhaps we should be surprised that he made it at all – but make it he did, spectacularly.

Early film roles included the standard background part credits such as a 'hotel guest', 'party guest' and, in Woody Allen's *Bananas*, 'subway thug' – as well as a regrettable dabble in softcore porn with *The Party at Kitty and Stud's*, a movie that would gain notoriety and be re-released as *The Italian Stallion* once Sly had found fame. Roles in *The Lords of Flatbush*, alongside Henry Winkler, *Capone*, alongside Ben Gazzara, and as a psychopathic driver in the futuristic and bonkers *Death Race 2000*, alongside David Carradine, gained him a little more attention but it was, of course, *Rocky* that launched him into the stratosphere.

Stallone was inspired to write his story of a down-on-his-luck club fighter getting a fairy-tale shot at the world title when, in 1975, he went to a cinema to watch a closed-circuit screening of Muhammad Ali defending his world title against Chuck Wepner. Wepner wasn't quite living in the same obscurity as Rocky Balboa when his chance came. He was a ranked fighter and had already been in with some respected heavyweights, including Joe Bugner and Ernie Terrell, but he was certainly a very heavy betting underdog against Muhammad Ali, who was in his second spell as world champion, having most recently defeated George Foreman in what was perhaps his most famous win of all time in 'The Rumble in the Jungle'. Wepner was known as 'The Bayonne Bleeder', because of his propensity for sustaining bad cuts when fighting, but he shook the world when he floored Ali in the ninth round with a body shot. Now we can spoil the fairy story a little here by pointing out that Wepner stood on Ali's foot as he threw the shot, which meant that the champ couldn't back away and take evasive action and, instead, hit the canvas. Or we can move on. It's up to you. Whatever the damage done to Ali's pride, he climbed off the floor and stopped Wepner in the 15th round, just 33 seconds before the final bell would have sounded – but not before Chuck had won a legion of new fans with his bravery and not before he had inspired the watching Sylvester Stallone.

Stallone biographer Marsha Daley says that 'Sly was fascinated by Wepner's story. One lucky break had raised

Wepner from the ranks of forgettable boxers and put him in the record books,' and that Stallone was inspired by the 'Cinderella story of an outclassed boxer granted one moment of glory'. Stallone immediately set about penning a script about a downtrodden boxer getting his shot and, within a few days, he had his script for *Rocky*, ready to tout around Hollywood. Studios were immediately interested in the film and pushed for James Caan or Ryan O'Neal to take the title role but Stallone wanted to play the part himself and stuck to his guns, eventually getting his way and justifying the decision.

His original script ended with Rocky taking a dive against Apollo Creed and using the money he was paid to fix the fight to buy a pet shop for Adrian. Stallone quite rightly saw sense and changed the script – though the new ending did lead to something of a clash with the film's director, John G. Avildsen. Stallone wanted it to be obvious that, at the end of the climactic fight, Creed was the clear winner. He wanted to show that Rocky's real victory was to do with his indomitable spirit and the fact that he had changed what people thought of him just by being there, still standing, at the end of a brutal fight against Creed, who acted as a proxy Muhammad Ali to Rocky's Chuck Wepner. Avildsen, however, wanted to blur the lines a bit more and, as Marsha Daley says, 'cut the film so fuzzily that audiences left the theatre without knowing which fighter was the champ. Sly lost that battle.' This is significant for two reasons, because, firstly, it shows a glimpse of Stallone battling with directors – something that would come to be a problem in ensuing years – and, secondly, because it shows that Stallone has an appreciation that there is more than one way to win. It explains why *Escape to Victory* may have appealed to him as a project, because, in terms of the football match, a draw is enough. They have proved their point and stood up to their German oppressors, with the penalty save being the last defiant act. There was an alternative ending that Stallone would have seen first, and which we will come to in due course, but when it was altered to the ending that we see, with the draw and the mass escape in the crowd, I think it's clear why Stallone could be supportive of the change, given his previous work.

One reason that *Rocky* struck gold, with audiences and critics alike, was in the inspired casting of American footballer Carl Weathers in the Apollo Creed role. Weathers auditioned for the part by boxing a few rounds with Stallone when, at that time, he believed he was only the screenwriter, not the star. As Stallone biographer Frank Sanello tells it: 'During the match, Weathers's enthusiasm overwhelmed him and he hit Stallone full in the face. The star didn't throw a tantrum but reminded Weathers "Hey, this is only an audition."' Weathers suggested that maybe he would be better off sparring the actual actor he would need to fight in the film and it was only then that Stallone revealed that he *was* the actor. Despite taking a few shots, Stallone warmed to his bigger, flashier opponent and gave him a part that would run through the first film and three sequels before breaking all our hearts in *Rocky IV*. I still can't talk about it.

Rocky broke box office records on its release and made a phenomenal amount of money for not very much outlay, thereby making it the Hollywood dream. It had gone on to enjoy huge TV ratings when it made it to the small screen, too, trailing only *Gone with the Wind* and *Airport 1975* in terms of a US TV audience for a film at that time. It also won best picture at the Oscars, as well as best director for Avildsen, who later went on to give us *The Karate Kid*, so you can file him under the same category as Brian Hutton – he'll do for me. Any dispute between Avildsen and his star can't have been a permanent rift, because the director returned to the franchise for *Rocky V* in 1990. That may not be anybody's favourite *Rocky* film but it is at least nice that Stallone and his director could put their differences aside and work together once more.

Problems on the original *Rocky* set seem to have stemmed from Stallone, by his own admission, over-stepping and upsetting people on the crew. However, this wasn't general star misbehaviour. It was, rather, born out of frustration at how his script and his characters were being treated. Stallone was closest to his creations and had his own ideas about how things should play out. Another Stallone biographer, Jeff Rovin, reports that: 'Nor did he feel any compunction about expressing these, often bluntly and at high volume.'

If the success of *Rocky* was able to draw a discreet veil over any on-set problems, his next film had no such luck. *F.I.S.T.* was a union drama directed by legendary director Norman Jewison of *In the Heat of the Night*, *The Thomas Crown Affair* and *Rollerball* fame and, unfortunately, it flopped in every possible regard; leaving in its wake only tales of a battle of wills between director and star. Next up was *Paradise Alley*, which Stallone wrote and directed himself. Set in Hell's Kitchen, it tells the story of three

Italian-American brothers trying to make money from the wrestling career of the youngest among them. This also flopped and received savage reviews, such as from Frank Rich in *Time* magazine, who described it as 'an exercise in egomania'. Stallone's ego certainly seems to have been something of a problem around this time, when he was sampling his first flush of success. Marsha Daley says that: 'Hollywood could not help noticing the subtle change in Sly from a modest, appreciative, level-headed young writer/actor to a high-handed, arrogant egomaniac.' She says that the 'problem stemmed from the fact that he swung from an abject low to a dizzying height – losing his equilibrium in the process'. For his own part, Stallone admitted to a certain level of resentment about the extra attention he got after *Rocky*, saying: 'Now there's this great herd of people who are coming forth and saying "I like you". It happened to Rocky, too. I feel like saying to them, "Where were you when I was living in Hotel Barf, eating hot and cold running disease?"' Hotel Barf does sound horrible, to be fair, but, regardless of the circumstances that may have led to a bit of a chip forming on Sly's shoulder, critics were unforgiving. The excellently named Rex Reed wrote in the *New York Daily News* that 'instead of a head, Sylvester Stallone carries on his shoulder an ego the size of a 40lb eggplant', which not only seems a bit malicious but also doesn't even work that well. If it's 40lb, it could be anything, Rex. Why pick an eggplant? I don't want to tell you your job, Rex, but surely you should just pick something that already weighs about 40lb?

In the fullness of time, Stallone was more than capable of recognising some of the ugly behaviour he displayed back in the early days, admitting in 2014 that 'I abused power badly' and saying that: 'I read some of the interviews I gave now and wish I could go back and punch myself in the face.' Don't beat yourself up about it, Sly, literally.

The humbling experiences of *F.I.S.T.* and *Paradise Alley* must have been a consideration in his decision to go back to Philadelphia for another chapter with his boxing alter ego. *Rocky II* would have a far larger budget than the original and, this time, Stallone would direct it himself. It's a lovely film, which sees Rocky struggling to come to terms with his new-found fame and in some dark places at the side of wife Adrian's sickbed as she lies in a coma, before rallying to win a rematch against Apollo Creed. At one point, the film was going to finish with the fight taking place in the Colosseum in Rome, like Bruce Lee against Chuck Norris in *The Way of the Dragon*, but Stallone had a rethink and the film is none the worse for it. *Rocky II* was box office gold again and gave Sylvester's career a timely boost. 'It came at a time when I needed it most,' he said of the film.

However, he then followed up the hit sequel with *Nighthawks*, which did not do well, reiterating the idea that cinemagoers wanted to see Stallone as Rocky Balboa, not as Sergeant Deke DaSilva – or anyone else, for that matter – at this stage of his career. Although the box office failure of *Nighthawks* was not confirmed until after he signed on for *Escape to Victory*, you can see why the star would be tempted to try his luck with another sports film, to split the difference with his demanding audience. Jeff Rovin says of his decision that: 'Hungry for critical success, Sylvester had every reason to believe that it would at least be an artistic triumph. He was also delighted with the stature of his co-stars.' Also, if he was looking to keep his own ego in check, then spending a month with a load of footballers and their zero tolerance approach to nonsense could go a very long way to doing that.

Next on the billing is Michael Caine. We all know Michael Caine. He is always a reassuring presence in any film. Equally comfortable locking intellectual horns with Laurence Olivier in *Sleuth* or throwing Alf Roberts, of Coronation Street fame, off a Gateshead multi-storey car park in *Get Carter*. The man is an acting legend. He's also a perfect fit for Captain John Colby, not only because he carries the qualities of a working-class hero but because he seems so very British. The memory of *The Italian Job* lingers around him, with its football-tinged plot and the idea of him leading a team of plucky Brits in getting one over on foreign opposition. It's fair to say that both films have a whiff about them of the jingoism that gets invoked whenever a World Cup comes around.

By the time *Escape to Victory* came out, on video at least, I think I must have already liked Michael Caine. There was an odd bit of business in my early years at school whereby when we weren't playing football, having a generic game of 'War' or playing 'Mr Tickle' (don't ask) at break times, we would play films. By which I mean we would recreate scenes from films and play out bits of the story. There was a fair bit of *Star Wars* going on but I also recall making bemused friends play along with whatever films I'd seen the day before, whether they had the same reference points or not. I have vivid memories of re-enacting the ending of the Frank Sinatra war film *Von Ryan's Express*, which might make me unique among

British schoolchildren of the 80s. More pertinently here, I can also remember running around the field pretending to be in a Mini and singing 'We are the Self-Preservation Society' from *The Italian Job*, without knowing what any of those words meant. I also remember co-ordinating a mass opening of our blue or green parka coats to recreate the moment in *The Eagle Has Landed* when, as the result of an unfortunate water wheel incident, Michael Caine's men get rumbled and are forced to reveal that they are, in fact, German commandos, rather than the Polish paratroopers they have been masquerading as. The dinner ladies were as shocked as those Norfolk villagers in the film, I can tell you. We might also have wanted to play *Zulu* but it was always difficult to get enough people to play. The point is, Michael Caine was clearly already on my radar as a young boy and we can probably consider him a bit of an early favourite of mine at the time.

Caine exploded on to the scene in 1964's *Zulu*, despite not getting the part he went in for. He initially auditioned for the role of Cockney malingerer-turned-hero Private Hook but director Cy Endfield told him: 'Michael, you don't look like a Cockney, you look like an officer. Can you do a posh British accent?' The part of Hook went to James Booth and, instead, Caine was promoted several ranks and a couple of classes to play Lieutenant Gonville Bromhead and his performance blew away cinema audiences.

By 1980 and the shooting of *Escape to Victory* in Hungary, Caine had starred in several other war films and several other great films but he had also developed something of an unwanted reputation for making the odd clunker in amongst them – but unless you're Daniel Day

Lewis and choose your projects very sparingly, I can't help thinking that a patchy record is inevitable. It's fair to say that movies like *The Swarm* and *Beyond the Poseidon Adventure* are not top of anyone's all-time list but Michael Caine is never the problem with the film. You know what you'll see and that's Michael Caine playing it straight and giving the film a gravitas, whether it deserves it or not. He's a man who can give the same level of performance and hold a film together whether he's acting opposite Elizabeth Taylor, Jack Nicholson, Batman, Miss Piggy or Bobby Moore – and it's why he's so beloved. Roger 'nearly Colby' Moore put it better than I ever could when he said: 'What I think sums up Michael is that he can do a film like *The Swarm*, be covered in bee shit and come up smelling of honey. I think it's absolutely bloody marvellous. Good on you, Michael!'

Caine's view of his own career is equally legendary. *Time* magazine journalist Richard Schikel once wrote that 'it seems to be Caine's sad fate to go around being intelligent in dumb movies' but Caine has an answer for that accusation, saying: 'Early on, I did work that I was proud of and I got no kudos for it, so I thought to myself, "Now I've got to be artistic and wonderful and everything is going to be fine and I'll get great reviews and get an award." And I did that and I got bad reviews and no award, so I thought I might as well do it for the money, so I did.' Fair enough. He goes on to say that: 'I treated my career the way you treat a job. I'd say "I want that now" – like a new house or something – and I'd go out and do some films and get it.' This attitude is distilled in Caine's autobiography, inevitably called *What's It All*

About?, and his famous quote about the role he played in the truly rotten *Jaws: The Revenge* for 'a tremendous fee' in 1987: 'I have never seen the film but by all accounts it is terrible. However, I have seen the house that it built and it is terrific.'

For those wondering which bracket *Escape to Victory* falls into, it's fair to say that the man himself regards it as one for the successful side of the ledger. In a second autobiography, perhaps equally inevitably called *Blowing the Bloody Doors Off*, Caine tells us that: 'In the early 1980s, *The Island* and *The Hand* were both mediocrities but I followed them up with three successes: *Escape to Victory, Deathtrap* and *Educating Rita*.' Sir Michael has gone on record as saying that '*Educating Rita* is the best performance I ever gave' and I'm inclined to agree with him. He also says that '*The Man Who Would Be King* is the film people will remember after I've gone, if they remember any of them.' Self-deprecation aside and even allowing for the fact that this quote is around 30 years old and that Caine has been going strong in the intervening years, with the likes of *The Quiet American, Children of Men* and any number of supporting roles in great Christopher Nolan films, I'm inclined to agree with him again. There are bad films on his CV but the good significantly outweighs the bad.

The one he thinks he will be remembered for, *The Man Who Would Be King*, is based on a Rudyard Kipling story and tells the tale of two British soldiers who try their luck by taking their military expertise into Kafiristan and find fortune beyond their wildest dreams when one of them is believed to be a god by the local tribes. In 1975, it was finally made into a movie, with

Caine and Sean Connery in the starring roles. The film had long been the passion project of director John Huston, who had previously wanted to get the film made with Humphrey Bogart and Clark Gable 20 or more years earlier.

Caine described working with Huston on the film as 'such a joy' and the pair clearly got on well enough to work together once more on *Victory*. Caine recalled Huston being very minimal in his directions to his actors. One of his only notes to Caine as Peachy Carnehan was to '"Speak faster, Michael; he is an honest man." He believes, you see, that people who talk slowly are dishonest!' This is all well and good and may well have added to his characterisation. However, when we first meet the younger Peachy, he is stealing Rudyard Kipling's watch, so the honesty thing may have been a wrong steer. Nevertheless, the pair hit it off and it's easy to think that Caine might have been something of a lure for Huston when he came to choose *Escape to Victory* as a project to work on. When, in September 1979, *Daily Variety* reported that Brian Hutton had left the project and that John Huston was now the director, it also announced that Caine, along with Stallone, was already on board, a state of affairs confirmed by Freddie Fields.

The announcement of John Huston as director of the film was met with some surprise within the industry. Huston was famous for a string of classics such as *The African Queen*, *The Treasure of the Sierra Madre* and *The Maltese Falcon* and he was considered an unusual choice for a film about football. Although, to be fair, Hollywood didn't have too many directors that wouldn't have been an unusual choice for such a film. For his part, Huston was quoted as saying of the project: 'I only make pictures if I like the story or if they offer me a lot of money and, in this case, it happened to be both.' This shows that his philosophy over jobs was similar to that of Caine – at this stage of his career, at least. However, Clive Merrison is pretty sure it was simply the cash that swung it, telling me that: 'Huston did it for the money to finance his last film, *The Dead*, which is a masterpiece. And whatever anyone thinks of it, *Escape to Victory* is not a masterpiece.' Clive is in the film and I very much value his opinion and, in the cold light of day, he is probably right on this. None of us are pretending that *Escape to Victory* is a masterpiece. However, I know which of those films I would reach for 99 times out of a hundred and it isn't *The Dead*.

When he snagged John Huston to direct his film, Freddie Fields was in the middle of a very productive couple of days. He told ITV's *Clapperboard* during an on-set visit that he called Huston at his Mexico home. 'And I thought it might interest him and indeed it did. I sent it [the script] down to Mexico and I got an immediate response. "Best picture, best script; I must do it."' Fields flew to see Huston, who continued to make positive noises about signing on, before flying immediately to New York to meet with Pelé to sign him up, too. Next, he flew straight back to Huston's home in Mexico 'and we made a deal'. Carbon footprint aside, you cannot fault the work ethic of Freddie Fields on this movie.

Given football's reputation in the United States at that time for being at the gentler end of the sporting spectrum, it's easy to see why some people thought that *Escape to Victory* was something of a strange choice for Huston. Here was this bear of a man with a string of very muscular films in his back catalogue, with his voice that 'had a way of soaking into all the air in a room' according to daughter Allegra and with any number of legendary drinking tales and eccentric behaviour on set. On *The Bible*, he locked horns with the equally thirsty Peter O'Toole and the two of them found themselves drinking whiskey on horseback, wearing kimonos and shooting rifles until Huston fell off and broke his leg. All pretty standard for a Tuesday. On *Night of the Iguana*, he gave his cast, including another Hall of Fame drinker in Richard Burton, gold-encrusted guns and bullets with the names of the other actors inscribed on them. According to Robert Sellers in his very entertaining *Hellraisers*: 'It was Huston's way of saying, if you want to kill each other, use the designated bullet. Bonkers but the ploy worked; there were no problems between the cast.' Apart, presumably, from the deep psychological ones. With all of this in mind, the football film could be considered an unusual step for Huston. Or maybe not when you consider that *Annie*, the film he moved on to afterwards – and, in fact, had already begun pre-production on – was another unusual choice.

Actually, this wasn't even Huston's first or last brush with footballers. In 1973, the director made a film called *The Mackintosh Man*, which was filmed in Malta and, more specifically, also filmed on location at one point at the house of England football legend Sir Stanley Matthews. Furthermore, a mackintosh owned by Matthews was even used in the film after a wardrobe error left the scene without one and Stan stepped in and offered to help. So that counts, right?

A bit more on the nose, and even more odd, is the other film that Huston went on to make with Pelé – 1983's *A Minor Miracle.* Huston doesn't direct this one but he does star in it, as an irascible old priest with a heart of gold who is doing the best he can for the orphan boys in his care. The orphanage is in financial trouble and those bloody city bean counters want to knock it down – you know what they're like. So, he gets actual Pelé to come and help them out because, get this, Huston's Father Cadenas is the man who 'taught him everything he knows'. It's an unusual film, to say the least. If it had any budget at all, then it must have all been spent on securing Huston and Pelé, because I cannot see where else it was spent. The two men do share an emotional scene in the hospital as Pelé visits his ailing mentor, who is dying from cancer. The music swells and tries to convince us that we really should care but, if we're being honest, it's neither man's best work. The end of the film is a mixed bag, as Pelé inspires the boys to win a football match that somehow means that the orphanage can stay open but we lose Father Cadenas, who passed away while he was listening to the game in his hospital bed. Quite why this local orphanage football match was being broadcast live on the radio is not clear but, for some reason, it is. I promise I'm not making up any of this.

John wasn't the only Huston on the Budapest set of *Victory* in 1980, as he brought his reluctant teenage daughter, Allegra, with him as an assistant. Michael Caine says that John also needed a bit of help at that stage from his producer, saying: 'John was not at the height of his powers then, to say the least. A lifetime of fun was beginning to catch up with him but Freddie was so supportive of him.' Caine is full of praise for Fields, saying that he was incredibly supportive of a past-his-best Huston and that 'he was one of the best hands-on producers I have ever worked with; he was there on the set every day and leading from the front'.

While we're heaping praise on Freddie Fields and ignoring those nasty things Tom Stern said about him, it's worth noting how clever he had been with his casting so far. Sylvester Stallone would bring in an American audience, Pelé would attract a worldwide audience and Michael Caine would bring a bit of legitimacy and class to the film. However, that wasn't something Caine could do alone and another heavy hitter was needed alongside him to spar with. Step up Max von Sydow.

The Swedish actor came to prominence through his working relationship with director Ingmar Bergman, who cast him many times, including in the likes of *The Seventh Seal* and *Wild Strawberries*. When Hollywood recognised his talent and began to put him in films with broader appeal, he was never typecast. He showed his range by going straight to the top of the shop and playing Jesus in *The Greatest Story Ever Told*, then memorably playing a sinister bad guy in *The Quiller Memorandum*. Let's not forget that, a few years after those two, he was also Father Merrin in *The Exorcist* – I mean, he's the actual exorcist. By 1980, he was having a bit more fun with an outrageous and memorable turn as Ming the Merciless in *Flash Gordon*, working in rather broader strokes than in his Bergman films. As a child, the idea that Ming the Merciless and Major von Steiner were the same person absolutely rocked my world, so the fact that he did them back-to-back is very pleasing. *Flash Gordon* was directed by Mike Hodges, who had directed Michael Caine in *Get Carter* and *Pulp* (two films, coincidentally, in which Caine gets shot on a beach), so on arrival on set, the two would, I hope, have had plenty of stories to swap.

Curiously, this was the first time that the Swede had played a German officer in a war film. As you might expect, he had been asked once or twice before but it was *Escape to Victory* that finally turned his head. He told ITV when they visited the set: 'I've always tried not to do it, because I don't want to get stuck in that particular type. Me being Swedish and me having a German name, I'm sure it's very easy for a movie producer to get the idea that I should fit well into a German uniform and I don't want to do that forever. But furthermore, most of the Nazi officers in movies are clichés. I felt that Von Steiner in this story is not a cliché, not really.' He cites his character's apparent lack of Nazi sympathies as one attraction of the part and the fact that he is an ex-footballer 'who has been injured in the war' as another. Again, like Michael Caine, I think Von Sydow needs to be praised for his performance in what, in the wrong hands, could be a very silly film. He brings gravitas to the part. There's a lot going on behind those icy blue eyes of his. It seems like he was also quite into the football. 'It has been a great experience for me to meet all the soccer players from so many countries.' So, you see, it's a nice cast. Already, everyone seems to be buzzing at being there with everybody else.

Max von Sydow's reluctance to be typecast as a German officer, or indeed as anything, is admirable. But it's fair to say that it was not a sentiment shared by every actor. The World War Two film is a less popular movie genre now but for a long time, there was work to be had if you didn't mind playing a German soldier. I'm thinking partly here of Michael Sheard, who played Hitler, Himmler and almost every rank down in the German army in between popping up in *Auf Wiedersehen, Pet* to make Oz's life a misery, as Mr Bronson in *Grange Hill* (arguably his greatest monster), where he made Danny Kendall's life a misery, and *The Empire Strikes Back*, in which he annoys Darth Vader so much that he force-chokes him over a Zoom call.

Sheard isn't in the cast of *Escape to Victory* but two similar stalwarts are – those who take one for the team and play the baddies but get to wear the smart uniforms while doing so. One of these is Lithuanian-Australian actor George Mikell, who plays our camp Kommandant and whose CV has more Germans in it than a David Hasselhoff fan club. War films were clearly something of a speciality for him and he most notably crops up in *The Guns of Navarone* and *The Great Escape* – two classics of the genre. The other is Anton Diffring, who turns in a memorable performance as the biased match commentator when the Allies finally take the field against Germany.

Diffring, who was actually German and who fled the country before the war, had an interesting career. He was in a film called *Convoy* but, disappointingly, not that one, and a film called *Top Secret* but, disappointingly, not that one. But with his light hair, blue eyes and natural accent, he often found himself playing German soldiers. *The Guardian* said of him that his 'claim to fame rested on a talent for being thoroughly nasty. At least he was so very often on the screen, where he played a series of Nazi villains.' The ever-reductive *Sun* newspaper even ran with the headline 'Nasty film Nazi Anton dies at 70' for his obituary, so you get the idea. Most memorable for me is his appearance as Colonel Kramer in *Where Eagles Dare* (there it is again) as an SS officer butting heads with a Gestapo man he clearly despises and being twisted in knots by Richard Burton's Major John Smith (no relation). In the Stade de Colombes commentary box, Diffring cuts a despicable figure, thrilled by every German touch of the ball and playing in fake crowd noise to convince listeners that the French supporters are behind them. Curiously, Diffring's voice was dubbed for the film and it has never been clear why or by whom. Nevertheless, he leaves his mark on the movie and, when the finale comes, we are left hoping that some of the rioting French get to his box before he can leave it.

The casting for the British officers in the camp is equally enjoyable. They are headed by Daniel Massey as Colonel Waldron, the stuffy commanding officer whose mind is so pre-occupied with continuing to fight the war from behind the wire that he cannot see the value in any of this football nonsense – until of course, the football gets so beautiful that he finally has to see it for what it is. Massey was primarily considered to be a stage actor and a distinguished one at that. He can be seen on screen, however, in the likes of *Star!* with Julie Andrews, in which he portrayed his own real-life godfather, Noël Coward, and for which he won a Golden Globe. Daniel was part of the Massey acting dynasty; his father was Raymond Massey and his sister was Anna Massey but, between you and me, this is not the most interesting thing I discovered about his private life. You see, Daniel Massey was married to actress Penelope Wilton from *Ever Decreasing Circles* back in the day and then pulled off the high tariff manoeuvre of divorcing her and marrying her sister, Linda. Now, I didn't expect to have to read any *Hello!* articles as research for this book but I did and Penelope says of the arrangement that eventually 'it was perfectly fine when everyone got used to the idea'. She went on to marry Ian Holm from *Alien* and Bilbo Baggins fame and everyone was a winner. No judgement here.

Massey's Colonel Waldron is joined on the escape committee by Shurlock, played by Julian Curry, best known by UK viewers from his long-running role as Claude Erskine-Brown in *Rumpole of the Bailey* and Rose, played by Tim Pigott-Smith, who, by all accounts, had a lovely time making the film and was often a bridge between the actors and the footballers. Pigott-Smith was approached for the role while he was filming *Clash of the Titans* in Rome, by casting director Rose Tobias Shaw, who arranged for him to meet with Freddie Fields when Pigott-Smith's press tour for *Titans* took him to LA. The actor describes the meeting as being pure Hollywood, driving up to Fields's Beverly Hills home, which had all the showbiz trappings. By the side of the pool, Fields gave Tim a script and the big sell, telling him that Stallone, Caine, Von Sydow, Massey, Pelé and a whole host of other footballers were already signed on and that John Huston was directing. As Pigott-Smith put it in his memoirs: 'Who would not want to be part of such a Hollywood tutti-frutti? It was unreal, not to say unbelievable.'

Hanging around in the camp with Waldron, Shurlock and Rose is Pyrie, the scrounger, played by Maurice Roeves. He had already appeared in *The Eagle Has Landed* with Michael Caine and is no stranger to a football film, either, as we've also seen him as trainer Jimmy Gordon in the excellent *The Damned United*. Here, though, he gets nowhere near the pitch, besides one brief scene in which he is watching a training session, and he seems grateful for keeping his distance. He seems to have loved being around the players but was understandably in awe of them, telling the *Daily Record* of his experience: 'I didn't dare kick a ball. They would have halved me!' He was clearly very happy to get up close to Pelé in action, though, telling the tale of his introductory ball-juggling scene. 'He was asked "Could you say this line and keep the ball up in the air?" He started playing keepy-uppy, heading the ball, landing it on his neck, rolling it across his shoulders and delivering this whole speech. Then he'd say, "You mean like that?" He was one of the best human beings I've met in the business.' Apart from his sterling Jimmy Gordon work, I have a lot of affection for Roeves due to his memorable turn as an SAS officer in another film that made a bit of an impression on me as a youngster – *Who Dares Wins* – alongside the greatest James Bond that never was, Lewis Collins. If I recite his exquisitely delivered line 'Slowing down a little, Peter?' from that film, I can still raise a smile from my brother to this day. We spent hours and hours watching the last act of that film on video once we had recorded it off the telly.

The next cast member to address is the only non-footballer I was able to interview for the book. I spent a very lovely hour or so chatting to Clive Merrison, who plays the forger, about one of only two Hollywood films he made. Imagine how proud I was to be able to help him out with the title of *Firefox* when he was reaching for it – a film in which Clint Eastwood must think in Russian in order to fly a stolen war plane. You heard – I'm hardly going to forget something like that now, am I?

Clive is a very recognisable face from any number of TV shows, including his appearance as Mark's monstrous dad in *Peep Show*, and his portrayal of the meticulous and unfailingly polite forger in *Escape to Victory* is a brilliant one, which even got him a line in the trailer. Merrison told me that he had already worked with Massey and Roeves before and was very much into his football, so he was thrilled by having all the players on set. These days, fittingly, he's an Ipswich fan, having moved to the area some time ago, but back then he supported Arsenal.

He did tell me, however, that the financial arrangements on the film didn't exactly inspire confidence. When he arrived at the airport to fly to Hungary, no flight was booked for him and he was told to find and pay for his own, with Freddie Fields paying him his air fare in hand on arrival. 'Then at the end of the job, I had to go to this back office and Freddie Fields paid me the fee for the job in dollars. I think he was funding the film day by day.'

The only female speaking role of note in the film is Renée, a member of the French Resistance and fleetingly a love interest for Hatch when he is staying with her in the safe house. Renée is played by Carole Laure, the French-Canadian actress and singer, and would have been chosen, along with the rest, by legendary casting director Rose

Tobias Shaw, a woman whose credits included *The Wild Geese*, so she knew all about putting together ensemble casts. In the wake of *Victory* and into the 80s, Rose is credited with giving the career of Pierce Brosnan a boost after seeing him in his small role as an IRA gunman in *The Long Good Friday*, opening up parts in America for him.

It seems that while Rose Tobias Shaw's remit was to cast all non-football parts, the bulk of the football work was taken on by Peter Mason. Sometimes mentioned in the press as 'football consultant' and, at other times, 'soccer co-ordinator', Mason is something of a mysterious figure and it is unclear what qualified him for the job. It is entirely possible that because Freddie Fields was so in the dark about football, he reached out to someone he was confident knew more than he did – an 'in the land of the blind, the one-eyed man is king' kind of deal, perhaps. An American, Mason lived in Greece at the time the film was being made, having once played professionally, albeit only briefly, in West Germany. *The Times* reported that Mason attempted to recruit players and 'tried hard in West Germany, Italy, Spain and France but failed utterly', although, as we will see, he did achieve that aim in Norway, Denmark and Belgium. What Mason did have going for him was a friendship with Bobby Robson, which he utilised to the max.

If Mason was the football 'expert', then the production also required a military expert or, more specifically, some expertise on prisoner of war camps and *Escape to Victory* had not one but two such technical advisers. The first of these was Desmond Llewelyn, who we all know best as Q in so many of the James Bond films. Llewelyn had been a

Fusiliers officer in World War Two, was captured in 1940 and spent the next five years in prisoner of war camps, including Colditz, after an attempted escape from his first camp, Laufen. Llewelyn may have done his advisory work early in the production, because it seems that he wasn't present on set. The other adviser was, however, and it was someone who had gone one better than Llewelyn by actually escaping from Colditz – Major Pat Reid. He had escaped to Switzerland in 1942 and worked there in British Intelligence before leaving the army and writing *The Colditz Story*. Tim Pigott-Smith fondly remembers his presence on set, saying that: 'He was always happy to talk about his extraordinary exploits. Indeed, one got the impression that he had never again had such an exciting time as when pitting his wits against his German captors.'

With the football, the casting, the directing, the acting and the prisoner-of-warring all in place, the production just needed one more thing to top it all off and that came courtesy of Bill Conti and his score. It isn't certain how Conti came to work on the film but it isn't too hard to imagine that Sylvester Stallone had something to do with it. Conti had made his spectacular mark as a film composer with *Rocky* and since gone on to score *F.I.S.T.*, *Paradise Alley* and *Rocky II*, although, oddly, Conti himself believes that John Cassavetes may have suggested him to John Huston. Huston's hands-off approach to making the film seemingly extended to the score and Conti remembers having a free hand on *Victory*; being told by the veteran director to 'put it wherever you want' when he asked where the music was needed. Nor was Huston at the scoring sessions. It's a questionable policy but one that surely pays off. Even the biggest critics of *Escape to Victory* – and they are out there, you know – would have to concede that the music absolutely slaps (or bangs or whatever the kids are saying these days).

Now the film just needed some footballers.

5.

THE PLAYERS

HAVE YOU seen *Armageddon*? The Bruce Willis film about deep-core drillers being trained as astronauts to go into space and destroy an asteroid that's on a collision course with Earth? It feels like you might remember if you have but, regardless, there is a very enjoyable clip from the DVD commentary track of the film (remember those?) which occasionally goes viral. In it, co-star Ben Affleck tells us of the time on set that he was silenced for raising a very salient point: 'Why is it easier to train oil drillers to be astronauts than to train astronauts to be oil drillers?' Affleck, who doesn't appear to have enjoyed working on the film very much, says that the film's director, Michael Bay, did not take kindly to such questions and told him to shush his lips. However, the question remains and I'm afraid it will spoil the concept of that film for you.

In the early stages of development for *Escape to Victory*, it feels like the producers were faced with a similar question to that faced by the space boffins in *Armageddon*. Is it easier to teach actors to play football or to teach footballers to act? The choice they made, of course, was to bring in a whole host of brilliant footballers to take care of that side of things and let them do only as much acting as they were required to do. The pay-off for that was that the football looks far, far better than it would have done had actors been pretending they could play. Director John Huston agreed with the policy on this, telling *Film '81* that: 'It's much easier to teach an acrobat to act then it is to teach an actor to be an acrobat. And, as a rule, you will find fine acting talent among athletes.' Mike Summerbee, who plays Sid in the film, can also see the sense of it, pointing out that 'players act on the football field, anyway'. There's something in what he says.

That decision made, the question remained as to which footballers they could get on board. The brief for football consultant Peter Mason was to hire stars who would be box office draws in each of their countries, thereby maximising the appeal of the film all over the world. Pelé was evidently on board very early on and, as discussed, his presence would have had a huge influence on getting the studio backing for the film at that time. But who would join him? Producer Mario Kassar said that logistics and timings were the real barriers to finding the right people, rather than finding willing participants. 'All the football players are like stars,' he said, 'they don't mind being in a movie. Everybody likes being in front of the camera.'

One of the first players mentioned in the press when the project became public knowledge was Denmark's Allan Simonsen, who was something of a superstar at Barcelona at the time and a recent European Footballer of the Year winner. Ultimately, though, it came to nothing. Just a couple of years later, the signing of Diego Maradona forced Simonsen out of Barcelona and he opted to sign for Second Division Charlton Athletic, as he wanted to play his football and live his life in a less stressful spotlight –

so, perhaps not appearing in a Hollywood movie was for the best, after all.

The Times, reporting on Peter Mason's quest, said that 'he pondered thoughts of George Best and Denis Law and then dismissed them'. Denis Law feels like he might have been an entertaining presence in the film and he would have been more than capable of delivering a line or two but of all the potential people that could have taken part in the film, I've always found George Best the most likely candidate who never did. It's just my own flight of fancy, so I was delighted to read, during my research, that he had, indeed, been considered. I can't help thinking he would have been perfect and when I asked every player I spoke to if they knew of anybody else who was considered for the film but didn't take part, I always imagined they might say Best. It goes without saying that he had the immense skill and talent, plus the film star good looks and charisma to be up there on the poster, let alone in the film, and, by 1980, his playing circumstances were fluid, to say the least. He also had a profile in America, having already played for Los Angeles Aztecs, where Rod Stewart used to pop in and train with him, and Fort Lauderdale Strikers. He also returned to America in 1980 to sign for San Jose Earthquakes, who were then owned by Milan Mandaric, the future head honcho of Portsmouth. It was a less than happy spell in San Jose, although it was there that he scored that lovely goal where he dribbled through a maze of defenders – a goal that doesn't look unlike Pelé's famous chalkboard game plan in *Escape to Victory*. Of course, there was always a downside with George and I suppose it's possible that, given his drink addiction issues and reputation for being unreliable, he may not have been considered worth the risk. Filming days in the movies cost a lot of money and you want as few of them to go awry as possible. We do also need to consider the fact that he once punched Michael Caine in a nightclub and one has to wonder if that had anything to do with him not being recruited.

Best's Fulham team-mate and general shadow, Rodney Marsh, tells the story, in his autobiography, of an evening in London nightspot Tramp with George and his then wife, Angie, and Michael and his wife, Shakira (not the 'Hips Don't Lie' one). According to Marsh, Caine was chewing Best's ear off about football and George was tiring of it. 'Then Caine leant across the table and, with messy fingers, took some of Angela's chips from her plate. "Don't do that again, Michael, or I'll slap you," George said, but Caine took some more, so George got up, whacked him on the chin and knocked Caine off his chair.' Chips are lovely but, given this fresh information, maybe Best's absence from the film isn't so mysterious.

Another tantalising prospect came up when I interviewed Werner Roth, who plays Baumann, the German captain. His initial discussions about being in the film were not necessarily centred on him playing that part and he told me that: 'When John [Huston] first mentioned that he had difficulty casting Baumann, I did have the suggestion that maybe they should try and get Franz involved.' There was a moment when he and I were speaking when I briefly thought 'Franz who?' And then I realised that, in one of the coolest conversations I've ever had, Werner had just dropped Franz Beckenbauer's name into the conversation by first-naming him. Roth was recently retired as captain of the New York Cosmos, where Beckenbauer was a team-mate, and if Franz Beckenbauer is in your team and you're still the captain, you must be doing all right. Roth doesn't know if any contact was made with Franz; firstly, because he suspects that Huston, with his limited football knowledge, never 'understood what casting Franz could mean for the movie' but also because 'by that time John was so fixated on me being Baumann'. Ultimately, that was a good choice, as Roth is excellent as the German skipper, but he does also recognise that Beckenbauer might have been reluctant to take the part anyway, given the circumstances. 'It might not be something he would want to do, putting on a shirt with a swastika on it,' Roth told me. He then paused and chuckled to make sure I knew he was joking before finishing: 'But I had no qualms about it!'

As we know, a lot of the players involved in the film were recruited from Ipswich Town. However, it seems that there was a second opportunity for a team to get involved as a group. The Scotland squad were on a mini-tour of Eastern Europe in May 1980, narrowly losing games against Poland and Hungary, and it seems that an invitation was extended to the squad, suggesting that if they wanted to stick around and help on the film, they were welcome to do so. Aberdeen defender Alex McLeish explained to local newspaper the *Press and Journal* in 2021 that: 'Jock Stein said that any of us who wanted could stay on after the tour game, as the film-makers were looking for extras for the football scenes.' It's interesting that, at this stage, it was still just considered as extras work. There was no mention of speaking parts literally until the players who took the job arrived and were handed dialogue to learn. McLeish declined the offer because he wanted to get home but he does have slight regrets, saying: 'Whenever I see that film nowadays, I wonder whether it could have been enhanced by the appearance of a certain red-headed Scotsman.' Oddly, McLeish did eventually make his silver screen debut in 2018 when he appeared in the background of a hotel scene in the wonderful *Stan and Ollie*, which was directed by Aberdeen fan Jon S. Baird.

One man who had two opportunities to appear in the film, being both a part of the Ipswich squad that was initially approached and the Scotland team that was also asked, was Alan Brazil. In a 2013 interview, Brazil said that he is often asked, 'Why weren't you in the film, *Escape to Victory*?' and he appears to have mixed feelings about it. He describes it as 'a real corny movie. But having said that, every Christmas when it comes on, I think "I wish I'd stayed."' He explains that the game against Poland had been his Scotland debut and that he had already been away for a few weeks, so getting home appealed to him a bit more than staying. 'Hungary, in those days, was not like it is now. It was still the Eastern bloc and it wasn't a nice place and I had just had enough, to be honest.' In a more recent interview, he explained that he visited his Ipswich team-mates at the Hilton in Budapest after the Hungary v Scotland game 'and there were loads of the boys over there and they tried to get me to stay'. But, due to a mixture of wishing to get home and not wanting to get his admittedly magnificent hair cut for a role in the film, he couldn't be persuaded to stay.

When I spoke to Mike Summerbee, he was slightly sceptical about those who claim that they were asked but turned it down, telling me: 'If you're invited to make a film, a real film, with John Huston directing it, you don't say "no", do you? Simple as that.' Which leaves us with the lovely brave boys who did say 'yes' to taking on a real adventure and having the summer of their lives making this film that we love. Those fellows you see in the famous picture on the front of this book and a few more besides.

PELÉ (Luis Fernandez)

The first player identified, approached and signed up to appear in the film was, as we know, the living legend, Pelé. In terms of profile and status in the late 70s when the film was coming together, there was no bigger fish for Freddie Fields and his partners to land. Pelé was, at that point, inarguably the greatest to have played the game. Other contenders may have come along since – and that's for you to debate elsewhere – but I would put my foot down and insist that neither Diego Maradona nor Lionel Messi would be as much fun in this film or one like it; Leo's a bit quiet and anything could have happened with Diego.

Pelé had, of course, exploded on to the scene as a 17-year-old prodigy at the 1958 World Cup as Brazil swept to victory for the first time. They then retained the title in 1962, before Pelé was brutally kicked out of the 1966 World Cup with treatment from defenders that was not so different to that which his character endures in the film. Then, in 1970, he bounced back as a part of that beautiful Brazilian team which captured everyone's imagination due to a combination of the television coverage bursting into vibrant colour for the first time and some of the best football the world had ever seen. All the while, he was scoring a record-breaking number of goals for his club side, Santos, even if you don't believe quite all of them should count. He then spent three years at the end of his career playing in that star-studded New York Cosmos side alongside Werner Roth, Franz Beckenbauer and his Brazilian team-mate, Carlos Alberto, before finishing with that spectacular televised friendly against Santos, with Pelé playing a half for each team. In 1980, when *Escape to Victory* went into production, it's safe to say that Pelé was not only the most famous footballer in the world but also, perhaps alongside Muhammad Ali, he was the most recognisable sportsman on the planet. The movie production notes were keen to point out that he had recently been named 'athlete of the century' in a poll of international sportswriters and, as I say, you can't argue too much with that. Unless you're Muhammad Ali.

A *Times* article about *Victory*, while it was in production, claimed that 'Pelé plays an interned Portuguese seaman called Macuado' but that he changed the name to Fernandez one day during shooting, because he 'did not care for Macuado as a name'. This, however, is a curious claim. I haven't been able to find any evidence of Pelé changing the name or a character of that name ever being in a script and certainly the character was never Portuguese. As any fool knows, Pelé is Luis Fernandez, from Trinidad, where he learned football skills playing with oranges.

The great Brazilian is officially credited with co-ordinating the football scenes for the film and although, as we'll find out later, things were a bit more complicated than that, it's easy to see why the superstar got to score the most memorable goal on screen. However, you could argue that, with his simplistic team talk of receiving the ball and saying 'I do this … this … this … this … this … this … this …goal' (and yes, that is the right number of 'this'), he also provides the most memorable non-match moment of the film. The man has charisma.

He obviously caught something of an acting bug on *Victory* because, aside from his appearance in the aforementioned orphanage drama *A Minor Miracle* alongside John Huston ('really awful' – anonymous Rotten Tomatoes reviewer), he also appeared in *Hotshot* in 1987. In that one, Pelé plays former greatest player in the world, Santos, who is living as a recluse until he is tracked down by Jim Youngs, who played chicken with those tractors against Kevin Bacon in *Footloose*, and asked if he will train him. They develop a similar master and apprentice relationship to the one between Sean Connery and Christopher Lambert in *Highlander* but with more footballs than swords. It's fair to say that *Escape to Victory* represents the high point of Pelé's acting career, notwithstanding his cameo in *Mike Bassett: England Manager*.

BOBBY MOORE (Terry Brady)

If Pelé is the best player to appear in the film, Bobby Moore is, without doubt, the coolest. Either subliminally or overtly, Moore is almost certainly the reason that Michael Caine's Colby character is a West Ham player and, for that, I am personally grateful. The script for the film was written when England's World Cup win was still fresh in the mind, with Moore front and centre of all that it entailed. He was also putting West Ham on the international map in the 60s, when they won the FA Cup for the first time and followed it up with the European Cup Winners' Cup. It's easy to see Colby's backstory as being heavily influenced by all of that.

The smartest dresser in football was the next player to sign on for the film after Pelé, which is fitting, as the two men are inextricably linked in the minds of football fans because of that iconic photograph of the two of them swapping shirts and embracing after the England v Brazil duel in the sun in Guadalajara at the 1970 World Cup. There's so much love and respect in that one shot that it was a joy to see them together again when the film rolled around. As chirpy Terry Brady, Moore gets to score the Allies' first goal in the match and it's his pinpoint cross which puts Pelé's overhead kick virtually on a plate for him.

Bobby Moore will forever be associated with West Ham as their greatest ever player, playing almost 650 times over 16 years there. When he moved on, in 1974, he went first across London to Fulham and then on to an inevitable dalliance with the North American Soccer League, with San Antonio Thunder and Seattle Sounders. You see, everyone was at it. By the time filming for *Victory* came around, Moore was 39 and dipping a toe into management at non-league Oxford City, with former Hammers teammate and future *I'm a Celebrity ... Get Me Out of Here!* winner Harry Redknapp as his assistant. The Oxford City chairman, Tony Rosser, certainly had one eye on the publicity that such a flashy appointment garnered for his club and he was only too happy to allow Bobby to head off and make a Hollywood film over the summer of 1980, very formally telling the press that: 'Bobby has been given approval by our board to be free for this period.' Unfortunately, Moore's stint in the city of dreaming spires was more of a nightmare. City were relegated and Moore had left the club before the film came out. One Oxford City fan felt that the failure was inevitable given that 'it was a bit like putting someone who's run a five-star restaurant in charge of a chip van in a lay-by'.

Moore did give management another go with Southend United but, once he retired as a player, he never really found the place in the game that his status as one of England's greatest warranted. He enjoyed himself in his role as a radio co-commentator, memorably alongside Jonathan Pearce at Capital Gold, right up until his tragic death from bowel cancer in 1993 but it's fair to say that neither West Ham nor England utilised his legacy as much as they should have done while he was alive, even if it is his statue that greets you upon arrival at Wembley Stadium these days.

Escape to Victory wasn't Bobby's only foray into the movies, for he had already appeared as himself in *The Alf Garnett Saga* a few years earlier, even if, with his trademark self-deprecation, he told a journalist that: 'I don't think one could say I've done any proper acting.' He does himself a disservice. Moore is perfectly fine in that film, in which comedy bigot Garnett goes to see West Ham take on Manchester United with his son-in-law, who isn't Tony Booth from the *Till Death Us Do Part* TV version. They spy Alf's daughter, who isn't Una Stubbs from the TV version either, mixing with some celebrities in the poshest seats Upton Park had to offer and are inevitably racist towards lovely Kenny Lynch, who she is there with. In the bar after the game, Garnett tries to hassle some of the players and celebrities while they take a drink in the bar and Bobby does a lovely double take as Alf approaches and says: 'Yul Brynner's old man, innit?' You know, because of the bald head. Garnett asks him about the infamous Bogota bracelet incident, Bobby whispers 'piss off' in his ear and then disappears from cinema until he crops up in the PoW camp at Gensdorf. It's fine work.

MIKE SUMMERBEE (Sid Harmer)

When Bobby Moore was playing down his acting credentials to journalist Paul Donovan, he also told him that the *Victory* production was looking for 'one or two other English players', which clearly set him to thinking about which of his mates he wouldn't mind spending a summer in Hungary with. His thoughts inevitably turned to close friend and Manchester City legend Mike Summerbee.

The pair had already been mates for a long time and were even business partners for a while, with Summerbee saying that they enjoyed a lot of the same things in life and 'were both very smart and tidy men'. Moore's fastidiousness when it came to clothes and his appearance is legendary (think of him wiping the mud off his hands before shaking the Queen's gloved hand in 1966), so we can only imagine how tidy the room that the two men shared on England duty might have been. Summerbee has so many good things to say about Moore and, in his autobiography, recalls a lovely-sounding road trip after an England game in 1968. The two of them journeyed down through Italy from Florence to Rome, Summerbee holding a portable record player on his lap all the while: 'I spent four hours holding this thing and listening to Frank Sinatra while Bobby was in seventh heaven driving in the sunshine.' I would not have minded being in the back seat for that trip, I can tell you. I would have happily bought the snacks and even taken a turn holding the record player. Summerbee describes Moore as 'a proper fella' and the consensus tends to agree with him on that matter.

It comes as no surprise then that when the phone rang and Summerbee was asked if he wanted to be a film star, it was Moore making the call. They arranged a meeting at Langan's in London – Michael Caine's restaurant. Summerbee didn't need his arm twisting too much to see that the film might be fun to do and the money didn't hurt either, being 'far more than I'd ever earned as a footballer'. So, that's an emphatic 'yes' then.

Whatever Mike Summerbee did earn as a footballer, Manchester City fans will tell you it should have been more. The day I spoke to Mike was the morning after a statue of him was unveiled outside the Etihad Stadium. Notwithstanding their more recent successes, the club still look back on the 60s and 70s for some of their true legends and, just as Manchester United have their 'Holy Trinity' of George Best, Denis Law and Bobby Charlton, Manchester City have Colin Bell, Franny Lee and Mike Summerbee. Mike had been an integral part of the City team that won every major domestic trophy and the European Cup Winners' Cup and, at the time of writing, he still works with the club as an ambassador.

THE PLAYERS

By 1980, however, his playing days at City were behind him and he had been retired for almost a year following a spell as player-manager of Stockport County. At that point, he was concentrating on his commercial ventures, one of which was a shirt-making company, and he didn't switch off his business head once he became a film star. He managed to sell a lot of shirts to Michael Caine after working with him ('bespoke shirts, made to measure') and continued to supply him for many years afterwards.

I asked every player I spoke with if they had ever done any acting before and Mike was the only one who said he had, citing 'a couple of pantomimes for the football club at Christmastime but you couldn't count that ... a bit of fun' – but it was the closest any of them had got. Despite this inexperience, Summerbee, along with Russell Osman, has to do more heavy lifting on the acting side of things than any other player in the film and he's actually pretty good at it.

His reaction when he waits for Hatch to face the final penalty in the game has got everything it needs to have, as hope and defiance fight for space on his sweat-dripping brow. It's hard to imagine a trained actor being much more invested than that.

In a 1967 *Sunday Mirror* article, Summerbee was asked what he wanted from his life when he was finished in football. He listed a comfortable mortgage-free house, a lovely wife and kids and a business 'to keep the wolf from the door' – and he got every wish. It's pretty cool that he could also have added starring in a Hollywood film with Michael Caine and Sylvester Stallone to that wishlist if he had had the foresight.

KAZIMIERZ DEYNA (Paul Wolchek)

Manchester City fans had further interest in the film in the shape of Polish midfielder Kazimierz Deyna. He didn't play with Summerbee at City, arriving a little later, in 1978, as one of a clutch of impossibly exotic-seeming footballers from around the world who appeared in English football in the wake of the World Cup. This was an intake that also saw Alberto Tarantini of Argentina sign for Birmingham City, Ivan Golac of Yugoslavia join Southampton and, of course, Ossie Ardiles of Argentina join Tottenham alongside his compatriot, Ricardo Villa, as English football tried to go global.

Deyna was, perhaps, past his best by the time he arrived in England, having spent the bulk of his career at home with Legia Warsaw. Being an Eastern bloc country made it difficult for Deyna to leave Legia before he did, despite being courted by some of Europe's biggest clubs, including Real Madrid. When City did sign him, they had to first buy him out of the Polish army, in which he held the rank of captain, before they could discuss a transfer fee with his club. And there are even suggestions that the transfer fee itself involved a lot more electrical appliances than cold hard cash. The two clubs also played a testimonial for him in 1979 as part of the deal, with Deyna playing for both sides and scoring a sensational goal for each team – goals which are well worth looking up online. His time at Maine Road was also blighted by injuries but he showed enough flashes of brilliance to endear himself to the crowd and become something of a cult hero. What's more, he was a current player at City when he went off to Hungary to make the film.

Deyna had found international recognition as a star of that brilliant Poland team of the 1970s, which he captained for a long time. They won gold at the Munich Olympics, then finished third at the 1974 World Cup back in West Germany. That year, Deyna was beaten only by Johan Cruyff and Franz Beckenbauer in the Ballon d'Or vote – good company to be in. In 1973, he captained Poland in that infamous game at Wembley when Brian Clough branded the Polish goalkeeper Jan Tomaszewski 'a clown' and the whole country thought England would roll over their opponents on the march to the World Cup. It turned out that the team that defied England that night with a crucial 1-1 draw and sounded the death knell for Sir Alf Ramsey's career as England manager were really rather good, after all.

Deyna has a unique position in the film, insofar as he is the only one of the Eastern European players that arrive late, looking emaciated and beaten and calling Colby's wisdom into question, to play any football. The others are extras who only sit on the bench but Deyna's Paul Wolchek plays, scores and gets an assist. Clearly, I love the film very much but it seems like something of a failing that more isn't made of this plot point. More time could be spent on the fact that one of these guys, whose existence is initially denied by the Nazi regime, not only gets fit enough to play, having arrived at the camp malnourished and beaten, but scores one of the goals in their inspired comeback. As a whole, I'm full of praise for how the laissez-faire attitude to just letting the action flow and filming it makes the football look but it feels like once Deyna's goal had gone in and there was a chance of it being used in the final film, something else might have been filmed to draw more attention to the significance of it. It's an opportunity missed.

Søren Lindsted, who plays Erik Borge in the film, speaks well of Deyna, saying: 'It was great to meet him and play with him. I knew him from the Polish team at that time. A really good team.' He also says that he stood out in the piggy-in-the-middle games that would inevitably break out between takes on the set among a very talented bunch of footballers, telling me: 'We had a lot of playing with two in the middle and four or five on the outside and he was technically so strong. I'd never seen anything like that.'

Sadly, Kaziu Deyna's real-life story does not end well. After City, he moved to San Diego to play for the Sockers in both outdoor and indoor football for much of the 80s and it was there that he was killed in a car crash in 1989. In 1994, Deyna was voted as the greatest Polish football player of all time and even though, 30 years on, Robert Lewandowski might have a say in the matter, he would still be considered to be right up there. His statue outside Legia's stadium in Warsaw is also one of the very best football statues there is. They can often go wrong – face facts, Harry Kane.

OSVALDO ARDILES (Carlos Rey)
Osvaldo Ardiles was probably the highest-profile and most successful of that foreign influx that arrived in the English First Division in 1978. Like Deyna, he had been a star at the World Cup but, unlike Deyna, he had won it, with Argentina, in a memorable flurry of ticker tape on

home turf. He and Ricardo Villa arrived together at Spurs and they very quickly became the affectionately anglicised Ossie and Ricky. Both went on to be future inductees of the Tottenham Hotspur Hall of Fame but it was Ossie who stayed for ten years.

The call to Ossie about *Escape to Victory* came from 'a kind of agent that contacted me and he was coming from Bobby Robson'. Ossie was hazy on a name but I suspect this was Peter Mason, doing his job and trying to gather international stars without having to do a whole lot of international travel. 'He asked me if I wanted to be involved,' Ossie told me. 'He told me the people that were already involved, like Pelé and Bobby Moore, and I said "yes, lovely". I was very excited, because it was something completely and utterly different, being in a film with some of these stars. He told me we'd be filming in Hungary, in Budapest, and I said "yes, brilliant".' Ossie's enthusiasm is infectious. The man won the World Cup and is very proud of it but speaks with equal enthusiasm about being part of the film. He told me that he already knew Mike Summerbee ('I had seen him at parties'), Bobby Moore, 'most of the Ipswich boys and Deyna', so he was quite prepared to spend the summer with them when he was given the opportunity.

The production notes released to the press refer to Ossie as the 'flashy, exciting young player who led Argentina to its 1978 World Cup victory', which seems reason enough to approach him, but Ossie plays it down and gives his own reason for being the only Spurs player approached to take part: 'Maybe they asked me because I'm small and don't look so healthy.'

Joking aside, Ardiles summed up the casting process for me: 'The original idea was Pelé and Bobby Moore, basically, so they started to recruit people. They got the Ipswich guys through Bobby Robson, Mike Summerbee was a close friend of Bobby Moore and then they needed some international players from other nations.'

The issue with this policy is that, while it made sense to have players (and, therefore, soldiers) from Britain, Poland, Belgium, the Netherlands, Norway and Denmark, Argentina didn't actually declare war against Germany until 27 March 1945 – thanks for coming, guys. It is for this reason that Carlos Rey is, in fact, in the French Foreign Legion, which explains the uniform he appears in, and is Venezuelan. 'They told me my name was Carlos Rey and that I was from Venezuela. I questioned it, because Venezuela doesn't really play football, so how can my character be so good? But that's the way it was.' That's one in the eye for Salomón Rondón.

Fortunately, Ossie isn't called upon to demonstrate his Venezuelan accent skills, because, apart from muttering a "hello" and murmuring in agreement, he doesn't have any lines – which he's perfectly happy with. 'Our contract was not because we could act. It was simply to play football.' When has Ossie Ardiles ever let that stop him, though? I'm pretty sure that his Spurs contract would have only mentioned playing and not appearing on *Top of the Pops* with Chas & Dave but that didn't stop him singing and dancing next to Chas's piano and delivering his famous 'In the cup for Tottingham!' line, now, did it?

At least Ossie's Carlos Rey gets to shine brightly when it comes to the match. He scores a good goal and, of course, gets his own hero moment with a trademark rainbow flick, which, as I took great delight in telling him, was known as 'an Ossie Ardiles' round our way, on the rare occasion that anyone could do one in their school shoes – every bit as much as an overhead kick was called 'a Pelé'. 'I didn't have to do that, not at all,' he told me. 'It was just something I did before games, because it was nice. When they saw me doing that, they were filming and then I did it three or four more times, because it wasn't difficult at all and they chose the one that they liked the most.' Superb 'what? this old thing?' energy there from a very nice man who appears to have had a spiffing time making the film.

CO PRINS (Pieter van Beck)

Co Prins was an interesting choice among Dutch players who might have taken part in the film. Dutch football was the sexiest possible football in the 1970s and you must think that the Johans – Cruyff and Neeskens – or Johnny Rep might have been nearer to the top of any wish list the producers might have had than the avuncular vibe of Prins. He may have pre-dated the fashionable era for the Netherlands and missed out on the sideburns and love beads but he was, by all accounts, still a very good player, who spent the most and best years of a distinguished career as an attacking midfielder at Ajax and MVV Maastricht. He was also something of a pioneer as a foreign player in West Germany, with Kaiserslautern in the early 60s, and had spells in the USA with two short-lived teams, the Pittsburgh Phantoms (interesting badge, check it out) and the New York Generals in experimental leagues before the North American Soccer League came along and helped football take a bit more of a root in the country. He retired in 1974, back in his native country with Helmond Sport. Tragically, Prins died only a few years after filming *Victory*, suffering a heart attack during an exhibition match in Antwerp in 1987.

Prins was 42 at the time of filming and is the oldest of the Allied players, apart from Michael Caine's Colby, of course, but Caine had Kevin Beattie as his body double. The white hair and what the tabloid newspapers might call a 'dadbod' do serve a good purpose in the film, though; he bridges the age gap between Caine and the rest of his younger team. Co's age and fitness were slight issues when it came to filming the match and Ossie Ardiles intimated that his character, Pieter van Beck, 'got injured because he couldn't really move too much'. Pieter is the first of the Allied players to take a bit of a pasting and he spends the rest of the game on a stretcher or laid out in the dressing room. Which makes me wonder if anybody thought to go and fetch him when they were all escaping out of the gates at the end of the game. It might have been nice to see a post-credits sequence in which we cut back to the dressing room and Pieter is still laying there alone, wondering how he's going to get out if the French find him first or explain the big hole in the bath if he is discovered by the Germans.

PAUL VAN HIMST (Michel Fileu)

For their Belgian player, the producers went right to the top of the tree. If you close your eyes and try to think of one Belgian football club, I reckon a good amount of you will say Anderlecht – not out loud, I hope, if you're reading this in public, as it might look a bit odd. And if you asked

Anderlecht fans to name just one player to ever pull on the shirt for them, a vast majority would say Paul van Himst.

When I spoke to Paul, he casually told me that he got involved 'with my Dutch friend, Co Prins', as if he just tagged along as his wingman, but make no mistake, if the film needed a Belgian player, then Van Himst was the one to have. Voted in 2000 as Belgium's player of the century, he played his entire career in his home country, winning eight league titles and four cups with Anderlecht, as well as four Belgian footballer of the year awards. He led the line for Belgium from his debut at 17, right through qualifying for the 1970 World Cup and then finishing third at the 1972 European Championship. Even allowing for the more recent golden generation of wonderful players like Kevin De Bruyne and Eden Hazard, Paul van Himst would still rank high when considering Belgian greats – even if Romelu Lukaku did eventually smash his international goalscoring record. When Van Himst retired, his testimonial match attracted an amazing array of all-stars, including Johan Cruyff, Eusébio, Cloughie's 'clown', Jan Tomaszewski, plus our very own Pelé and Bobby Moore, which hints at the high esteem in which he was held.

His appearance in *Escape to Victory* didn't exactly give him a taste for Hollywood but he did also make a cameo appearance in 1994 Belgian knockabout comedy *Max*. It's fair to say, however, that his post-playing career was mostly taken up with the more conventional path as a coach. He became a manager, inevitably with Anderlecht, and won the UEFA Cup in 1983 before losing the following year's final on penalties to a Tottenham team which had Ossie

Ardiles coming off the bench. As manager of the Belgian national side, Van Himst then took his side to the last 16 of the 1994 World Cup.

A prolific goalscorer throughout his career, Paul van Himst had two nicknames and though both come from love, it's fair to say that one is rather more impactful than the other. The first was 'Polle Gazon', which translates in a mixture of Brussels dialect and Dutch to 'Paul Lawn', apparently because he spent so much time laying on the grass after heavy tackles – which is a compliment of sorts if you really look for it. *L'Equipe*, with more of a flair for these things, called him 'The White Pelé', which is obviously much more complimentary but it does leave me wondering if it ever came up in conversation on set between him and the real Pelé.

HALLVAR THORESEN (Gunnar Nilsson)

Hallvar Thoresen has a very special place in English football folklore. It may be one that the hardcore fans won't enjoy but I can't help thinking that it is one that those with a sense of fun, those with a sense of perspective or Scotland fans will enjoy. We have all seen that grainy, early 80s footage of Norway beating England in Oslo, haven't we? You know, the one when Norwegian commentator Bjørge Lillelien absolutely lost his mind with joy and started telling Lord Nelson, Lord Beaverbrook, Sir Winston Churchill, Maggie Thatcher and anyone else who was listening: 'Your boys took one hell of a beating!' Well, guess who was Norway captain that night and scored the winner – you guessed it, Hallvar Thoresen. Imagine if it wasn't him after I gave it all that build-up.

In scenes that we can't imagine taking place now in an age of mobile phones and Citizen Media, England defender Russell Osman, who played at the heart of England's defence that night, went out on the town with the Norway captain after the game. The match took place very soon after *Escape to Victory* was released in September 1981 and the pair were obviously firm friends from the experience. Osman told me: 'We had a good night out after that, even though we lost. He was treated like royalty that night.' And Thoresen confirmed it, saying: 'The whole of Oslo was celebrating, of course. So, I took him with me. After a couple of beers and all the celebrations, he thought that he had won the match. It was a nice time.' Good luck to them, I say. The bonds from the movie they made together were clearly strong.

Hallvar told me a familiar story of how he got involved in the film, saying: 'Peter Mason contacted me when I was at FC Twente and asked this strange question if I wanted to join the production for this movie.' And, of course, he didn't hesitate to say 'yes', telling me: 'It sounded very funny and interesting, of course, to get that experience.' He reinforced the idea that the plan was always to get players who were high profile in a number of countries to drive up interest in different territories, saying: 'I was captain of the Norwegian national team and played for a top team in Holland.' More than one, as it turns out. Although Thoresen was with FC Twente at the time of filming, he moved to PSV Eindhoven the following summer, in 1981, winning three league titles and playing alongside a young Ruud Gullit. The former attacking midfielder is still involved with PSV, for whom he is head of recruitment in Scandinavia, which sounds like a lovely job.

Hallvar says that he only knew his Allied team-mates by reputation when filming began. 'I had never met them. But, of course, the Ipswich players were well known at that time, because they were really good in Europe. Also, the legends like Mike Summerbee, Bobby Moore, etc.' Luckily, in case he was shy, Hallvar was able to take a friend along with him.

SØREN LINDSTED (Erik Borge)

Denmark's Søren Lindsted was also playing for FC Twente at the time Peter Mason made his approach to Hallvar Thoresen and, as the Norwegian told me, Lindsted got the nod, too. 'We could travel together and do this together. That was also good for us. It was in a time where we had a vacation from professional football.'

The very affable Lindsted was yet another player kind enough to speak to me and another who was very effusive about the time the players had making the film. It's all very heart-warming to hear first-hand how excited everyone was to get involved and how much they enjoyed the experience. Søren is perhaps not the biggest name to take part in the film and was only too happy to entertain the idea that he, perhaps, wasn't first choice among his countrymen. 'I've heard that other players from Denmark were asked first. I wasn't playing for my national team then but Hallvar was and they asked him and, a week later, I was asked. I think they asked some of the other players on the Danish national team. I don't know which ones but it's what I heard.' This tallies with the Allan Simonsen rumour but, whoever else was asked, I put it to Søren that he must be glad they said 'no'. 'Yes, it was a nice holiday.'

Lindsted was in no way overawed in the company he kept on the film set. He says that Kazimierz Deyna was a bit of a hero of his and he was, of course, delighted to be rubbing shoulders with Pelé. 'He was absolutely fantastic and really nice and welcoming.' Nor was he overawed when it came to filming the match and he scored several goals on the day, even if they didn't make the final cut of the film. 'But then I at least got an assist in the match,' he explained in a 2022 interview with the Danish Coaches Union. He's quite right. It's his cross from the left that Bobby Moore's Terry Brady steers home with a cushioned volley on the stroke of half-time.

Lindsted scored plenty of goals of his own in a playing career as a forward, a career that took him from the Netherlands to Belgium, before he rounded things off back in Denmark, where, by the way, the film was called *Fangelejrens Helte*. That translates as 'Prison Camp Heroes' and who among us could argue with that?

RUSSELL OSMAN (Doug Clure)

I will be forever grateful to Russell Osman for being the first player to speak to me for this book. I drove up to Suffolk not long after I began my research and we had a very pleasant chat. I've worked in television for a long time, been around a lot of famous people and I like to think that, for the most part, I've taken it in my stride but I must confess I have a tendency to go a bit giddy around footballers. Thankfully, I managed to stay composed that day. At the time, I was still trying to contact some of his former Ipswich team-mates and I can't help thinking that some of that same infectious 'let's go back, we can win this' enthusiasm from the tunnel under the bath in the film meant that he was able to reassure one or two of them that I was on the level and might be okay to speak to about this book.

Osman had arrived at Ipswich as a teenager in the mid-70s as part of their drive to find the best young talent from all over the country. Buses full of wide-eyed kids with boots and a dream would be driven down for trials from the north-east and elsewhere, including, in later years, a young Paul Gascoigne. Once Bobby Robson's brother had seen Russell play for Repton Casuals in Burton-on-Trent, Osman was a part of that initiative – and the club were certainly keen on him. 'My youth coach, Charlie Woods, used to do a 200-mile round trip to pick me up for youth games,' he told me.

Once there, he made rapid progress through the youth teams into the reserves, 'which really opened your eyes as a 16- or 17-year-old playing against seasoned professionals on a Saturday afternoon'. The opposition would often include older pros making their way back from injury and 'trying to make an impression. It was the best learning experience ever, because you had to grow up fast.' He recalled a particularly bruising encounter against Bill Garner of Chelsea, which he recalled with a faraway look in his eye that suggested that he might still be able to feel it on cold mornings. He said: 'I remember he battered me for 90 minutes and you realise you've got to give as good as you get.' That fearlessness which clashes with the likes of Bill Garner instilled in him would stand him in good stead for the future. By the time he started making first-team appearances at Portman Road, as Allan Hunter and Kevin Beattie picked up more injuries, he was ready for anything. Not least acting alongside Michael Caine.

'First time we heard anything was when Bobby Robson just called a meeting one day in the changing room,' he told me. 'He said he'd been approached by a company who were making a film about a prisoner of war camp and they needed some half-decent footballers for the background football scenes.

'That was basically how he sold it to us and he said if any of you aren't doing anything in the summer and want to go, I will give you permission to go and play.'

Quite what motivated Bobby Robson to go all-out to help the production is up for question. One wonders if there might have been a drink in it for him or, to put it more plainly, if he was paid for his services. And if so, good luck to him; he earned every penny. Russell put his hand up and he was joined in Budapest by John Wark, Kevin O'Callaghan, Paul Cooper, Kevin Beattie, Laurie Sivell and Robin Turner, who all went there in a variety of capacities and roles. So, what on earth would they have done without Bobby and his permissive attitude to show business?

Not everybody went, however. Alan Brazil has already been discussed, Terry Butcher had just got engaged, while Mick Mills and Paul Mariner had the valid excuse of being in Italy with England for the Euros (although Mariner might have been reluctant to trim his flowing locks even if he hadn't been on international duty). But for Russell, the adventure was on. 'Five weeks we went out there for. I wasn't doing anything else that summer. I hadn't planned a holiday, I was single, so I went.'

I think we can all agree that he made the right choice.

JOHN WARK (Arthur Hayes)

John Wark remembers the same meeting when the issue of the film was raised but remembers 'a chap in the movie business who knew Bobby Robson' being in there alongside him. I have read some articles that claim this was Freddie Fields but I think it's far more likely to have been Peter Mason. It was Mason who contacted Ardiles and Thoresen– player recruitment was within his purview and it seems to have been him who had the connection to Bobby Robson.

Given Mason's trials and tribulations in populating the squads on screen, it seems that he struck gold with Ipswich. Not only did he pick up a great bunch of lads, all keen as mustard to give this film lark a go, he was also able to chalk off a few nationalities in one fell swoop. Such was the make-up of a lot of Division One squads at the time that Wales, Northern Ireland, England, Scotland and the Republic of Ireland were frequently all represented within their ranks and, with Russell Osman, John Wark and Kevin O'Callaghan signing on for the film, Peter Mason was able to chalk off the latter three in one visit. He might also have harboured hopes of boosting the Dutch contingent while he was there, because Ipswich's own exotic signings around this time were the Dutch duo Frans Thijssen and Arnold Mühren. Thijssen would have been unavailable, as he was off to the Euros with the Dutch squad, but Mühren wasn't a part of that. Perhaps he simply didn't fancy the film or maybe, with Co Prins already on board, Mason didn't feel the need to push it. 'Anyone who said "yes" would have had a chance of going out,' says John Wark, so it's possible he just had other things on that summer. He might have been useful supplying crosses for Pelé's overhead kick, though – it was his over-hit cross that got him an assist with an arguably even better goal by Marco van Basten in the European Championship Final eight years later.

John Wark had no hesitation when he was asked to join the cast in Budapest, telling me: 'When I was asked, I was straight in, because it's the sort of thing you dream about.' His attitude of 'this sounds good, I'll have a go' sounds like words to live by.

Wark, like Osman, had joined Ipswich at youth level and worked his way up to the first team, where he scored goal after goal, despite playing in almost every position on the pitch at one time or another. It was a boom time for Ipswich under Bobby Robson's stewardship, during which they won the FA Cup in 1978 and the UEFA Cup in 1981, with Wark winning the Footballer of the Year award as they did so. After leaving Ipswich, Wark joined Liverpool and won the league twice. He briefly played for Middlesbrough but twice he returned to Portman Road. Wark was even Ipswich's representative in the famous 'Alive and Kicking' Sky advert to launch the brave new world of the Premier League in 1992.

It's interesting that the film was a shared experience for all these Ipswich lads, because it must have made something so out of the ordinary feel ordinary. Understandably, however, once out of that bubble, it becomes an oddity once again. As John remembers: 'When I moved to Liverpool, people took the mickey and wanted to know the stories.' Now, personally, I don't think you can have it both ways, Bruce Grobbelaar and Alan Hansen (it was probably them, right?) – either you make fun of him for being in the film or you gather round, pull up a chair with a cup of tea and listen to John's stories about it. Not both.

KEVIN O'CALLAGHAN (Tony Lewis)

Everything was still a bit new to Kevin O'Callaghan in the summer of 1980. He was just 18 years old and had only signed for Ipswich from Millwall for £250,000 in January of that year. It stands to reason that the 'have a go' spirit was riding high in the tricky winger when the Ipswich squad were called into that now legendary meeting about the film. He says that they were told: 'There's a film being made and they need some players to do the football scenes. It will be a four-week shoot. Your girlfriend or your wife can come out for a holiday. So, he just said "Who wants to do it?" and we all put our hands up.'

I asked Kevin what he would have been doing that summer if he hadn't said 'yes'. 'I was just about to move into a new house, so I'd have been doing bits and pieces, pottering around, playing a bit of golf.' Do you fancy unpacking boxes or being in a film with Ming the Merciless? It sounds like one of the easier decisions he would have had to make.

After Millwall and Ipswich, O'Callaghan went on to play for Portsmouth, Millwall again and Southend – the man absolutely loved playing in blue. He also represented the Republic of Ireland, making his debut in 1981, a landmark sandwiched between shooting the film and its cinema release. And, of course, there was the Ipswich UEFA Cup win in that period, too. What a time to be alive.

Kevin said that he 'didn't have a clue' about what the film would involve and that the players were not told anything other than they were needed to play a bit of football and be filmed doing it – but, given the names involved, he didn't need asking twice. 'I grew up in a block of flats overlooking West Ham Football Club, so obviously Bobby Moore was a bit of a hero.' For the record, as a kid, I always wanted to live in those flats myself. I couldn't think of anywhere better to be.

So pleased was he to be mingling with his new co-stars – and, I hope, best friends – that he didn't even mind that he eventually got cast as a goalkeeper and had to do some real acting opposite Michael Caine. In fact, the two of them probably share the most heartbreaking, not to mention wince-inducing, scene in the film when Colby is forced to break young Tony's arm because of reasons. But don't rush me. We'll get to that.

Although no one is quite sure why Ipswich were chosen as the go-to club for the *Escape to Victory* producers, it seems that, as already discussed, a key factor was that Bobby Robson, a well-connected man, had a pre-existing relationship with Peter Mason. However, an overlooked element of their involvement is quite how good they were at the time. They had won the 1978 FA Cup and were a constant presence in Europe for a few seasons afterwards. They finished sixth in the First Division in 1978/79 and, at the time Peter Mason came calling, were in the process of improving on that by finishing third in 1979/80. So, if you were looking at a Division One table for where to go shopping for football stars, you didn't have to go far down the list to get to Ipswich. Liverpool and Nottingham Forest were both right up there around this time and some Liverpool stars would go on to have their own brushes with the small screen in years to come. Graeme Souness appeared in *Boys from the Blackstuff* and Kenny Dalglish and several others were in *Scully*, both written by Alan Bleasdale, so maybe Liverpool players might have done just as well if they had been asked. However, it just might be the case that Ipswich had the most approachable and amenable gaffer of the three clubs in question.

The Ipswich contingent was bolstered by four more players who went along to take part but didn't end up as part of the Allies' squad.

KEVIN BEATTIE (Michael Caine's body double)

Kevin Beattie was an England defender who all right-thinking people agree would, had it not been for the injuries he suffered, have won a lot more than the nine caps he accrued. Those injuries – which gave Russell Osman and John Wark their early chances at Ipswich – meant that, through no fault of his own, he never quite fulfilled his potential. However, in the summer of 1980, he was just as keen as the rest to go to Hungary, saying that 'I nearly fell off my bloody chair' when he was asked.

Although he more than played his part in many of the on-set stories, he can only be seen in the film if you look really hard for him in some of the longer shots during the match or in the odd melee or scramble for the ball in which you can see Colby but not his face.

Russell Osman told me he was glad that things worked out as they did. 'Kevin had a slight likeness to Michael Caine. You know it could have been Kevin playing alongside Bobby Moore and me playing left-back as Michael Caine, so I'm grateful for that.' You've got to wonder whether, had Roger Moore taken the part as Colby, those roles would, indeed, have been reversed.

PAUL COOPER (Sylvester Stallone's coach and body double)

We're going to pay closer attention a little later to all the goalkeepers that became involved in this film but Paul Cooper might just be the unluckiest among them. Cooper was a great goalkeeper who played well over 500 times for Ipswich at a time when it really felt that teams had one goalkeeper for a number of years and that was just the way it was. At Ipswich, it was always Paul Cooper, so he was another player that I was thrilled to speak to. His dual role on the film, however, involved coaching for Sylvester Stallone, as the actor looked to improve his ability between the posts, as well as being his double for some of the action, for which he was given a full Stallone mask to wear over his head. The trouble was that the first job was probably hard work and the second job was barely a job at all.

Like Beattie, Cooper says that he can be glimpsed in some of the long shots from the commentary box during the match action but those are few and far between. Stallone was keen to do as much of the action himself as he could, which is admirable, but it left Cooper – like Tom Cruise's stunt double – on the sidelines.

Cooper remains circumspect about it all, saying that 'Budapest was lovely' and that 'I was quite happy getting money for nothing. I've got some lovely memories from it.' He was more than happy to go along with the gang and says that team-mates of the Ipswich seven 'heard enough about us talking about it when we got back'.

These days, Paul has a golfing company and divides his time between Tenerife and the Algarve, so maybe he isn't that unlucky after all.

LAURIE SIVELL & ROBIN TURNER (German players)

The final two Ipswich players who took part in the film were Laurie Sivell and Robin Turner, both of whom ended up on the German team for the match – but nobody seems to have minded. Unfortunately, Turner eluded me for an interview, as nobody seemed to be in contact with him, but Russell Osman told me: 'I think Robin was quite happy to participate on the German side. We got five weeks' extra money.'

I did speak to Laurie Sivell, who was a goalkeeper for Ipswich for 15 years, partly as understudy to Paul Cooper, and he endearingly referred to 'Mr Robson', rather than 'Bobby', calling that initial meeting when 'some of us put our hands up and went'. Again, it's funny how repeated telling of the tales of this film to any number of interested people has taken some of the novelty out of it for these players. Don't get me wrong; each and every one of the players I spoke to is glad and grateful for the experience of making the film but the casual way in which they describe getting involved belies the fact that one week they might have been playing away at The Dell and then, practically the next week, they were standing next to *Alfie* and being directed by John Huston.

Sivell says that all they were told was 'that it was a football film and they were going to have a game in the film but that was about all we knew'. In fact, on arrival, Sivell was given the part of Schmidt, the German keeper.

Of course, Sivell and Turner couldn't take on the might of the Allies alone in defending the honour of the Fatherland, could they? They were joined on the team by eight Hungarian players, including midfielder Béla Kovács, Imre Boda, a striker who went on to be a top scorer in the Greek league, and József Gáspár. All three played for MTK at the time, so the stadium used in the film was their home ground. Kovács already had two caps for Hungary and the other two went on to earn some, too. Curiously, Gáspár, who went on to coach MTK in the 90s, was a goalkeeper but he must be playing outfield in the game because, of course, Laurie Sivell donned the red shirt as Schmidt in the German goal.

Also on the team was midfielder Ferenc Fülöp, another MTK player, who is the father of Marton Fülöp, who went on to be a goalkeeper for Sunderland and, in a bit of a full-circle moment, Ipswich Town.

Russell Osman says that filming the match was a joy. 'From the footballing side of things, there were absolutely no egos at all, which was amazing. Nobody was the big "I am". Even Werner Roth, who was captain of the German side and had to play against the best players, was absolutely fine with it all.' Ah yes, Werner Roth.

WERNER ROTH (Baumann, the German captain)

Although Max von Sydow's character, Von Steiner, is the most prominent German in the movie, he can in no way be seen as the villain of the piece. For that, we need to look no further than Baumann, skipper of the German team. He dives, he fouls, he cheats and, annoyingly for the Allies, he's very good. All of which makes him a worthy protagonist for Hatch when it all comes down to the penalty at the end of the game. He exudes menace throughout his time on screen and, ultimately, he gets his two-shot, going face-to-face with Stallone in close-up, putting him in good company in that regard with the likes of Carl Weathers, Mr T and Dolph Lundgren in the *Rocky* movies.

Just as Bobby Moore got Mike Summerbee involved in the project, so Pelé secured the involvement of his friend and New York Cosmos team-mate, Werner. Having been born in the former Yugoslavia, Roth was a naturalised American citizen and went on to captain both the Cosmos and the US national team. The production notes for the film describe him as 'America's most famous soccer player'.

He was another player who was good enough to speak to me and he explained how he became involved. 'I heard about it from Pelé. We were both retired for a few years already,' he told me when we spoke. 'I had gotten involved with the Special Olympics, helping to develop their international soccer programme.' See … he's not really a bad guy. 'We were at dinner catching up one evening when he told me about *Victory* and said that the producers were looking for football players who wanted to do a bit of acting.' Uniquely among the footballers who took part in the film, Werner 'had an interest in acting at the time' as an area he might pursue now that his football career was over and, based on his Baumann performance, I would say that he could, perhaps, have given it a good go had other things not got in the way.

He had already appeared on screen in another film, *Manny's Orphans*, though that was as himself. Orphans again. Why is it always orphans?

'That was another one that Pelé got me involved with. They originally cast Pelé as that character to play himself, then Pelé had some scheduling conflict and he asked me if I was interested in doing it. So, Pelé got me a lot of work.' Sounds like, for lots of reasons, Pelé was a good man to know.

Roth appears in that one as a coaching guru figure who is training in his full white Cosmos kit at Giants Stadium when one of the young orphans, Billy, breaks into the ground and tells him he needs help with his soccer skills. The very accommodating skipper agrees to help and there then follows a training montage which would have stood Werner in good stead for working with the king of the training montage, Sylvester Stallone. Roth then turns up at the big match finale to deliver a half-time team talk that inspires a comeback. So, in movie terms, he can consider himself one-all in terms of second-half comebacks.

Aside from Pelé, Roth had another link to *Escape to Victory* via Ahmet Ertegun, the former boss of Atlantic

Records and a co-founder of the New York Cosmos. According to Werner, he had been helping Freddie Fields with casting suggestions for the footballers, so, between the two of them, Roth was a shoo-in for a meeting with Fields. 'So, I went out to LA and I spoke to Freddie Fields but there wasn't really an idea to cast me in any particular role at that time and Freddie said "Well, read the script and come back to me. These are the characters that still have to be cast." I was thinking about a member of the Allied team. I never thought too much about the German side.'

Indeed, Roth's part was still not set in stone before he flew to Budapest ahead of filming and met Pelé at the hotel. He recalls: 'There was a dinner arranged for Pelé, myself, John Huston and Freddie Fields and my luggage was left, inexplicably, in London. So, I had nothing but the clothes I was travelling in. I tried to get out and buy clothes but it was difficult in Budapest at that time, so I went as I was and the first thing I was thinking was that it was a very fancy restaurant. It was the penthouse of the hotel they were staying in and the waiters were dressed in tuxedos, so I was worried that I'd be underdressed. But when I got to the table, I saw that John was dressed in a Mexican kaftan, so I thought I was okay.' Nothing puts you at ease like arriving for your business meeting and finding someone in a Mexican kaftan. 'We had this meeting and John was explaining how they hadn't been able to cast Baumann yet. He felt that Baumann could be a pivotal character in the film as the major bad guy.' Which is very astute of the veteran director because he's quite right, despite there being no discernible dialogue for him to work with. Roth was unsure, as he had his heart set on another role. 'But John kind of sealed the deal with this hand gesture. You know how film directors use their thumbs and their forefingers to make a frame? He said, "I'm going to give you and Stallone a scene at the end that could make your career." And he put the frame over my face and then Pelé's face and he said, "It's going to be you ... and Stallone ... and you ... and Stallone." I saw how enthusiastic he was for me to have that part and I certainly had the look for it – it was a bit of typecasting. So, that was that.'

The casting of Roth as Baumann shows that the intention was never just to have these players play out the action and keep quiet. Plenty of them, including Roth, Moore, Summerbee, Osman, O'Callaghan, Wark (albeit dubbed) and, of course, Pelé get to inhabit their characters, share scenes with Caine and Stallone and make a pretty good fist of this acting lark throughout. The wisdom of the decision to go with acting footballers, rather than actors pretending to be footballers, is, I think, there for all to see on the screen. Ben Affleck might approve.

6.

THE FILM – PART II

IN THE hut on the camp reserved for the highest-ranking British officers (probably an en suite), the assembled escape committee await the arrival of Hatch to pitch his latest plan to get out. Waldron is supported here by Rose and Shurlock, kind of the Crabbe and Goyle to Waldron's Malfoy, as well as Maurice Roeves, as Pirie. The colonel is portrayed in this scene as a fair man but one with little to no capacity for nonsense. He quickly dismisses a proposed escape plan from unseen prisoner Peter Bailey, which Shurlock reads aloud as if it's the postbag section on a consumer affairs TV show. The ambitious and fun-sounding Bailey's plan would have involved pole vaulting the fence but the idea is turned down, thereby denying us what would have been a very interesting moment in the film. And thus, after volleyball, pole vaulting becomes the second sport to get sidelined here in favour of football. It's a shame, as Peter Bailey sounds like a right laugh. However, when Hatch suggests something altogether more reasonable for himself, Waldron is all ears. The escape committee also serves as the exposition committee in this scene, as we quickly learn that, although he is American, Hatch had crossed the border and enlisted in the Canadian army – thereby explaining why he's the only American in the camp.

THE FILM – PART II

Hatch's plan involves climbing up and out of the wash house during shower time and relying on two of the less fastidious guards, Hans and Anton, to assume they have miscounted the number of prisoners, which would give him cover until the following morning. It's a plan that he will, in due course, retain elements of, despite the proposed football match putting a spanner in the works.

Back out on the dusty exercise field, Pirie tells Waldron that Colby has insisted on seeing the other ranks in the camp play against the rest of the officers so that he can pick the best team possible for the game he is arranging with Von Steiner. Fearing that Colby can't, at this point, see the war for the football, Waldron raises a quizzical eyebrow and asks to see Colby at the earliest opportunity. It's already clear that a clash is coming about the real purpose of the match against the Germans. Waldron will see it as a chance to stage an escape and to give 'Jerry a bloody nose', while Colby pretty much just wants to have the best game of football they can possibly have. Both are admirable in their own way. It does raise a question about Waldron's priorities here, though. If he is intent on getting maximum escape bang for his buck, should he not be starting a selection process of his own, wherein the football squad is packed with those men who could do most damage to the German war effort on the outside? Demolitions experts, code-breakers and the like? It doesn't matter if you can kick a ball straight – if you can steal and fly German aircraft, then you're in at right-back, that sort of thing. That might make for another good film but, for here and now, in this movie, it's Colby's picks that we're focused on. And so, his selection process begins.

As dust flies up among the clatter of army boots, Sid Harmer (Mike Summerbee) is the first to shine as he scores a diving header in the trial game – very brave on that surface. Colby approaches him, asks his name and if he would like double rations for a month. Sid quips back with 'whose mother do you want me to strangle?' and he's in. In terms of footballing ability and banter, it's clear he's a perfect fit for what's to come. This is the first example we see of one of the footballers having to master a bit of dialogue. It isn't pages and pages, by any means, but it's worth a reminder here that none of the players were expecting to have to handle anything of the sort but, rather, just turn up and play. Summerbee acquits himself well here and continues to do so throughout the film, whenever called upon. The Manchester City legend has fond memories of filming this scene with a very generous Michael Caine, recalling: 'Michael said to me, "I'll tell you what to do; follow me around and I'll keep you in camera. They see enough of me. It'll be nice for them to see you for a change."' In the start of a running gag, Hatch runs into shot, keen to magnanimously accept his own place on the team, too, only to be shut down by a less-than-impressed Colby. It's fair to say that at this stage, certainly, Hatch's thinking might be more in line with Waldron's view that this is an escape opportunity, rather than for purely footballing reasons. Either way, Colby isn't having it.

Next to impress is Arthur Hayes, played by John Wark. Ipswich fans might already be able to recognise his sweet feet as he dribbles through and scores before the camera tilts up to reveal that it's him. It's enough to get him on to the team and when Colby tells him, he cryptically answers: 'It's not quite like playing for Manchester but it's better than not playing at all.' Now, by this point, you've probably realised that I think about this film more than most but it is only a slight stretch of the imagination to say that I have woken up screaming about this line – it troubles me so much. Does this mean that it's always been his dream to play for 'Manchester' or that he did, indeed, play for 'Manchester' before the war? On top of that, by Manchester, does he mean Manchester City or Manchester United? What kind of psychopath says Manchester when referring to one of those teams? Well, I've looked into it. The novelisation of the film by Yabo Yablonsky does reveal several delights about the film and warrants its own chapter but on this issue, it is disconcertingly vague. Annoyingly, the line is the same and just says Manchester, so we are none the wiser about whether the talented Arthur wore the sky blue or the red. However, it does tease us with a line saying: 'John knew the man. He had played against him and knew him as a hard-driving back.' This does at least suggest that Colby had crossed swords with Hayes in professional games before the war, so it confirms that Hayes was a player and lends his line a bit more poignancy. Now, if you wanted to be really nerdy about this, then you could have a look and conclude that Manchester City are the more likely team, as they were in Division Two with West Ham at the time, but I can't say for certain that this will help you sleep at night. Saying he played for Manchester is still a bit odd and it still surprises me that it survived into the final script, with nobody picking up on it during filming. I did ask John Wark about it and he was also unsure. Understandably, he would just have said the lines he'd been given to say off the back of nailing the little dribble he had to perform. He suggested that, as Manchester United were the more successful team at the time the film was made, it was possibly written with them in mind but, either way, it seemed to bother him less than me.

The thing that bothered John Wark a little more was that, in the moment of his crowning acting glory, his voice was taken away from him. For whatever reason, the film-makers decided to dub Wark's voice, with someone with a little more of a clipped Scottish accent. It seems unnecessary and John, unfortunately, didn't find out it had happened until he watched the film for the first time at a special premiere in Ipswich; settling in to watch it, no doubt with stars in his eyes, pride in his chest and popcorn in his lap, only to reach his big moment and let slip: 'Oh my god, that's not my voice.' He says that his team-mates, Alan Brazil and Eric Gates, who had missed the boat with *Escape to Victory*, were only too happy to rib him for it and make sure everyone else knew, too. Wark has two lines in the film. This one and 'I'll take the top one' when bunks are being chosen in the team dorm room. Both are dubbed with what he says is 'a posh Edinburgh accent' rather than his own Glaswegian one.

This, of course, puts him in the same good company as Dave Prowse, who as the man in the Darth Vader suit, happily delivered all of his *Star Wars* lines in his West Country burr, only to find out when he sat down to watch the film for the first time that he'd been dubbed over with the voice of James Earl Jones. I would stand by that decision to use one of the greatest voices in cinema to give

Vader the presence and gravitas that he might not have had if he had sounded like he came from Bristol but dubbing out John Wark's perfectly nice voice in *Escape to Victory* feels a bit uncalled for. I will, however, always be grateful to this book for giving me the opportunity to be the one to tell John Wark about Dave Prowse and his Darth Vader voice. They will never take that away from me.

Next, we see Colby standing, bewildered, as the escape committee fuss around him, running through the options for making a break for it that are offered up by the proposed match – one of which is loosening the boards and dropping out of the truck that takes them to the game. Despite being reminded that it is his duty to attempt to escape, the captain stands firm, saying that he has no interest in getting anybody killed and that, to these guys, escaping is 'just some bloody upper crust game'. As if to ram home the point, Tim Pigott-Smith's Rose plays chess throughout the scene. Something he was apparently keen to do for real during downtime on set, with Ossie Ardiles, among others, speaking fondly of him as a chess opponent.

Colby says of the lads that 'they've done their job and they just want to be left alone until the war is over', which certainly chimes with my own world view, if not that of Waldron, who dismisses his officer with a weary 'I'll pretend I didn't hear that' tone in his voice. There's that class element of the film again, carried shoulder-high by Caine's Colby. It's often overlooked in what is viewed by some as a one-dimensional film but it's there, all right.

On the German side of things, Von Steiner is fighting his own battles to keep the game in its purest form. I guess it's the curse of the propaganda officer that even your simplest idea might, if it's a good one, get blown out of proportion. He takes his scheme to his superior officers and, while some are sceptical, one sinister man at the back of the room gets behind it and shoves. He is wearing a brown uniform with a swastika band on the arm, which can't be good. It may indicate Gestapo or it may indicate SS; I'll be honest, I didn't want to research it too much in case my internet search history meant that I ended up on a list somewhere. What it does show is that he has some clout. We also know this because he's got his feet on the table. And you don't have your boots on the desk unless you're pretty comfortable in a situation. This is Herr Lorenz, who, in another of my favourite moments, describes Von Steiner's scheme as 'Fantastisch!', which is translated in the English subtitles as 'Brilliant!' That can't be right, can it? I'm a long way from fluent in German, having only ever sung along to 'Wooden Heart' and once managed a panicked 'Ich spreche nicht Deutsch' having missed a connecting flight in Frankfurt but, surely, he's saying the word 'fantastic' here. Let's not get bogged down in it, though.

The Germans discuss the fact that their country has never beaten England, although there will have been a few notable scrapes. In real life, England had most recently played Germany at the Olympic Stadium in Berlin in 1938 when things were certainly brewing, war-wise. Before the infamous game, the England players were ordered to give the Nazi salute at the insistence of FA officials, who told them that the delicate political situation needed 'only a spark to set Europe alight'. Amid a no doubt high-pressure atmosphere, Sir Stanley Matthews says in one of his autobiographies that the England players took inspiration from two English fans, who were behind one of the goals, displaying a Union flag in among the swastikas. Now, the seasoned football fans among you may have travelled away to Millwall or faced the odd hairy situation in Europe but THIS, my friends, is a tricky away trip. Göring, Goebbels and other members of the Nazi hierarchy were in attendance at this game but left early as England, in trying circumstances, romped to a 6-3 win. It's tempting to imagine these two absolutely hard-as-nails lads in the home end singing 'we can see you sneaking out' as the Nazi top brass left. Within the world of *Escape to Victory*, it's even more tempting to think that both Von Steiner and Colby could have been playing in this match.

Back at the camp, we get our first glimpse of the lovely Bobby Moore as Terry Brady. In the cut and thrust of a game, he easily robs the hapless Hatch of the ball and fires in a goal. It's nice that it was decided to include a tackle, as well as a goal, in the eye-catching moment that marks Moore's arrival in the film, because it evokes memories of him in his England pomp, stopping Jairzinho against Brazil at the 1970 World Cup. Although Sylvester Stallone would no doubt happily concede that he is no Jairzinho, it's all sufficiently impressive that Terry Brady is quite rightly immediately invited on to the team by a reinvigorated Colby, no longer watching passively from the sidelines but now in amongst things with a clipboard, avidly making notes.

Colby asks how Terry would like to come and live with the officers and, taking a leaf out of Sid's book, he replies: 'Only if you've got a chaperone, mate.' All suggestions of impropriety on the part of the officers aside, can you call a superior officer 'mate'? When you're a legendary defender for West Ham and England and the bloke you're talking to is pretending to be one, I suppose you can. Colby may outrank him but I guess that this, once more, establishes Caine's character as an approachable man of the people and not one to stand on ceremony; although I gather that a bit more discipline is quite important in military life and one hopes that Colby ran a tighter ship when he was leading men into action. Hatch is once again lurking and looking to get noticed, like a 12-year-old me at a school disco, but, just like a 12-year-old me at a school disco, he is completely ignored as Colby looks for better offers.

Just as in *The Magnificent Seven*, each of the recruited men gets their introductory moment to shine. Next up, it's Pelé and it's what we're all here for. A very loose pass runs out of play to where Pelé's character, Luis Fernandez, is spectating. Why he isn't already playing in the game, we don't know and we're not told. We can only hope that he's waiting his turn to play in the next trial game, because the possibility of such a talent going unseen by Colby had that ball not happened to go in his general direction is unthinkable. He stops it and flicks it up and launches into some very enjoyable keepy-uppies that have always made me wish I was one of the extras sitting there behind him. Colby is no fool and you can practically see him licking his lips as he looks on.

In his memoirs, Michael Caine speaks fondly of his own work in this scene. He often speaks of the acting he does while his character is seemingly doing nothing or, at least, doing nothing on the scripted page. He says that throughout this scene: 'I'm noticing him. I'm watching him with growing interest. My mind is turning over what I'm seeing and what it means. What I am definitely not doing is standing there doing nothing.' And therein lies the beauty of the film. We have a scene where a player is required to show off their skills but instead of that being an actor pretending in close-up, we have a footballer to do it properly. And not just any old footballer but Pelé, the best possible option.

Yet, Michael Caine is right there bringing his 'A' game to the scene, even though he is playing second fiddle. He isn't resting on his laurels, letting the football do the work. It's the same approach that makes *The Muppet Christmas Carol* as good as it is. Not for a minute am I comparing footballers to Muppets, so you can wash your grubby minds out if that's what you were thinking. What I mean is that just as it would be easy to sit back and let Pelé's trickery carry the action here, it would surely be just as easy to walk through a Charles Dickens adaptation filled with the Muppets and let them do the heavy lifting but Caine absolutely doesn't. He quite rightly points out that his role in making that comedy so good is that he has to play it absolutely straight, as if it is completely natural to have a puppet frog working for him and for that puppet frog to be married to a puppet pig. Caine says he did his research for that role by studying Wall Street bankers on CNN and 'played Scrooge straight, as though I was playing him for the Royal Shakespeare Company at the National Theatre'. And that, in my opinion, is why both films are much better than they have any right to be.

Suitably impressed by the sideline display, Colby eventually asks Luis where he learned to do it. Delivering some exposition of his own, while dazzling his prison mates with a show of skills, Luis tells us that he got good at football by practising with oranges as a child in Trinidad, thereby making his presence in the camp far more likely than if he were Brazilian. Colby asks if he would like to play against the Germans and Luis says 'Sure, why not?' in a very casual 'if I haven't got anything better to do' way that is at slight odds with the ostentatious display he has just put on as a clear 'come and get me' plea. I'm sure we'll see more of this guy later.

Hatch's obvious frustration at being ignored by Colby boils over here and he starts showing off like a toddler. He performs an American football tackle on someone who is so bad that referee Colby stops the game completely and everyone traipses off like their delicate sensibilities have been abused and that bringing an end to the match is the only option available. Hatch and Colby clash about the incident and, despite not having a leg to stand on, Hatch shouts 'You play English, I play American' and declares football 'a game for old ladies and fairies' before leaving the field. It's not very right-on and I'm not sure it's a word that would have a place either now or in 1943, if we're honest – but at the time of filming in 1980, it got his frustrated point across.

When we next see Hatch, he is being told by Shurlock that his own escape plan is all systems go, so he gleefully runs to find Colby to tell him where to stick his football team, as he no longer needs it to get out; not stopping for a moment to consider that the guard escorting Colby might understand English and could blow the whole thing

THE FILM – PART II

wide open. Colby, however, has other things to worry about. He's about to be taken off in a German staff car to visit Von Steiner in his office; although, as the two men mostly chat about football and, the last time they spoke, the German offered him free beer, perhaps it holds no fears for him.

The office is decorated with a discreet photograph of a 1930s German international football team and a relief map of Europe that is exactly the same as one which we had on the wall in the stairwell at my primary school. You can believe that or not and I don't know where it gets us but it's true, you know.

Von Steiner introduces Colby to Hauptmann Reinhold Müller, who is coach of the national team. Müller is played here by the much-missed Gary Waldhorn – David from *The Vicar of Dibley* or Lionel from *Brush Strokes* for those seeking a slightly deeper cut. There's a nice moment in which the two men recognise one another from an England v Germany game in London, some years before, and the flicker of a smile from Michael Caine is enough to convey the idea that all things being equal with the world, these two men could have a nice chinwag about all of that instead of being literal enemies. Müller is here because, as Von Steiner reveals, their shared idea of a local game for local people has got out of hand and has been co-opted by higher powers. The match will now be between the German national team and a combined team of Allied prisoners of war at Colombes stadium in Paris. Things have really escalated quickly.

The good news is that Colby is presented with a list of players he will be getting for his team – internationals from England, Norway, the Netherlands and France. The bad news is that when he enquires about Polish, Czech and other Eastern European players, he is regrettably informed by Von Steiner, with his head bowed, that he cannot have them because 'officially they do not exist'. It's another of those moments when the reality of the war comes crashing into the story that's unfolding and brings us up sharp. There are those who complain that the weighty topic of the labour camps isn't dealt with sufficiently in the film and it is definitely something that could be expanded but it is there, ever present in the background, and, given the tone of the rest of the film, you can see why the decision was made to keep it in the background. The German promises to see what he can do about the Eastern European players and Colby tries to lean on his opposite number a little here by saying that, as an officer and a gentleman, he is duty bound to give him some chance of winning. By the time I saw this film, the movie *An Officer and a Gentleman*, starring Richard Gere, would have been out and I can only imagine the confusion that this line would have caused me, being familiar with the film but not the saying. You can't go bandying around the titles of other films in your dialogue and expect a young man to cope. These days, of course, I'm familiar with the phrase 'an officer and a gentleman' but, at the time, Colby may as well have said 'as a *National Lampoon's Vacation*' you have to give me a chance, for all the head-scratching it caused me.

Back at the camp, the Germans are looking for the right drill bit and trying to make sense of the instructions as they put up a new flat-pack hut for the football team. Chances are they will have some screws left over that they're not sure what to do with but the hut looks good. Waldron is less impressed, though, remarking to Colby that 'collaboration pays' as he continues to disapprove of Colby's approach to the game and the prospect of his team being 'paraded in Paris like performing fleas'. He also warns Colby about what London might think about all this when they hear about it and Colby is momentarily rattled as his commanding officer walks away with his entourage, before Colby rallies himself either with his faith in the process, the overpowering warmth that his love of football gives him or the prospect of all the meat, eggs and beer he's been promised.

Next comes Clive Merrison's time to shine in a wonderful scene, alongside Hatch, as the forger. He is a bundle of efficient energy throughout, delivering delicious lines like, 'It's my busy time. Everybody wants to escape in the good weather,' all the while gathering his camera equipment and assembling the intricate contraption with the air of a man more than comfortable with the danger hanging over them of getting caught at any moment. When I spoke to Clive, he told me that he based his performance in this scene on Cyril Cusack's work as the gunsmith in *The Day of the Jackal*. Now, there's another eye-catching performance in another very good film.

Despite his own fine work in the scene, Merrison says that working with Sylvester Stallone 'wasn't a pleasant experience. I mean, he turned up late for the scene, as I remember. He had this kind of rope and he used to do exercises on a beam while I was trying to work my stuff out. Then, during the scene, he wouldn't talk to me in person.' Clive says that Stallone would prefer to talk to one of his people, who would then relay to Clive that he was talking too fast for him, which seems odd. The dialogue is hurried from both of them but the idea of the scene is that all of this subterfuge has to take place quickly while someone keeps watch for any approaching guards. There's a nice contrast here between the clipped English accent of the slight forger, who is obviously a bit of a genius, and the American brogue of the brash, physical Hatch. It's a reminder of Allies of all stripes being brought together by the war and works well in the scene. Still, Stallone doing pull-ups in the middle of preparing for it must have been annoying.

We often hear actors talking about the filming of close-ups as a measure of the professionalism or kindness of another actor. Some actors will stick around behind the camera and deliver their lines so that their scene partner can faithfully react to them. Others will see their work as being done and simply let somebody else do it. Guess which option Sly chose.

'We'd done Stallone's close-ups and they turned around on me and we were waiting for an hour and eventually John Huston said, "Boy, would you like to do the scene with me?" I said, "I would consider it the greatest honour of my life." So, he did all my reversals.' It's disappointing to hear this about Sylvester Stallone, as we like to imagine a happy, collaborative set for the whole film but we can't have everything and, ultimately, Clive got to work even more closely with John Huston, for whom he had such affection, so maybe it worked out for the best.

Within the scene, the forger sits Hatch down for his fake passport photo and is informed that the American wants to pass himself off as Marcel Dupin, a Frenchman travelling home for a funeral. Warming to his task, the forger also offers to knock him up a forged letter about the funeral to go with the passport. This is a man who clearly loves his work and we're left to shake a rueful head at the thought of his meticulous efforts on the passport of Williams, the tragic failed escapee from the opening scene, going to waste.

As Hatch leaves the forger's hut, he notices that his favourite guards, Hans and Anton, have been moved from their regular duties to guard the football team and he realises that, without their slack habits and shoddy attention to detail at the wash house, the wheels have very much come off his escape plan. Shurlock is on hand here with a bit of a catty, uncalled-for remark that he never thought it was a good plan anyway, which is all Hatch needs at this point.

Hatch must now think again and realises that he needs to be a part of that football team, after all. This will, of course, involve going to Colby and convincing him that, despite earlier telling him where to stick his team and notwithstanding the slurs he made against the beautiful game of football, he really rather would like to join in, after all. The moment he chooses to do this is just as Colby is moving into his new team digs along with Sid, Terry, Arthur and Luis. How he got here to just walk in with them, we don't know but it's bound to have something to do with that slack pair Hans and Anton, who, frankly, seem lucky to still have a job at this point, war or no war.

Hatch comes in with his bag of belongings and announces that he is more than happy to be the team's trainer and look after them all because he knows everything about 'bruises, strains and Charley Horses'. Aside from this being the only reference to Charley Horses I've ever heard outside of the game *Operation* (it's American for cramp, apparently), Colby isn't convinced and unceremoniously throws Hatch and his cool bag of stuff out of the hut. In one of the sweariest moments in the film, he calls 'bullshit' on Hatch as he does so. Outside on the steps, the two men have a confrontational conversation in which Hatch explains his predicament and pleads with Colby to allow him to join the team to facilitate his escape. Colby says that he doesn't want to be responsible if Hatch gets shot but he eventually relents and lets him in after Hatch insists it's his own choice to take the risk. This is a slightly odd scene. In the book of the film, which I promise we're getting to, the relationship between the two men is much closer. They are friends, rather than simply prisoners together, and that closeness means Colby's decision makes more sense. Given what we've seen pass between Colby and Hatch in the film so far, there seems little reason for the British officer to acquiesce here. He's been against the team being used as a means of escape, he's obviously concerned about anyone getting killed as part of this whole endeavour and the American clearly gets on his nerves – and yet, he now agrees to let Hatch use the team for his own ends. It jars slightly but I feel Caine manages to sell it. Just a flick of Colby's head gets Hatch inside; no smile or welcoming open arms, in case too much humanity pokes through, but he's in, nevertheless.

It does mean that Hatch is on hand for the next scene, to greet the new players who have arrived, supplied from other camps by Von Steiner. They arrive in the back of a truck covered in chicken wire and one can only imagine the logistics involved in picking them all up from their respective camps. The driver must have had the patience of a world-weary Sunday League football coach, going around picking up all his players for an away game, but on a much larger, Germany-wide, prison-based level.

The arrival of the players causes a bit of a frisson. We're treated to the first strains of the more stirring stuff that Bill Conti has put together for the soundtrack, while Waldron, Rose and Shurlock all clamour for a space at the window to get a glimpse. They may be motivated by things being taken up a notch and the game becoming more of a reality or they may just want to gawp at the famous footballers. If these new arrivals are the ones on Von Steiner's list, then we are led to believe that they must be well-known players from pre-war football. In the case of Tim Pigott-Smith, you get the impression that if this were, indeed, his first look at these stars, there would be genuine excitement there.

The truck pulls up, the back door is unlocked and out hop the new players. First off is Kevin O'Callaghan as Tony Lewis, who Colby greets warmly as if he's an old friend. The rest he greets as if he might know them by name or reputation but it's only Tony who gets the special treatment. The other players are Russell Osman as Doug Clure, Paul van Himst as Michel Fileu, Hallvar Thoresen as Gunnar Nilsson, Søren Lindsted as Erik Borge, Ossie Ardiles as Carlos Rey and Co Prins as Pieter van Beck. It's a pleasing blur of faces and different uniforms that conveys the idea that this lot are a mixed bag, who will soon become a team. Inside, they eat and drink ferociously as Colby briefs them. He tells them that there is no rank within the football team, although, handily, he is captain in both military rank and the football team, which will, no doubt, make it easier for everyone involved. Russell Osman has been in the film less than a minute but gets to show some acting chops with a quick exchange with Colby outside before delivering his line between bites from a generous chunk of bread. 'Well, I don't know how you did it but cheers, anyway.' Colby has a team.

There is one more character who emerges from the truck besides the listed players and it's one with an interesting story. This is Benoît Ferreux, as Jean-Paul Remy. You might have missed him but he's the one with the beret on and, though we only get the odd glimpse or three of him during the film, his character has a much bigger role in the book of the film, which is full of interesting things.

See, I told you we'd get there.

7.

THE BOOK OF THE FILM

FILM NOVELISATIONS can be a tricky proposition. They sit in an uncanny valley between source material novels and the film itself. They lack the initial inspiration of an original novel but never seem to adhere quite closely enough to the actual film to give you the same comfort that you want from them. In a case like *Jaws*, for instance, differences between Peter Benchley's original novel and Steven Spielberg's film adaptation are interesting but easy to accept, as choices have been made in the interpretation. With a film tie-in novel, however, those differences just look like anomalies. It's like someone has tried to fit the film into a suitcase and some bits and pieces are left sticking out of the sides. Original scriptwriter Yabo Yablonsky's book of *Escape to Victory* is a good case in point. There is much fun to be had from those bits sticking out of the sides, as you will see.

    I myself have something of a patchy history with books of films. I'm not swinging it about here but I was a pretty good reader in primary school. I voraciously tore through everything the school library had to offer and eventually gained the exalted position of 'free reader', which meant that I had gone beyond the confines of the colour scheme reading stages, leaving *Billy Blue Hat* and *Roger Red Hat* in my wake and had a free rein to read whatever I fancied and could lay my hands on. This was all well and good until I decided to read the novelisation of *Ghostbusters* by Larry Milne, which I suspect I would have bought with a WH Smith's voucher. I grew up in the 80s and I'm not made of stone – of course I chose *Ghostbusters*.

I'm sure it was the same at your school but, periodically, we would be called to the front of class during quiet reading time to read to the teacher, so that she could monitor how individuals were getting on. One fateful day, when it was my turn, up I went amid the near silence of 20-odd other kids reading to themselves, some running fingers along the page to help them, others just freewheeling it and having fun.

I should have been aware of the looming problem, because I had seen and laughed at that scene in the film, P-word and all; but whether it was the innocence of youth or the arrogance of the free reader, I was unlucky with the timing and didn't give a thought to the impending danger. The section I was called upon to read was the moment early on in which Dr Venkman is running telepathy tests on two of his students – one an attractive female and the other an increasingly annoyed male student. Even if I got away with reading out loud to Miss Name-Redacted the bit about 'the girl bites the sexiest lower lip on campus', I was never going to get away with the bit where Venkman gives the other student one too many electric shocks for failing and he shouts: 'It's pissing me off!'

There was an awkward moment between me and Miss Name-Redacted as the forbidden swear word hung in the chalk-infused air of the classroom. I was probably ten years old and even if we were starting to dabble in swearing in the playground by then, we certainly weren't doing it in front of teachers. A ripple of shocked giggling darted across the front row of desks, there was some brief telling-off and it all resulted in my reading list being a bit more closely monitored. But I'm mostly over the incident now, honestly. I suppose it could have been worse. I could have had to read out the bit where Venkman says: 'This man has no dick.'

Inappropriate school moments aside, printed versions of films have always held a bit of a fascination for me, because they tell you the things that could have made it into the film but didn't. Take *Star Wars*, for example. I know that, if we want it, there are now countless sequels, prequels, books, TV series, cartoons and fan fiction that mean we have the backstory to pretty much everyone who ever lifted a beaker or smoked a weird pipe in the Mos Eisley Cantina but even the original novelisation of the 1977 *Star Wars* film has plenty going on. George Lucas is the named author but, in fact, it was ghost-written by Alan Dean Foster and it contains several details for fans of the film to get their teeth into. There's a reference to 'the later corrupt Emperors', which suggests there have been more than one Emperor rather than just Chancellor Palpatine seizing control like he does in the films; and Luke and Leia definitely fancy each other, with lines that suggest that, at this stage, Lucas was not secretly planning to later reveal that they were actually twins. The very cool 'parsecs' haven't been thought of yet as a spacey unit of measurement and Han Solo talks, instead, about the much duller 'timeparts'; he also definitely shot Greedo first – without question. Then there's the odd reference

Obi Wan Kenobi makes about ducks, telling Luke that, 'even a duck has to be taught to swim', which prompts Luke to ask, quite rightly, what a duck is. Are there ducks in *Star Wars*? Are there any regular Earth-type animals? I have wondered about this before, because, if pigs exist in *Star Wars*, then Porkins the big lad pilot could have had a terrible time at school, whereas if pigs don't exist in that galaxy, then he got away with it. It's possible I think about things too much.

What this all means, though, is that, as a bit of a superfan of *Escape to Victory*, I am going to gobble right up every last nugget of information that found its way into the book. And I hope you will, too. The time has come to deal with Jean-Paul, the mystery French character who appears in the film, then disappears without warning.

There are clues that indicate that the character of Jean-Paul was, at some point, a much bigger deal in the script, not just the book. The fact that French star Alain Delon was mooted as a potential headliner in early reports of the film's production suggests to me that a French character might have had greater prominence than any that survives into the finished article. We also have Werner Roth and his acting ambitions. It seems that, after Roth was initially invited to read the script by Freddie Fields, Jean-Paul was the that Werner had his heart set on. He told me: 'There was a French character that I kind of liked. He never made it to the final match but he had some interesting scenes before that. So, I called Freddie at the time and said I would like that part and he said "fine".'

However, as we know, upon arrival in Budapest, earlier than much of the rest of the cast, John Huston dazzled him with his kaftan and his finger framing and convinced him that he was, instead, perfect for Baumann the German captain; meaning that Roth reluctantly let his dream part go. 'In fact, my knee-jerk reaction wasn't about being on the German team or being a Nazi. As an actor, you do what you have to do but I was so invested in the French accent that I had worked on so diligently for the months prior, more than anything else.' Roth got over it like a true professional, left his own mark elsewhere on the film and still describes making it as 'one of the more interesting experiences of my life'.

It's unclear whether Huston was already considering cutting back on the Jean-Paul story thread by the time he successfully steered Roth towards the Baumann part. But, if so, he was doing him a huge favour, as the German skipper gets a lot more screen time than the Frenchman in the finished film.

Aside from his arrival with the rest of the players from other prisoner of war camps, the moments that Jean-Paul, played by Benoît Ferreux, does appear are brief. When Colby gathers his players to decide whether or not they should play on in light of the state that the Eastern European players have arrived in, he is front and centre, insisting that they must play the game. When Hatch makes his escape by clambering above his team-mates in the showers, he can be seen once more. He can also be glimpsed in passing in one or two of the training shots, though never with a ball at his feet. And there is a good reason for that.

Although one or two cast members that I asked did not even remember Ferreux being on set, Russell Osman told me: 'Yes, I remember Benoît; nice fella but never going to get away with being a footballer, very uncoordinated.' Søren Lindsted went even further in saying: 'I remember he couldn't play any football at all. He was so bad at football.' In fairness to the French actor, if he was the only non-footballer that was ever called upon to play a bit of football on the Gensdorf set, then he was bound to stand out as being not good enough. This takes us back to the argument of getting footballers to act rather than the other way around. It's interesting that this one casting choice slipped through for what could have been a big part in the film, though it isn't clear at what point Ferreux was chosen. Presumably, if Werner Roth arrived in the country for filming believing that the part was his, it was quite late on.

Years before his lack of footballing ability was a concern for him, Benoît Ferreux had emerged as a child actor in Louis Malle's 1971 coming-of-age drama *Murmur of the Heart*. He plays 14-year-old Laurent, who experiences his sexual awakening in the film, partly by being taken to a brothel by his older brothers to lose his virginity and partly, I'm sorry to have to tell you, by having sex with his own mum. You heard me.

One person's exploration of 'excessive love', 'a love affair between mother and son' and an attempt to 'de-dramatise incest or at least this form of it' – all quotes from director Malle – is another person's mucky film and, understandably, the movie caused a great deal of controversy upon its release, with calls for it to be banned. A 1989 *New York Times* article on the film explains that: 'In some of the angriest French press reactions to the film, such as in the conservative *Le Figaro*, critics worried aloud that young Benoît Ferreux, the actor, might wind up permanently scarred by the film.' However, despite the questionable subject matter, Ferreux insisted that he was fine on *Murmur of the Heart*, saying that, having been chosen after an exhaustive casting process to star alongside his own brother in the film, Louis Malle looked after him like a 'big brother'. Although on a film about incest, that might be less reassuring than it otherwise could be.

One of the young Benoît's co-stars on his unforgettable screen debut, also known as *Le Souffle Au Cœur* and *Dearest Love*, was Michael Lonsdale, who appears here as a priest but is more famous for his menacing role as Drax, the megalomaniac villain being thwarted by Roger Moore's James Bond in *Moonraker*. This is significant, because one of Benoît's few Hollywood roles came in *Moonraker*, a film which rivalled Sylvester Stallone's *Rocky II* at the box office in 1979. Ferreux appears, albeit briefly, near the start as a henchman or contractor of Drax, stowing away on board the Moonraker shuttle and wordlessly stealing it with a colleague. Beyond this sequence, he is never seen again in the Bond film, so we should have been prepared for his characters leaving films prematurely.

The final sight of Jean-Paul in *Escape to Victory* comes as the players file across the screen to board the train which will take them to Paris for the match. Once the team reach the other end, Jean-Paul is never seen again. Not on the pitch, not in the dressing room, not at all. And there is a very good reason for this, because the main difference between the film and its paperback equivalent is that in the book, Jean-Paul uses that train journey as an opportunity to attempt to escape.

Looking through the train window, his first glimpse in a while of the French countryside gives him a rush of blood to the head. He experiences visions of his mother, standing high on a hill. No, not the one from *Murmur of the Heart*. You can stop thinking about that now. Or try, at least. Inspired by his visions, suddenly all Jean-Paul can think about is freedom. As Remy catches the scent of freedom and goes for it, this isn't the meticulous planning of Hatch on show here or even the have-a-go pole vault fantasies of Peter Bailey; instead, it is pure emotion and spontaneity. Requesting a trip to the gents, he catches the guard and a German officer unawares, stealing a gun and dragging one of them into the toilet. The alarm is raised and the train comes screeching to a halt, jolting everyone on board: 'Jean-Paul's head shattered the toilet mirror. The sudden pain and loss of gravity pulled his body stiff and he touched the trigger and blew the German's face away. He smashed the Luger through the window, then kicked out the remaining glass.'

As the players watch through the train windows, their team-mate jumps down from the train and plunges into the wheat fields alongside the track. He runs for his life as the German soldiers fire after him. Yablonsky has him zigzagging and dancing between the bullets and it looks for all the world that the desperate prisoner is going to make it, until he is finally caught by a bullet or three and he falls, dead, 'like a marionette ending a performance for children'.

It's all very dramatic and you can imagine how it might look on screen. As fans of the film, we can read this and not feel much emotion, because we barely know this character. However, if the original script had been preserved and this whole character arc had played out, then the death of Jean-Paul would be devastating and would completely change the tone of the film. The team wouldn't just shrug and wonder how to fill the gap on the pitch created by being a man down. Instead, every kick of the ball would be motivated by revenge for their fallen comrade and the football match would be given a whole different perspective. Without this scene, and anything with Jean-Paul Remy that really sets it up, that fine line between the horrors of war and a football adventure movie can continue to be trod. The murder of an escaping main character would certainly tip things away from the jauntier end of things.

So, if it's understandable why the scene was left out, the mystery remains about the point at which it was cut. Werner Roth confirms that: 'The escape attempt was in the script I read. It was one of the reasons that I thought that was an interesting character.' On Benoît, he says: 'I do know that he was cast and he was on set, but I think he was mostly left on the cutting room floor. I don't know if they filmed the escape scene.' And here is the curious thing. Nobody I spoke to remembers the scene being filmed. Russell Osman told me: 'I don't think that we filmed anything about him overpowering a guard on the train. I remember the train scene but they could've done something in a different carriage in the train, unbeknown to us. There was so much going on at the time, it was hard to keep track of everybody. People were flying in to do a few days' filming and then disappeared, so, when we didn't see Benoît again, it wasn't a surprise, as so many came and went.'

It seems unlikely that a big sequence like this would have been filmed and then left out of the completed film. I imagine that it would have been expensive to shoot, if you'll forgive the pun, and if there were any doubts about including it, it would have been much more cost-effective to exorcise it from the script than try it to see what it looked like. It's clear that John Huston wasn't sure about including it, because he talked Werner Roth out of taking what was a meatier role in the script. That said, why was Benoît Ferreux cast and included in the film at all, if the escape attempt was never going to be filmed?

But wait. It's true that nobody I spoke to could remember the scene being filmed but there is photographic evidence to the contrary. There are production stills, one of which you can find among the pictures included somewhere around the middle of this book, that show a concerned Colby and Hatch, staring in horror through the train window, while being held back by a guard. This suggests that they are witnessing something horrific taking place outside the train. Could that something be a team-mate being gunned down as he runs across a field towards freedom? More than likely. And if they got as far as filming the reactions, they must surely have filmed Benoît Ferreux's big moment. In some ways, this makes me sadder for Benoît and even more baffled that the people responsible for continuity thought that nobody would notice he was missing.

What we are left with in the finished film is a character who has joined the team, trained with the team and been sufficiently involved with the team that he is a voice to be listened to when it comes to making crucial decisions – and, yet, he gets on the train in Germany and never gets off of it in Paris. And his disappearance is never explained. I would like to think that he successfully jumped off and made a run for it during the journey but the book of the film tells us different. And that isn't all it tells us.

Strewn throughout the book are gems of information about a whole host of the characters we meet in the film. We discover that Doug Clure, portrayed by Russell Osman in the film, should actually be Scottish, as the novel mentions his 'deep Highland burr'. We also learn that the forger's name is Captain James Lawry, that he had been a watchmaker before the war and that he and Hatch 'had been taken together at Dieppe', so the two should be firm friends rather than having the purely transactional relationship that survives into the film. There is a hint that some of this may have been in the script at one point, as Clive Merrison did recall filming a scene with Sylvester Stallone in which Dieppe was mentioned. He remembered it because he recalled that Stallone kept mispronouncing Dieppe for take after take. Obviously, such detail as this might be cut for time but it does mean that we're robbed of a touching moment in which Lawry puts his master craftsman skills to sentimental use and makes a beret for Hatch to wear once he has escaped. Accepting the gift, 'Bobby's eyes filled with tears'. That's right, Hatch's full name is Robert or Bobby Hatch.

In fact, we find out a lot more about Bobby Hatch from the book. He has been in prison camps for three years at the time our story takes place and he had already escaped four times, getting as far as Stuttgart on one occasion, which certainly adds to the idea that he is a character similar to Steve McQueen in *The Great Escape*. We learn that he had been a pre-war American football star who almost made all-American as a half-back, which I think is the same as a running-back for those of us less well versed in American football terms. In a further bit of backstory, we find out that his mother died just before his graduation, his American football dream faded when he didn't make the grade and a close friend of his who had volunteered for the RAF had been killed in action. On the plus side, however, Yablonsky gives him a saucy interlude in which he beds a local girl, Carrie Thompson, and her sister, Pamela, at the same time, so it's not all bad news for the lad.

Yablonsky doesn't stop there with his sex scenes. Aside from Hatch's threesome reverie, we also get a saucy interlude for Von Steiner with Emma, a 'dark-haired beauty' whom he meets at a party. The German major isn't portrayed in the film as a man passionate about anything other than football but here he seduces Emma with the promise of chocolate and her 'erotic acquiescence' plays out over a few pages, despite an interruption for an air raid siren. Modesty forbids me from providing further details but suffice to say that these scenes place the paperback firmly in the airport pot boiler fiction bracket and take us away from the football into very different territory. I didn't want to have to think about Von Steiner having sex, but now you do, too.

The film naturally eschewed any of this kind of stuff but maybe all of this was in that original script which

Jack Nicholson, among others, considered to be too long. One thing the movie does skip discreetly over is the liaison between Hatch and Renée when he escapes and finds himself as a guest in her Paris safe house. All the film shows us is a bit of flirting on Hatch's part and a tender moment as he leaves, which implies that something has happened during his stay, but it's all we need. The suggestion of a fleeting moment where two lost souls find and take comfort from one another in the middle of this crazy war. We don't need to see it; the subtle hint is more than enough to add significance to Renée watching on from the stands when the match comes around. She's invested and so are we. In the book, however, Yablonsky goes all in and leaves nothing to the imagination. He lays it, and them, bare.

Yablonsky infuses the scene with some emotion, as Renée the widow is clearly looking for a brief substitute for the husband she has lost and longs for but it all gets a bit buried beneath talk of 'Belgian lace' and 'silken mysteries' and what goes on isn't left to our imagination. The right decision was made to leave anything gratuitous out of the finished film, because the mention of it in the book detracts somewhat from Hatch's noble mission and, instead, puts us in mind of the equivalent scene in *McVicar*, when Roger Daltrey's main character is placed in a safe house with a woman looking after him and asks his mate: 'Will she stand for it?' All a bit grubby.

Significantly upping the sauciness levels is not the only way in which Yablonsky's novelisation is a bit more adult than the film. With one eye on the cinema certificate, decisions would have been made on the production to keep the swearing to a minimum and give what there is to Michael Caine, because he's so good at it. In the book, however, everybody gets a go. Colby ups his game and, throughout, delivers several F-bombs to anyone who will listen but we also get an exasperated 'As the Lord is my witness, I'll have that bastard shot' from Waldron about Colby when relations between the two are particularly strained and a wonderful 'Kiss my black arse!' from Luis. It's a shame that they didn't let Pelé have this one, although the thought of some kid somewhere having to read it aloud to their own Miss Name-Redacted at the front of the class sends me cold.

Some of that fruitier language is used in scenes between Colby and Waldron as they argue the toss about the merits or otherwise of the match that Colby has got them involved in. It really ramps up the tension and shows that Colby is happy to go toe-to-toe with his superior officer over the matter. We also get some significant backstory for Cedric Waldron, for that is his name, which in part explains why he might find the brusque working-class nature of Colby difficult to tangle with. Waldron is painted as a career soldier from well-bred stock; we are told all about his father's military training and record. We learn that Waldron himself graduated third in his class from Sandhurst before a family friend, Brigadier Wentworth, requested his presence at a consulate in 'Black Africa' and then he moved through the embassies and up the ranks as far as good breeding could take him. The colonialism is strong in this one and it's easy to see why Colby might bristle against him when he calls his loyalties into question.

While we're in the escape committee hut, it's worth mentioning that Rose and Shurlock get mixed up in the transition from film to book. In the film, Julian Curry's Shurlock wears the blue uniform of the RAF, while Tim Pigott-Smith's Rose wears the khaki army fatigues. In the book, however, Yablonsky talks about Shurlock wearing bifocals and looking 'more the college don than the leader of a band of commandos'. Still, even if we take this to mean the Rose character in the film, it's still nice to think of him out there doing his spectacular bit for the war effort before he settled down to his games of chess and his withering stares.

All this, though, is skirting around the bombshell I've been waiting to unleash. Are you ready? Settle in. Here goes. Colby is supposed to be Welsh. I was prepared to find out some background history on our main man when I picked up the book but I was not ready for that. If it was ever a note or a consideration that was suggested to Michael Caine at any point during production, it doesn't seem to be one that he took on board for very long. There is no nod to the accent from Caine, although critics might ask 'when is there ever?', apart from *The Cider House Rules*. It may be that Caine or Huston or the production as a whole decided to disregard this original character note. You see, Yablonsky does seem to have it slightly confused. He describes Colby as an England international but says that he's Welsh. That, along with the whole Arthur Hayes–Manchester debacle and another moment in this book when he has Colby say that 'Red was my winning colour when I played for Glasgow', makes me think that Yabo wasn't, perhaps, quite as across British football as he could have been. Who would even begin to talk about their time at Rangers or Celtic as vaguely playing for Glasgow and who on earth in the city is playing and winning in red shirts? It's either done wilfully to obfuscate for fun or these are errors on the author's part.

Another indication that any of these character notes were thrown out the moment that Michael Caine was cast is the fact that he is described as 'the Welsh flyer' and there are constant allusions to the bombers that Colby flew before capture. Yet, in the film, he wears an army uniform, not one of the RAF, and he's a captain, which is an army rank. So, the film version of Colby is not Welsh and not a flyer, yet the book has him watching birds in the sky and imagining himself 'behind the stick of his Lancaster' being shot at by Messerschmitt fighters. The book includes an elaborate description of the character being shot down and captured with his crew on a mission to bomb Stuttgart.

One element we know and love of the Colby character that is reinforced in the book, however, is how bloody good at football he is or, at least, was. When Von Steiner arrives at the camp and observes his first game, Colby is playing and Yablonsky waxes lyrical about his ability, saying: 'The ball was his to do with as he damn well pleased.' And when Colby and Von Steiner meet, the German is slightly in awe of his British counterpart. Later, when he is defending Colby and trying to persuade his superior, the sinister Herr Lorenz, not to have him shot in the wake of Hatch's escape attempt, he explains that Colby is the best player and the main attraction and that: 'If we kill him, there will be very little to show the world, very little to please our Führer.'

For his own part, Von Steiner seems to have been not so bad himself. In the book, when he first meets Rose at pitchside at the camp, he tells him straight away that he was once a player and when Rose fully recalls him later, he tells the others that: 'He's "Dancer Steiner". Remember him? He was part of Jimmy Hogan's "Wunderteam" in 38 and played for Germany in 39.' This means that Von Steiner was, in fact, Austrian and would have been co-opted into the German team after the Anschluss when Nazi Germany annexed Austria. Do you like the way I casually dropped Anschluss in there like my main reference point for it isn't *The Sound of Music*?

We also learn that Von Steiner has wound up as a reluctant propaganda officer because of injuries he sustained in combat. All of which makes him not really a propaganda officer, not really a Nazi, not really a German and perhaps, therefore, not nearly enough of a baddie. Hence the need to bring in Baumann as an antagonist once the match starts. In the book, the German captain is called Rheingold rather than Baumann and has an interaction with Colby before the game when the British officer is taken to the German training camp. The arrogant Rheingold points out that the Allies will play in red shirts and no doubt be nicknamed 'The Cardinals of Gensdorf'. He then tells Colby that the red kit was his idea so that the Paris crowd 'could see the team we've beaten'. All wars aside, there is no need for this sort of trash talk, Herr Rheingold. And let's also give thanks that the film-makers ditched the idea of red shirts for the beautiful kit we did end up with.

That brings us to the game and, of course, the book comes up trumps once again, with some wonderful extras for us. We will, of course, get to the match that we all know and love from the film in due course but, for now, let's spend some time in this alternative universe and enjoy the match served up by Yablonsky's book version. It's like one of those timeline variants from the Marvel films but hopefully like one from back when you still cared about them.

First, we learn that one of the German players is called Kuntz and some of us will remember how much fun we all had with the real-life striker of the same name at Euro 96 – until he scored against England in the semi-final. We also find out that the ref is called Vogel and that he is a bad man who is willing to cheat to help the Germans win. The other big revelation of the first half is that it's Sid Harmer – or Sid Harmor (the surname is spelt both ways throughout production material and credit lists) – who scores the face-saving goal just before half-time.

At the interval, the same option to escape plays out as you would expect, with the same tunnel under the big bath, but there's good news and bad news. The good news is that injured goalie Tony (Lewis in the film, Morrell here) has been allowed to travel to the match with the rest of the team. The bad news, for Hatch at least, is that it's Tony who begins the dissent about running away at half-time. Hatch is standing there, having carried the injured Pieter van Beck down the hole, when Tony pipes up to tell everyone that they should play on, saying: 'From where I sat, you people looked as if you were just warming up.' Then, having sown the seed of doubt in the minds of the escapees, he then waves them off with his remaining good arm and scarpers down the tunnel himself. Fine work.

Hatch responds to the change of heart by telling them they are 'fucking crackers', which gets him on the sweary scoresheet but sounds like something an American wouldn't say. Crackers sits in that distinctly British vein for words meaning crazy, along with barmy, daft and loopy. Maybe we should give it the benefit of the doubt and say he's spent too much time around British soldiers. Then we get a bit of dialogue from Colby that I can't help thinking should have survived into the script and the final film, as he lays out the dilemma before his players. 'The Resistance is down there and there are boats that can carry you safely to Spain. Out there,' he says, gesturing towards the field, 'are a bunch of big Nazis who will possibly kick us all to death. Now make your choice.' There could also have been a bit of dialogue for Ossie Ardiles at this point, as Yablonsky has Carlos Rey invoke the Foreign Legion motto, 'March or die!', as a rallying cry to inspire the team to go back.

Back out on the field, Colby gets his moment as he dribbles around the goalkeeper to score and make it 3-2, then Carlos Rey scores a disallowed equaliser (rather than Doug Clure), before Colby and Sid combine to physically assault the referee. Yes, you read that right – they duff him up. In a moment they contrive between them, Colby goes down and drags the ref with him, then Sid goes down on top of them, throwing cheeky punches until the ref is carried off with his ribs broken and a linesman has to take over. It's understandable why this moment wasn't included in the film, as I suppose it might portray the otherwise fair team in an unsympathetic light; although I would argue that battering one little referee in revenge for what the

Nazis did in the 1940s is fair enough. As an audience, I think we would have accepted it.

When Luis Fernandez gets his equaliser to make it 3-3 – instead of 4-4 – it comes in the form of a 30-yard chip rather than an overhead kick, which simply suggests to me that, if this was also in the original script, Pelé was a much better player than they ever hoped to recruit for the film. Pelé is credited as the football co-ordinator, so fair play to him if he has seen a 30-yard chip on the page and said he would prefer it to be an overhead kick.

Then we come to the finale and the very different ending to the game that Sylvester Stallone would have read when he was first given the script while viewing Freddie Fields's beach house. With the clock running down and passions running high: 'Bobby abandoned the goal and ran with his team. The Allies drove towards the goal.' You know what's coming here, don't you? You guessed it. Hatch comes out of goal, runs upfield and scores the winning goal. He backheels the ball to Colby, who shoots and hits the bar, only for the ball to land in a crowd of players until 'Bobby found it and, with a banshee yell, drove the ball into the net!' And then the pitch invasion begins, which whisks the players away from their German captors, just like in the film.

And that is your lot. Apart from a brief epilogue in which Hatch sits in a Montmarte Resistance safe house, where he is, no doubt, trying his luck again with a generous hostess, and muses on the possibility that he will never again see his comrades or team-mates. That's it. There is no further explanation or speculation about what happened to the rest of the players and we are just left to deal with the idea that this story ends with a goalkeeper charging up the field in open play and scoring the winning goal.

Would we have all still loved the film as much if they had decided to keep that ending?

8.

BETWEEN THE STICKS

IT IS fascinating to me that the script for *Escape to Victory* existed for around ten years before it was made and was passed around Hollywood without anybody pointing out that having the film finish with a goalkeeper charging forward in open play to score the winning goal was a bit daft. This means that Yabo Yablonsky and any other writer who looked at the script, plus Tom Stern, Jack Nicholson, Mario Kassar and Andy Vajna, Freddie Fields and even Fields's French co-worker, who knew her football and spotted the potential in a film about the sport, all waved that through and thought it was okay. It was certainly in any script that Sylvester Stallone got to read and it isn't entirely clear how far into production the film was when it was discarded in favour of the climactic penalty save, although that moment seems to have been the first time some of the players got a look at it.

In his autobiography, as part of an uncharacteristic and largely unnecessary dig at his co-star, Pelé tells us that: 'Stallone, for example, wouldn't let anyone else sit in his chair on the set and the story went round that he insisted on his character being the player who scored the winning goal.' John Wark also said to me that Stallone asked 'can I score the winning goal?' before being set straight by John and the other players. However, while these recollections both suggest that the big finale moment was something that came up during filming, the opposite is true. It was there at the start of the production and was subsequently taken out. Paul Cooper remembers, 'The script said that Stallone got the ball, dribbled to the other end of the pitch and scored the winning goal but we all looked and said "You can't do that." So, they changed it and gave him the penalty save instead.' Jeff Maguire is credited in a recent *Telegraph* article as the writer who inserted the penalty scene as a replacement and, specifically, Paul Cooper credits the two biggest-name players with nixing the original idea: 'Bobby Moore and Pelé said "You can't do that, it's impossible."' It's an indicator of the clout the pair carried on set.

We can see the survival of such a silly idea so far into the production as a failing or we can see the fact that experts were allowed to step in and point out a better way to end the film as evidence that the process was all collaboration and love. There certainly seems to have been plenty of flexibility throughout. If Stallone signed on for a film in which his character had such a heroic ending, there is no evidence that he was too bothered when it was changed. Given some of the stories of diva behaviour around this time, there doesn't seem to have been much of a problem here, at all. It feels like once it was explained to him, he was happy to go with the new finale and put the work in to make the penalty save look as good as he possibly could. He still had his goalkeeper-as-hero moment, after all.

It is interesting to me that, having finally come around to the idea of making a movie about football, Hollywood should pick a story with a goalkeeper, of all positions, as the hero of the piece. Given that a large proportion of the potential audience, in the all-important American market at least, may at that stage have only had a passing familiarity with the game, putting the man in goal as the main protagonist might be considered a tough sell.

In the real football world, how many goalkeepers get to have heroic moments? Sure, there are some, like the Gordon Banks save from Pelé for England against Brazil at the 1970 World Cup, but, ultimately, England lost that game. Emi Martinez's stop from Randal Kolo Muani in the last minute of extra time against France in the 2022 World Cup Final is as good a save as you will see and came at as important a time as you could ever see and, yet, it feels like plenty of other things from that final will live longer in the memory – not least Salt Bae infiltrating the post-match celebrations. David Seaman made countless awe-inspiring saves but, unfortunately, he is only as likely to be remembered for them as he is for being lobbed by any number of people from Ronaldinho to Serge from Kasabian. Goalkeeping can be a thankless task.

All football fans will have keepers they admire but how many match-winning performances by those keepers can we hang our hats on? Appreciated? Sure. Held in high regard? Certainly. Loved? By all means. But headlining a Hollywood movie seems an unlikely fate. Of course, there was Jimmy Glass, who came up for a corner and scored a last-minute winner for Carlisle against Plymouth Argyle to keep them in the league but that kind of makes the point. He had to score a goal to become the hero.

In his definitive book on the subject, *The Outsider: A History of the Goalkeeper*, Jonathan Wilson takes some time out from real-life tales to ponder the role of various goalkeepers in fiction. He points out that Bill Naughton's classic 1961 children's book, *The Goalkeeper's Revenge*, sets out the stereotype in its first paragraph. 'Sim Dalt [the goalkeeper of the title] had two long, loose arms, spindly legs, a bony face with gleaming brown eyes and, from the age of 12, was reckoned to be a bit touched in the head.' There are other examples of the goalkeeper as something other, existing on their own plane, a specialist operating only on the fringes of the rest of the team. Michael Hardcastle's *Soccer Special*, Andy 'Streaky' Styles in *Roy of the Rovers* and Harvey from 80s kids' TV show *Jossy's Giants* all contribute to or conform to the stereotype of the goalkeeper as a maverick outsider, not quite one of us. Probably most formative in indoctrinating myself into this mindset is Colin McNaughton's children's book *Football Crazy*. If I got this book out of my local library once as a kid, I must have got it a dozen times. It features new bear in town Bruno joining a football team called Tex's Tigers, despite his very limited ability, and being allowed to be sub. When Roberto the pig gets injured late on in the big match, Bruno gets his chance but only in goal. He saves a last-minute penalty, then hoofs the ball downfield and scores a winning goal to become the hero. It's all there. The outsider, the worst player, the unusual moment of heroism and the goal. Even then, they only let him go back to being sub for the next match. A pattern is emerging.

When Jonathan Wilson turns his attentions to *Escape to Victory*, he points out that Colby agrees to let Hatch be his goalkeeper: 'In part that's because of the hand-to-eye co-ordination he's developed playing US sports but it's also because, as a goalkeeper, he would not disrupt the team unit.' It's a fair point, because goalkeepers are something slightly other. Part of the team but working to their own rules. This comes into play when Colby needs to appeal to Von Steiner to allow Hatch to rejoin the squad after his escape attempt. He can't demand to have him back with the team in his role as trainer and to ask for him as a valued and needed outfield player is too far-fetched – but the idea of him being the best available goalkeeper rings true enough for the plan to work.

In an on-set interview, Stallone agreed with this suggestion, as it applies to both Bobby Hatch and to Sylvester Stallone. He told the interviewer: 'It was the only position that I could have portrayed with some authenticity.' Though, in saying that, he isn't suggesting that anything was easy. 'I like it a lot but the position to me, itself, is the ultimate challenge of nerve and speed and just all-round courage. I have tremendous respect for soccer players in general now.' The word 'now' is doing a lot of work there, because it seems like there was a time when Stallone might have thought it would be easy.

Speaking in a 2022 Q&A, Sly told the crowd that his initial attitude towards the football was 'how hard can this soccer be?', before going on to recount a story of Pelé and a World War Two-era ball that 'looks like a cannonball' that disavowed him of any notion that it might be a walk in the park. The two men had an early conversation in which Pelé asked an over-confident Sly to stand in goal and try to save a shot from him on the dusty training ground of the prison camp set, telling him: 'Okay. You stand here in the goal. I'm going to put the ball right there and I'm going to score and there's nothing you can do about it.' To which Stallone said to himself: 'Yeah, right.'

Pelé took his first shot and it whooshed past the actor before he even saw it, so Stallone told him to try and do it again, now that the element of surprise had gone. When he was telling the same story to *Newsnight* when the film was released, he said: 'It went so fast that I thought I was trying to stop a meteorite.' And it was a moment that clearly stayed with him until that 2022 recounting, when he remembered: 'This time, I managed to get my hand out and it snapped my finger, tore a hole through the net and shattered the barracks windows that were covered in wire mesh.

'And I went: "I'll never say that again."'

Having Pelé taking shots at your star must have been an insurance nightmare for Freddie Fields and John Huston but that broken finger wasn't going to be Stallone's only injury on set.

Given that goalkeeping is so fundamental to *Escape to Victory*, it seems only right to give everyone involved in it a closer look. On the surface, it seems like a mess. Sylvester Stallone accepted the part on an ultimately false promise of scoring the winner; Ipswich provided two goalkeepers, one of whom ended up as the German keeper and the other as a coach and body double for Stallone; a teenage winger who also came along from Ipswich was cast as the chosen Allied goalkeeper; and the German team contained a Hungarian goalkeeper playing out on pitch. It's a lot to untangle. And that's before any mention of the England legend who was involved before filming even began.

Gordon Banks was England's World Cup-winning goalkeeper playing behind Bobby Moore in 1966 and is not only regarded by many as England's greatest-ever keeper but also as, perhaps, one of the best the world has ever seen. So, the fact that Sylvester Stallone had him coaching the basics of goalkeeping in the months before filming began means he went right to the top of the shop for advice. Gordon Banks is sadly no longer with us, having died in 2019, but such was his commitment to goalkeeping that, at his funeral, he had four keepers as his pallbearers, representing his career – Jack Butland (Stoke City), Joe Anyon (Chesterfield), Kasper Schmeichel (Leicester City) and Joe Hart (England) – which is quite something. I was lucky enough to speak with the keeper of the Banks flame – his daughter, Wendy.

Wendy speculated that it may have been Bobby Moore who suggested her father for the job with Stallone. 'All these football players are very cliquey. So, they would recommend each other for all sorts of things. It was just the way they did stuff; you know, "Call Banksy".' Gordon was on the periphery of football at that time and trying to find his feet again. A car accident in 1972 had left him with sight in only one eye and, prematurely, effectively ended his career at the top level. He had attempted a comeback but found it difficult to adjust to the angles and dimensions and timing that had previously come so naturally.

Initially, he became a youth coach at Stoke but his playing career was offered a lifeline by, you guessed it, America. Banks spent a year playing for Fort Lauderdale

Strikers in the NASL, where, despite understandably not being able to perform to his previous levels, he won the goalkeeper of the year award and was named in an all-star team that also included George Best, Franz Beckenbauer, future Wales manager Mike England and Pelé. At one match, Banks was required to engage with the glitz and glamour of it all by taking part in a western-themed match and entering the field riding a white horse. Banks was not a gregarious man and just how comfortable he was with such gimmicks is open to speculation but, on the whole, he seems to have had a nice time in America.

Certainly, he enjoyed it enough to divide his time between there and home. He attempted management, unsuccessfully, at Telford in England's non-league but also coached young players in the USA at the excellently named Camp Kikinthagrass and when the call came from the producers of *Escape to Victory*, he and his family were in something of 'a transition period' and he was only too happy to help.

It seems like the relationship between Stallone and Banks was an uneasy one to begin with. It may not have been helped by the fact that Stallone was, at the time, trying to lose 40lb to better portray a prisoner – perhaps he was hangry? To be honest, Sylvester Stallone and any British footballer of the 70s would seem like uneasy bedfellows but I guess that Gordon was at the vanguard here, before Stallone had a chance to get used to being around the rest of his team-mates on set. The coaching sessions took place early in 1980 in Stallone's breaks between filming *Nighthawks*, which conjures the pleasing image of him being heavily bearded throughout training in full-on Deke DaSilva mode.

Wendy Banks told me that 'Dad had developed a lot of his own coaching ways and methods because when he started goalkeeping, there weren't a lot of specific goalkeeping coaches about', so he was a good man to have around. But it seems that Sylvester was reluctant to take on board his words of wisdom – at least to begin with. He struggled to pay attention to what he was being taught, with diving a particular problem. When he hurt himself attempting it one day, there was a change of attitude. Wendy told me: 'I think then he started to pay a bit more attention. I think he thought he could do everything. And it wasn't quite as easy as it looked. Dad said he started to get better then.'

As Gordon Banks took the lead on coaching Stallone, it has always seemed odd to me that he wasn't subsequently involved in the film and Wendy told me that she thought her dad might have had mixed feelings about it. She said that it never really came up that he was asked to take part and that he was, perhaps, a bit put out by the lack of an offer. However, she happily concedes that he was no kind of actor, 'didn't ever want to make a fool of himself' and that he might have been a little out of his depth if he had taken on a role. Which brings us to those lads who did come on board.

As we know, both of Ipswich Town's goalkeepers, Paul Cooper and Laurie Sivell, joined the party but neither of them ended up in the role of the Allies' unlucky first-choice goalkeeper, Tony Lewis. That honour went to young winger Kevin O'Callaghan and nobody really seems to fully understand why, although Russell Osman has a theory.

'I think Laurie Sivell was going to play Kevin's role but Laurie's got a very croaky voice – he sounds like he's got laryngitis all the time but it's just the way he talks. So, I think they were worried that people wouldn't understand what he was saying.' Whether it was the croakiness or Laurie's distinctive Suffolk accent, it does seem that the voice may, indeed, have been the reason, because O'Callaghan also recalls that: 'We just went and did the voice test. Then, the next day, they told me "You're Tony Lewis."'

It seems that O'Callaghan was more than happy to do it, from acting scenes with Michael Caine to being in goal while some of the world's greatest players fired balls at him in shooting drills for the training sequences. 'I loved it. It was a sandpit. If you watch it, I make some pretty good saves in that bit.' Indeed he does.

What's interesting to me here is that the voice was all-important for the character of Tony but, seemingly, not the look. That's not to say that Kevin O'Callaghan doesn't look like a goalkeeper, because, as he says, he acquits himself well in the training sequences. But the part of Tony the goalkeeper should clearly be an older man.

In the book of the film, which I'm clearly not quite done with yet, when goalkeeper Tony Morrell arrives, he and Colby recognise one another and embrace like old pals, because they clearly know each other from their playing careers before the war. Even when the action is transposed to the film version – in which Tony is now called Lewis – the nod of recognition between him and Colby remains.

And Von Steiner also knows who Tony Lewis is. So, quite why you would go to the lengths of finding the right voice but cast an 18-year-old to play somebody who is supposed to have had enough of a football career, at least four or five years earlier, to be considered the best keeper available in Europe, I don't know. Paul Cooper could have been an option for the role but he told me that he doesn't think he was ever really in the frame for it. Although he originally thought he would be playing the role of one of the keepers in a match situation, he arrived in Budapest slightly later than the others. He recalled: 'We were just told that Kevin O'Callaghan was the goalie and he gets injured and Stallone takes over.'

It is true that whoever got the Tony part would have to endure his fate of being sacrificed to allow Hatch on to the team in his place and have Colby break his arm in a scene that, to this day, is difficult to get through with your eyes open.

Although 'book Tony' gets to escape, 'film Tony' is left behind at the camp, nursing a broken arm. In the moment the Allied team are being swept into the streets of Paris under the cover and protection of a sympathetic crowd at the end of the match, poor old Tony is back on his bunk fearing the worst. And, as Jonathan Wilson puts it in *The Outsider*, 'nobody, not the players, probably not even the viewer, gives him a second thought: he's only a goalkeeper, barely part of the team at all, for all his courage and self-sacrifice'. When I asked Kevin O'Callaghan, even he didn't seem to have wondered about his character's fate. When I pressed him, he told me: 'He just stays in prison, I expect. I broke my arm, went to hospital and stayed in prison.' However, he did enjoy my suggestion that they should have made a sequel called *Escape 2 Victory: The Tony Lewis Story* and I stand by it.

With O'Callaghan cast as Tony Lewis, that left Laurie Sivell on hand to be cast as the German keeper, Schmidt, and he doesn't seem to have minded at all, saying: 'I was out in Budapest for a month and they took our wives out, so I wasn't too displeased.' Fair enough. Sivell does claim to have also chipped in a little with training Sylvester Stallone, telling me: 'I had to give him a couple of goalkeeping lessons at the start because I think he thought he was a basketball player.' But once Gordon Banks had finished with him and Stallone had arrived in Hungary, the responsibility for the bulk of his training fell on Paul Cooper.

The consensus is that Cooper had a thankless task as Stallone's coach on set. Russell Osman said of Cooper: 'He tried to make Stallone look like a goalkeeper, which was hard work.' John Wark said, in his autobiography, that: 'Stallone was coached briefly by Paul Cooper but quickly decided that he could manage without him.' Kevin Beattie went even further in his own candid book, *The Beat*, saying: 'I went over to see how "Coop" was getting on with Sylvester Stallone but he wasn't. "Coop" told me that Stallone had said in no uncertain terms that he didn't want him as his understudy. Mind you, Stallone still wanted "Coop" to teach him how to dive properly as a goalkeeper does. From what I saw, Stallone might have been a star actor but he was an awful goalkeeper and an arrogant sod into the bargain.' However, the struggle here might be slightly overstated.

With regards to the understudy situation, it simply seems to be the case that Stallone was keen to do as much of the physical work as he could for the film, which I think is to be admired. Stallone's take on it was, 'I really believe that I'm paid a good salary and I like playing sports.' He also wanted to strive for realism wherever possible: 'I hate it when you see a shot of someone diving and then, when he lands, he lands in close-up and it's the star's face. We know it's not him so, I just wanted to make sure it was authentic. Otherwise, I wouldn't even attempt to do the role.'

As a director in his own right, Stallone may also have doubted how effective the idea of Paul Cooper in a Sylvester Stallone mask for some of the shots would be. For his part, Cooper seems unbothered by his reduced role, telling me down a phone line from a golf course in Portugal that: 'I was quite happy getting money for nothing. And then they did create this role as an adviser.' As far as Stallone being 'an arrogant sod', Cooper does suggest that Stallone 'thought it was going to be easy'. However, he also describes Stallone as 'very accommodating', says the star was nice and that they got along really well. Furthermore, in a heart-warming touch, he told me: 'I've got some lovely memories from it. I've got a picture of me and Stallone together, which he signed "To my guiding light". I've still got it in the toilet.' I really want to go for a wee at Paul Cooper's house now.

As previously mentioned, Hungarian goalkeeper József Gáspár also pops up in the film as an outfield player for the Germans but these guys nearly weren't the only goalkeepers involved in the production. The 'Goalkeeper

Union' almost had one more representative – Scotland's Alan Rough.

Rough says that he was approached to join the show while on that Scotland trip to Poland and Hungary and would have been sorely tempted to do it had he been told that Pelé was taking part – but he wasn't. He does say that it was mentioned that part of his job might have been to coach Stallone on 'free kicks and penalties' – and you can do your own jokes here. Apparently, it wouldn't have been Rough's only brush with the movies, as, along with his Partick Thistle team-mates, he coached Dee Hepburn a little for her role in the superb *Gregory's Girl*. However, ultimately, he turned down the chance to stay on in Hungary, as he just felt it would have meant he was away from home for too long. When I told Russell Osman that Alan Rough had gone on record as saying that he could have been involved if he had wanted to be, he smiled and said: 'Well, Stallone was a better keeper than Roughie.'

Paul Cooper says that most of what he taught his pupil was 'coaching him on how goalkeepers would have worked in the 30s and 40s. You know, there was no four-step rule, you would have bounced the ball to the edge of the box and booted it'. However, what he still needed to learn was how to dive properly without hurting himself.

Bravery was not a problem for Stallone. On *Nighthawks*, which he had just finished, he had committed to film a stunt that had him dangling on a cable above New York's East River, 250ft in the air. *Escape to Victory* may not have required anything as death-defying as that for him but it did need him to take his fair share of knocks. But that was something he was used to from his *Rocky* films. Biographer

Marsha Daley says that Stallone and Carl Weathers weren't pulling punches in their famous fight sequence for the first film – or in rehearsals – and, as a result, they battered each other significantly, although without causing major injuries. On *Rocky II*, the pair came back together and did the same. This time, Stallone did suffer injuries, tearing his 'pectoralis major, the muscle anchoring the ribs and holding the arm in place. He also suffered a bruised kidney but it was the torn chest and abdomen muscles that caused real problems.' The lack of movement it left him with meant that some of the big fight scenes had to be restaged to cover it. Do you remember in the film when Mickey decides that Rocky, famously a southpaw, should fight the Apollo rematch with an orthodox stance? In the film, Mickey says it is to protect his fighter's eye and they use his reversion to southpaw as a tactic in the final round but Stallone's injuries were the real reason they adjusted the narrative.

The pain doesn't seem to have been a hindrance to Stallone in *Rocky II*, though, and *Escape to Victory* brought its fair share of injuries. Aside from the broken finger sustained from Pelé's net-buster, Stallone damaged other fingers, broke a rib and dislocated a shoulder throwing himself between the posts. The last two of these listed injuries were sustained on day one of filming, which meant an enforced break and some rescheduling. Stallone described himself as 'a walking blood clot' a few weeks into production. In fact, he suggested to the *Clapperboard* cameras when they came to the Budapest camp that his *Escape* injuries were worse than those suffered on his boxing films: 'I had a lot of injuries on *Rocky* but never as many as I've had in jumping on the ground and trying to make some kind of authentic portrayal of a goalkeeper. I think it's a much more ferocious position than I ever imagined.'

It seems that, as with his training under Gordon Banks, his early injuries forced Stallone to focus and change his attitude to learning. He certainly appeared keen to get things right for his character, despite never having played soccer before his role as Hatch was mooted. The actor spoke with the zeal of a convert to anyone who would listen, saying: 'It's a game of such finesse and speed and dexterity and I really wasn't prepared for that much work in the beginning. They say that goalkeeper is quite a difficult position and now I'm convinced of it.' He referred to himself as a 'Johnny Come Lately' when it came to learning his new trade and told a reporter that he wished he had started when he was 'about ten years old'.

Although traces of that old arrogance might have been there on set and he may have rubbed one or two of the players up the wrong way, Stallone grew to respect and admire the game. His commitment to the physical nature of the role cannot be faulted and it's good to stop and appreciate how difficult it must have been to do much of his learning on the job in front of some of the best players to play the game. He admitted to being intimidated by it and said that: 'In boxing, I spent many, many months preparing but it was always in private. I was never under the scrutiny of the best in the world, like having the first sparring partner as Muhammad Ali.' He told *Film '81* about a moment on set when 'Michael Caine says "fire!", so I have Pelé and Bobby Moore and all these people just firing balls. I mean, I bent my finger, I broke one knuckle already and I think I've chipped a bone in my back from doing all these dives. I have tremendous respect and now I know why they say most goalkeepers are a little squiffy.' A little squiffy makes him sound more like Margo from *The Good Life* than Rambo but I get his point.

In the same report, Pelé complimented Stallone's progress, saying: 'He could be a good goalkeeper because he has nice hands and he throws the ball well and he has the vision to get the ball.' And while Pelé was always prone to a bit of hyperbole about people's chances, especially whenever a World Cup came around, Stallone also drew praise from Bobby Moore, who commended the amount of practice he was putting in and said that 'you can see he's improved since the footballers have been here'.

In public, at least, Stallone always played down any progress he had made, saying that he had the advantage of learning to be a goalkeeper rather than an outfield player, which he conceded would have been impossible. He also said that he had the advantage of playing 'an inept goalkeeper', which he described as being 'about the extent of my ability'. Hatch doesn't need to be portrayed as a good goalkeeper. He needs to be portrayed as an enthusiastic amateur. Someone who enjoys a kickabout on the camp and, when he's called upon to pretend to be a goalie, learns the basics and gives it a go. Above all, he needs to be portrayed as being brave. And Stallone worked hard to be able to do all that.

The star was self-deprecating enough to tell *Newsnight* that acting was easier than playing football, enthusing: 'Ooh yes! And a lot less painful and you save a million dollars on ointment.'

Sylvester Stallone takes an unfair amount of criticism from audiences for his role in the film. But the problems that people have with him seem, to me, to be Hatch problems, not Stallone problems. Here is this brash American thinking he can play our sport – that kind of thing. I think it stems from a form of snobbery. America is often accused of being insular around sports, elevating those national games that other countries barely play, while paying less attention to sports that are played worldwide. Think of the consternation Olympic champion sprinter Noah Lyles caused when he said that, while he was a proper world champion because he took on any number of nationalities, NBA winners were 'world champions of what?'

Obviously, there has been a Stateside thawing in the attitude to our brand of football over the years but one suspects that back in 1980, people still didn't want Americans interfering in our game. But you can't have it both ways; surely the Americans who do take an interest in our sports are the ones we have common ground with? The idea of a Hollywood star being cast as the goalkeeping hero in a football film may have got backs up to some extent but my feeling remains that the character is essential to making the film what it is and that Sylvester Stallone worked very hard, took his knocks and generally did everything in his power to give the part everything it needed. The originally intended finale might well have taken things beyond the pale but, ultimately, that was rejected and, instead, we're left with a perfectly reasonable penalty save. Yes, the Hollywood star still gets the glory moment, despite the wealth of footballing talent on show but that is not the fault of this Hollywood star, who took the late change to his character's heroic moment in his stride and got on with it. Stallone is everything he needs to be as Bobby Hatch – the brash, brave, low-ability goalkeeper capable of occasional moments of brilliance. His penalty save at the end isn't about skill, it's about will and I, for one, am buying it.

9.

THE FILM – PART III

A NEW day dawns in the camp and Colby's squad have woken up together in their own barracks as they take their first steps towards becoming a team. We find Colby delivering his initial address to the players before training commences. Bill Conti's strings stir underneath Michael Caine as he tells his assembled squad that: 'It's been a long time and none of us feels like or looks like world-class players.' The smile to himself at this point might be Caine's rather than Colby's.

He suggests they get started with some easy stretches and he kicks the ball away, saying: 'We won't be needing that for a while.' A wide shot from a gun tower then shows everyone trotting through a gentle lap of the training ground. Hatch stands in the middle, barking instructions and not joining in, which is ironic given that, when the cameras stopped rolling, Stallone would be the one spending most breaks between shots exercising and generally trying to hone his physique.

Next, we have a lovely scene in which all the training equipment promised by Von Steiner arrives. Anybody who has known that thrill of a load of free gear arriving and piling in to get your share will relate to the glee among the players here. Red tracksuits, white training shirts and boots you might have a hope of controlling a ball in are all here. There is not yet any sign of the matchday kit, however. We are not told when that arrives or if it is, perhaps, just laid out for them at the stadium but you think if it were among the kit to have just arrived, at least one player would be pulling it out of a box with an excited 'Cor!'. The scene also offers an opportunity for Hatch to get on Colby's nerves by endlessly prattling on about injuries and illness, including the curious choice of 'anal bleeding'. It moves their relationship on from the loaded scene outside the hut when Hatch pleaded to be involved, with all the personal dangers that entailed, and on to a more fun plane where Hatch is a minor irritant to him, purely due to their very different personalities.

Once dressed in their new kit, we see Colby and his players emerge from the hut resplendent in all red, to wolf whistles and catcalls from the other prisoners, who have assembled to watch. Caine flicks the Vs a few times and throws in a lovely 'Take no notice lads, they're only jealous,' in addition to a well-timed 'Up yours!' at the goading prisoners, with both comments smacking of improvisation on his part. It is true that while Caine isn't a frequent improviser of lines, John Huston was known to let him freewheel a little bit. Caine recalls that the wonderful scene in *The Man Who Would Be King*, when he is drilling troops and becoming increasingly exasperated at the ineptitude of one particular recruit, was improvised. And it is very funny. On *Escape to Victory*, the veteran director once again allowed Caine to play with his dialogue a bit because 'he was the Limey we wanted'.

This is where Bill Conti debuts his football theme, as we move into a new phase of the film, and it's an absolute banger. The military drums remain but the brass is far more playful than the earlier music and it is saying 'we have a job to do but we'll have fun doing it'. Quite why this music isn't played before every professional football match that ever takes place, I don't know. It's stirring stuff and it would make me want to run through a brick wall if I was a player – although, while that's a phrase we hear a lot, I'm never sure how it would help in a football situation. Much better in a prison camp situation, if anything.

The music taking centre stage can only mean one thing – it's a montage. It swells over shots of the team, resplendent in white training shirts and their fancy new boots, bending, stretching and doing that odd move where they do sit-ups, leaning back over a partner's raised knees. There is head tennis and piggy in the middle, which we are these days duty bound to call a rondo, as if we're all too grown-up to call it piggy in the middle anymore. You get the impression that these games of head tennis and keep-ball are just what would have been going on anyway, regardless of whether cameras were rolling. At times, the joy on the faces of the players looks genuine.

Benoît Ferreux can be glimpsed within this montage doing the more rudimentary skills and admiring the shooting of others, so, although his lack of footballing ability is being masked by better players and some clever editing, he is still very much there in the mix at this stage. We also get the shooting session in which Kevin O'Callaghan gets to look the part of a capable goalkeeper and, of course, we get a first glimpse of Pelé's acrobatics. We've heard of Chekhov's Gun, the principle which means that any narrative element introduced to a story should be important to the plot later on; well, here we see Chekhov's Overhead Kick – with Luis Fernandez giving us a glimpse of what he's capable of, just in case he needs to do it later.

After the training montage comes perhaps the most famous scene in the film. In the hut, Colby is stood at the tactics board with the chalk, making a lot of sense about making sure his unfit players let the ball do the work instead of running themselves into the ground. Incidentally, it's a tactics board which has, written along the bottom under the pitch, 'Prisoner FC Motto: Win or Lose, On the Booze!!!', which is either confirmation that Colby was always more about the beer than the eggs and fresh fruit and vegetables when he was making his demands to Von Steiner or a lovely in-joke that a cast member has slipped in. Certainly, if it was an in-joke by one of the team, it rings true with some of their downtime tales, which we will come to.

Luis is more about the flair than the tactics and decides that this stuffy old nonsense isn't for him. He jumps down from the bunk, where he has been sat with Søren Lindsted's Erik Borge, and ambles up to the front to interrupt Colby's chat. He grabs the chalk and memorably draws his own mazy dribble towards goal, showing that he can win the game on his own if his team-mates will only give him the ball. Everyone in the hut enjoys the moment so much that nobody feels compelled to tell Luis that he has drawn his mazy run heading in the opposite direction to Colby's sweeping passes, so, effectively, he's just described an own goal. An audacious one, for sure, but an own goal, nevertheless. Werner Roth claims that Pelé improvised this moment and that John Huston liked it so much that he got him to give it another go for a take. If so, it's further evidence of collaboration between the players and the film-makers. Well done everyone.

The jovial mood is halted when Rose comes to the door and interrupts the laughing to request Colby's presence with Waldron. When Colby steps outside, we see that Waldron is standing about 10ft away, so, all rank aside, he could probably have gone knocking himself. However, there is no time to quibble because we are about to get the biggest gear change in the entire film.

The Eastern European players have arrived, to Waldron's bemusement and Colby's regret – because they look, understandably, like completely broken men. Whatever the war has seen them face in their own prison camps, it isn't fresh vegetables and grog. Somebody might want to rub off that 'on the booze' motto before these guys go in, because it doesn't feel so appropriate now. The five men are made up of four extras, who have open uniforms to show their skeletal frames, and, at the back, another who has full uniform on to disguise the fact that he was probably in very good nick, because the man at the back is Kazimierz Deyna, of Manchester City and Poland.

Obviously, Deyna's Paul Wolchek is Polish and, appropriately, with the Eastern European prisoners. However, it isn't clear if it was always the intention to have him arrive at this stage or whether he might have got there earlier with the previous truck full of players. Ossie Ardiles remembers that Deyna arrived on location later than the rest of the footballers and had reservations about appearing on screen in this state.

Ardiles told me: 'He had to arrive with blood on his face and with his hair cut to look terrible. But he came back from make-up and the director said "that's no good", because his hair was still as long. He sent him back to have more off.' I've never been a prisoner of war but I distinctly recall my mum sending me back round to the barber to ask them to take off some more hair when she wasn't happy with it and, let me tell you, it's a humiliating experience.

Ardiles continued: 'So, when he appears, he has blood all around and a black eye and his hair is badly cut, so it's long in some places and short in others and looks terrible. He wasn't very happy, as you can imagine.' Unhappy he may have been but the five of them standing there, with Colby insisting that they are, or were, great footballers, as we see the damage that has been done to them, is a rare powerful note in the film. Coming so soon after the fun and laughter of Luis Fernandez's alternative team talk, it stops us in our tracks.

Waldron blasts Colby for his naivety and tells him that London has heard reports about the match and can't quite believe that any British officer would be involved in such a scheme. Caine's Colby is left looking vulnerable here. Is he doing the right thing or has he got lost in it all? Sylvester Stallone made an interesting point when he drew parallels between Colby and another iconic British officer from the movies: 'This football game, to him, is not just being played for the men's spirit, it's like what Alec Guinness went through in *Bridge on the River Kwai*; it's like a private war.' Any comparison between Colby and Alex Guinness's Colonel Nicholson is high praise, indeed. In trying to give their men something to be proud of, both men are unintentionally helping the enemy war effort. Of course, while Nicholson's bridge would either be built or not, Colby's football match can take place or not but it's the result which will decide who it helps.

Hatch shows compassion here by taking charge of the situation and offering to get the new arrivals cleaned up and deloused before they mix with the rest of the team. Once they are inside, they sit silently in their training kit and enjoy their first square meal in who knows how long. The relief on their faces is palpable and heart-breaking. Colby takes the opportunity to gather his troops for a consultation. He knows that he has messed up in insisting on bringing these damaged footballers in but knows that if he now decides not to play, they will be sent back to the hell from which they came. He therefore resolves to play but invites his team to make their own decisions about defying high command and playing the match. It is Jean-Paul who answers first and most decisively, saying 'We play. What else can we do?', which keeps him at the centre of the action for the time being, making his subsequent disappearance when the football starts all the more baffling. Did the producers just think that we wouldn't notice him or not notice that he was gone? They might have been right. To be fair, I don't think it is something I noticed until I was several viewings into the film. Jean-Paul is followed up by Sid, then Luis, then a host of murmured assenting noises – some of which must surely have been added in the Mayfair additional dialogue recording (ADR) sessions the players had to attend after filming, because there is a resounding 'Yeah come on, let's play' in here from Bobby Moore that we cannot see him say.

Matter resolved, the training continues the following day, with renewed determination. When trainer Hatch goes to speak to Waldron and Shurlock as they look on from behind the goal, the first seed of his goalkeeping exploits is sown. Colby puts him between the posts and the whole team fire shots at him. Some of these he saves and others he doesn't but all the while he is talking a good game and Colby playfully asks him if he can do it with his mouth shut. The session ends with Luis dribbling round Hatch to score and leaving the American face down in the dirt. As he picks him up, despite humiliating him, he assures him that he could be a good goalkeeper and Colby agrees. As the prospect of Hatch playing in goal in the match has yet to come up, we must chalk this up as an entertaining aside – for now.

Hatch has no time for such frivolities as goalkeeping just now, though, as he's off to collect his freshly forged passport, only to be told by the forger that Colonel Waldron has taken it for his own reasons. Clive Merrison's forger helps out Hatch with a bit of French vocabulary he might need while on the run and then there's a lovely exchange in which he reminds the American to take his identity tags with him because he won't want to be shot as a spy, to which Hatch quite rightly quips: 'I don't want to be shot as anything.' It's lovely stuff and it plays into a universal truth that every schoolboy who watched war films knows. I wouldn't claim to have known very much about the world as a kid but I knew, for sure, that if I ever got caught by Germans without my own uniform or at least my identity tags, I would be shot as a spy. Thankfully, it never proved to be necessary in 1980s Basildon, where it was all much

THE FILM – PART III

more of a synth pop vibe than a behind enemy lines one, but it's still useful to know.

Hatch makes his way to the escape committee hut and when he's right outside the window, Rose announces that he's on his way, which rather suggests that Rose's main job in this command structure is to be Waldron's eyes and ears but only when really close to doors that Waldron is, himself, already quite close to.

Hatch enters and Waldron hands him his Marcel Dupin passport, which contains a photograph of Hatch which looks nothing like the one the forger took at their session. It's almost as if all that fiddling with the camera equipment was just good acting. Waldron, Rose, Shurlock and Pirie then work together to soft soap Hatch and smarm him into doing them the huge favour of escaping, making his way to Paris, contacting the Resistance and arranging the escape of the football team, instead of just scarpering off somewhere on his own. Although they do give him a cup of tea while they do it, so things are just about even. The American agrees to do it and then, as he leaves, he truly joins the ranks of all football people everywhere when he says: 'This frigging game is wrecking my life.' It's a sentiment that fans of most clubs have shared at some point.

The plan swings into action, with Hatch using the team's shower time to make his escape on to the wash house roof, as he had planned all along before stupid Hans and Anton swapped shifts. It's a curious scene which uses lots of that ADR, possibly too much, to create a feeling of general hubbub and camaraderie among the showering players, while Colby distracts the guards with cigarettes.

But when it comes to looking up and delivering actual lines wishing their comrade good luck, it once more falls to Mike Summerbee and Russell Osman to deliver the goods. These two are naturals. Once out on to the roof, Hatch waits until darkness falls to make his next move.

At roll call, held at dusk, Terry and Pieter carry a very impressive dummy between them to cover for the missing Hatch as the guards take a head count. I cannot stress how good this dummy is. I mean, it doesn't look like Hatch but a lot of work has gone into it and I would love to know which prisoner made it, when and with what materials. I would gladly have watched several scenes showing it being built. The move recalls another war film, *Albert R.N.*, in which the same trick is pulled, albeit with an even better dummy. That's another film in which our commentator and prolific on-screen Nazi, Anton Diffring, plays a German officer. You're never more than 10ft away from an Anton Diffring war movie, so they say.

In the team hut that night, after lights out, Luis plays a plaintive tune on a harmonica as the camera pans from player to player to show their shared deep concern for the welfare of their escaped comrade. It demonstrates the level to which Hatch has truly been adopted as part of the gang.

Night has fallen and Hatch, now fully dressed, goes to work clipping the wire and dropping down into the German side of the compound. There's genuine tension here, helped by Bill Conti going all suspenseful. Hatch skilfully evades those sweeping searchlights that did for Williams at the beginning and manages to jump on to and cling to the side of a car, which is taking a visiting woman out of the camp and presumably back to the local town. Quite what she was doing visiting the German camp command and leaving so late at night is for you to speculate on but I'm going to assume that she was the Avon Lady. Once out through the gate and unseen, Hatch drops off the runner and scampers into the trees, where he presumably spends the night. In the morning, at the local train station, his new passport is good enough to blag his way past two German soldiers and get himself on to the train. He gives himself extra cover by helping a woman and her child on to the carriage with their bags and acting like he's with them. He hops up on to the moving train as it leaves the station – and he's away. Remember when we could all jump freely off and on moving trains in stations, before health and safety went mad? Happier, simpler, far more dangerous times.

The whole train station scene inevitably evokes memories of the similar transport scenes in *The Great Escape*, with the escapees slipping aboard with their forged papers. With that and *Albert R.N.* in such quick succession, our film is wearing its influences on its sleeve around this point.

Back in the camp, the team continue to work out themselves, even in the absence of their trainer, which suggests he wasn't doing much. The lads are mostly tops-off at this point, working in the sun and doing an exercise which consists of getting up off the floor as quickly as possible and booting the ball as hard as they can. It's a strange one but Hatch isn't there to oversee it. He's off on his own adventures around Paris.

Now, if there is a section of the film that sags a little, then, hand on heart, it's this bit, as Hatch goes on the

Metro and finds the right bar in which to contact the Resistance. It isn't that it is dull at all, just that it feels like it belongs in a different film. Or perhaps it's simply that now I know all the other guys are playing football in the camp, I just want to see more of that. Even in montage form, I would take it. Hatch signals his intentions to the waiter by sketching a quick V for victory on the table, although he could be playing a game of Hangman and starting with the legs. Either way, the landlord wipes away his daubing and before you know it, he has linked him up with the plucky Resistance.

Certain elements of Hatch's time at the safe house were discussed in a previous chapter about the novelisation of the film and we won't dwell too much here on what does or doesn't happen between him and Renée, played by Carole Laure. In the version we see, Renée tells her guest about the life she has chosen in wartime and the husband she has lost and the two do no more than flirt. After all, her sleeping son is in the flat. If you want it any muckier than that, I'm afraid you'll have to go for the paperback version.

Before Renée even speaks, however, Hatch has been discussing the possibility of an escape for the team on matchday with three Resistance members. André is played by French actor Amidou, while Claude, who eventually pokes his head up through the bath at half-time after doing all that digging for nothing, is Jean-François Stévenin. Viktor, the third man, is Zoltán Gera. Not the West Bromwich Albion and Fulham winger of the same name, you understand. Although this film is full of footballers, none of them, unfortunately, are time-travelling ones. This

THE FILM – PART III

Zoltán Gera is considered Hungarian acting royalty. He also provides a nice link for us here, because he is one of the stars of the 1961 film that *Escape to Victory* took inspiration from, *Two Half Times in Hell*. It all fits.

After initial doubts that such an escape would be possible, Viktor reacts to a mention of Stade de Colombes and, suddenly, everything is looking more positive. The sewers under the ground are discussed in French and the three men head off to find a big hole and look into it, so to speak. They leave Hatch to Renée's hospitality and he immediately tries to chat her up a bit, over another cup of tea, or possibly coffee. Either way, his escape seems to be going well so far and the situation he finds himself in tonight is far better than the previous night he spent in the woods or the night before that spent bunked up with about 14 farting footballers.

Roll call in the daylight is a different proposition to the bedtime one and the Hatch dummy ceases to cover for him when its head drops off and hits the floor with a thud, alerting the camp Kommandant to what has been going on. Where is Luis and his keepy-uppies now? Surely he could have flicked the head back up to where it should be with a touch or three? Even with a sinister patch over one eye, the Kommandant can see that one of the prisoners that has been counted is headless and the game is up. There's a lot of schoolboy sniggering from the team at the revelation and Waldron does a lovely 'what are they like?' style clutch of the head and it is all very knockabout for what might be the serious matter of aiding and abetting an escape. Indeed, Colby is summoned by Von Steiner for a bit of a telling-off for making him look a proper Charlie but that's about all it is. The novelisation may have had Von Steiner having to convince Herr Lorenz not to shoot Colby at this point but the film settles for much more of an 'I'm not angry, just disappointed' tone.

Caine and Von Sydow do play the scene with a bit of creeping antagonism that hasn't been there before, as the reality of war threatens to encroach on their football ideals, after all. The German asks for Colby's word that there will be no further escape attempts and the Englishman, or Welshman depending on who you believe, says he cannot give it to him. The possibility of everyone escaping or everyone getting shot is suddenly in the air; before now, the concerns of these two men were more along the lines of who might play right midfield. Von Steiner tells Colby that the team will be very well guarded and sends him on his way. This, I feel, is a warning that would have more weight to it if the Jean-Paul Remy escape attempt from the train had stayed in the film.

While, back at the safe house, Hatch is developing his relationship with Renée, the poor Resistance lads are poking around in the Paris sewers, trying to find a way into the Stade de Colombes through the pipes. When they tell Hatch that they think they have a way, André, the leader, tells Hatch that the only way to let everyone in Gensdorf know that an escape attempt will be on for half-time is for him to get recaptured and go back. With Renée onside and all the tea he can drink, Hatch is reluctant to go along with such a plan and raises the possibility that he might get taken to a different camp. André insists that he will be returned to whence he came as an example to others that his escape was a failure. Hatch begrudgingly accepts that he might be right and once more curses what football is doing to his life, which lightens the mood for the viewer a little and, again, is something many of us can relate to.

Hatch says his goodbyes to Renée until the match, then it's a hard cut to Hatch standing on the back of an army truck as he is transported back to the camp. Now, I know that I said that the Hatch-on-the-loose section sags a little but, at the same time, I feel like we've been robbed of a scene in which we would see him get recaptured. How did he do it? Surely he can't have just wandered up to a German soldier and tapped him on the shoulder, put his hands out and said: 'It's a fair cop?' Was there running, was there chasing, was there fighting? I guess we will never know – Hatch is back and that's that.

As the escape committee watch on through a fence, Shurlock beats Rose to the prize for stating the bleeding obvious by saying 'He's back' but it's Rose who is smart enough to interpret Hatch's flapping hands-on-head gesture as meaning Mercury – Messenger of the Gods – and that he has got information for them. The rest of Hatch's triumphant return, from the cheering prisoners to the wordless way the goons toss him into the cooler, is once again very reminiscent of *The Great Escape*, with Stallone mirroring the cool Steve McQueen role. They are both in the cooler but, for my money, Steve McQueen was just a little bit cooler.

Colby is summoned by the escape committee to discuss the team's escape plans, which Colby has remained oblivious to, and to work out how they can possibly get Hatch out of the cooler to receive his message. Waldron,

Rose and Shurlock, who really do operate like a three-headed beast in these situations, fire information at the beleaguered captain, who just wants to be left alone with his football mates. Waldron reminds him that it is his duty to escape if he can and that he already faces a possible court martial, if and when he ever gets home, for collaborating in what they regard as a German propaganda stunt. Colby pleads ignorance and is all out of ideas for getting Hatch released. Waldron suggests insisting to Von Steiner that they need their trainer and Colby says they won't buy it. At this point, the door is creaking open for Hatch to end up in goal, as the plan will need to be taken up a notch, but nobody has said it out loud yet. As he walks away, Colby looks across to the cooler, where Hatch lies sweating up a storm, and says 'Crazy Yank', with a smile and more than a glimmer of affection for the man who has escaped, given up being shacked up with Renée and got himself recaptured just to give him and his team a chance to get home.

In the next scene, somebody finally says it out loud. In the camp Kommandant's office, Von Steiner lays out some ground rules for the match, telling Waldron that he and Major Rose must travel to the match to represent the camp, which is, to be frank, one in the eye for Shurlock. Then Colby tells Von Steiner that he needs Hatch out of solitary confinement, not because he is the trainer but because he is his goalie. An incredulous Von Steiner, who knows his football and is well aware of the internationally renowned reputation of the 18-year-old Tony Lewis and all the work he was doing five years ago before the war started when he was at school, says that Lewis is the keeper. Despite presumably having had some time to think about it and not just make it up on the spot, Colby says that Tony Lewis broke his arm that morning and Hatch is needed to replace him. Von Steiner's initial reaction of 'put someone else in goal' takes us right back to that slight disdain we all subconsciously carry for the craft of keeping but, eventually, he concedes that the switch can be made if the camp doctor verifies the broken arm. It does leave me wondering, though, why Colby couldn't have just said that Tony had a stomach bug or a concussion or something that he could feign, without having to get his arm snapped in half. Even a finger or two would have been enough to keep Lewis out of the game, but no. Colby goes all in on the arm.

Which brings us to the single most brutal scene in the film. Forget the messy death of Williams, all tangled up in the barbed wire at the start, because now is the moment that Tony Lewis gets his arm broken. Although I've been critical of casting such a young player in the role of Tony Lewis, maybe this was the scene that the casting director, Rose Tobias Shaw, and whoever else made the decision had in mind. Because Kevin O'Callaghan's callowness and baby face really sell the tragedy of what is about to happen. Tony agrees to go along with it and, despite muttering a plaintive 'I won't even get to see the game, will I?', places his forearm between two bed slats and lets Colby put his big army boot through it. This is some proper acting from O'Callaghan. Obviously, he is helped out in the scene by Michael Caine – and who else would you rather have smashing your arm to pieces on camera? – but I can't imagine anybody else being able to sell it any better than Kevin O'Callaghan does here. His team-mates can't look and nor can I. Honestly, I've heard people talk about Mr Blonde cutting off Marvin the cop's ear in *Reservoir Dogs* as something you have to look away from. In truth, the cameras cut way from both and you don't see either moment but, for whatever it says about me, I've always found poor old Tony having his arm broken and being left behind in the camp to fend for himself to be by far the more traumatising moment of the two. Now, about that Tony Lewis sequel?

Squad finalised by the last-minute freak injury, everybody is off to the train station to make their way to Paris on what seems to be the same day as the match. No pre-match night in a hotel for this team; no training session on the pitch; just bus, train, bus, ground, kick-off for the Allies. As the boys all board the train in silence, Benoît Ferreux is still unmistakably there as Jean-Paul and, yet, he absolutely is not when they arrive at the other end. I will not let this go and I hope that, after reading this book, neither will you.

At the stadium, the Germans are carrying out their – frankly inadequate – security checks, deciding that they will post a guard at the dressing room door and another at the dressing room window but not one inside. Now, I'm not saying that anyone could have had the foresight to know that the French Resistance were going to come tunnelling up the plug hole but I am saying that a guard inside the door would not have hurt as a security measure and might have nipped any naughtiness in the bud. I'm not here to tell Nazi Germany their business but I would just have expected greater attention to detail, that's all.

THE FILM – PART III

The commanding officer decides that the Allies should have the visitors' dressing room, which they are in the process of inspecting, and that the conquering Germans should take the home dressing room. It's a controversial decision designed to antagonise the occupied French but I can't help thinking they have other things to worry about. After a cursory question about both dressing rooms being exactly the same, the officers are away, having taken the stadium worker at his word. But what if it's like 'Crazy Gang' Wimbledon in the 1980s and the hot water and light switches only work in one dressing room? They might have walked into the other one to find that the thermostat was deliberately broken and all the seats had splintered wood. Again, it's worth a check, I think.

Wait, what's this? It was only on what might have been my 43rd viewing of this film that I realised that the stadium worker is, in fact, our Viktor from the Resistance. How have I missed his cheeky grin before as he places the 'visiteurs' sign on the door for the Allies and scuttles off to tell his colleagues which one they will be in? Imagine if poor old Claude came up in the wrong bath. He would have a tough time explaining that to the German team. Four-one up at half-time or not, they would have spotted that something was up.

On the train journey, most of the players are sleeping but an anxious Hatch cannot. He asks Colby the perfectly reasonable question of where he should stand for a corner kick but Colby just laughs at him and brushes him off. We live in a time when set-piece coaches have murals outside the ground and any kind of throw-in within 40 yards of the goal represents a clear and present danger, so maybe

I'm being over-sensitive, but it feels like even in the 1940s it was worth your goalkeeper knowing where his captain or manager wanted him to stand to best defend a corner. This is poor from Colby.

Cut to the stadium, where many troops are arriving to take up their places in the stands and along the surrounding rooftops. There are so many here that it has an air about it of the cops in *The Blues Brothers*, but it does leave me wondering quite where all these guys disappear to at the end of the game. We see a few guards overpowered but not a single shot gets fired. Maybe they left the game early; you know, the way that some people do.

The Allies players arrive in a bus that looks suspiciously exactly the same as the one they got off at the other end of their train journey and they file into the ground, with no sign of Jean-Paul, who I've now decided fell asleep on the train and simply went back the other way again. It can happen to the best of us.

The players make their way into the dressing room and nervously start to get changed. Colby and Hatch, as the only ones aware that an escape attempt has been planned, throw furtive glances at the bath and at one another, then we're back outside, rattling along in a van with the Resistance lads, who make their way to a Parisian junction, put some cones out and pretend they are working in the sewers. Just to show that I'm balanced and not only worried about Nazi security, this set-up also seems, to me, a bit flimsy. What about permits and traffic? What if these guys get challenged by the authorities? It worries me sick. Perhaps there will be no attention on them because everybody is at the stadium? We already know that half the German army are there and then we see the fans start to arrive. Inside, Renée and her son have taken their places on the terrace, while, in the posh seats, Waldron and Rose sit with other British representatives and Von Steiner takes his seat alongside his superiors – one of whom sidles up to him and confirms that the referee is bent, just in case that sort of thing is needed. The Corinthian spirit of fair play runs strong through Von Steiner's veins and he is horrified at the very idea but, at this stage, he realises that this whole thing has got way bigger than him. Maybe he longs to be back on the camp pitch chatting to Colby or even further back before the war, when football was all he needed to think about?

In the 'visiteurs' dressing room, the Allied lads sit around looking terrified and paying no attention at all to the fact that they have just dropped the smartest football kit of all time. Hatch asks for advice on corners once more and, this time, Colby tells him what he wants from him, marking a final thawing in what was once a frosty relationship between our two lead characters.

And as, beneath the ground, the Resistance boys continue to do what will amount to a lot of pointless hard graft in the sewers, the stage is set for our match.

10.

ON SET

PRINCIPAL PHOTOGRAPHY for the film began on 26 May 1980 and the cast began to assemble in Budapest accordingly. Werner Roth remembers arriving early and being greeted with the dinner he described, with Pelé, John Huston and Freddie Fields in attendance. However, if Pelé was already there, then Werner was not particularly early, because most of the cast were already there, too, having arrived hot on the heels of the Brazilian superstar.

Ossie Ardiles recalls the flight that brought him in, along with some of his co-stars from the English game. 'When we arrived in Budapest with the English guys, we were on a private plane and we were all dressed in jeans, very casual. As we landed, the pilot said to Bobby – because, although he wasn't our captain, he was so clearly the leader – "Oh look, there are thousands of people waiting for us on the tarmac." So, Bobby moved like a flash. I've never seen him move so quickly. He went to the toilet and he changed and he came back out in collar and tie and a lovely jacket. That was Bobby all the time.' Bobby Moore there, like a dinner party Superman, ready to save any social occasion with a change of clothes and a splash of aftershave. This time, however, it was all in vain. Ossie continues: 'But when we got off, there was nobody there and we asked what was going on? They said "Oh, they were waiting for Pelé and he already arrived, so they all followed him to the hotel." So that was it. There was nobody waiting for us.' Hopefully, Bobby won't have seen this as a waste of a good shirt. It clearly made an impression on Ardiles, who claims that Moore even washed and changed after filming the half-time tunnel scene so that he would still look immaculate for any more football shots they might have to do.

Mike Summerbee remembers being on that same flight with Bobby, with the pair of them sampling the Hungarian wine. He says it was 'like drinking Domestos' but they showed admirable perseverance to keep drinking the terrible drink anyway, because what else are you going to do? Customs and airport formalities only briefly halted their session, because they hit the gin and tonics as soon as they got to the hotel – or presumably after they had unpacked and positioned everything just so in the wardrobe. They were in a pair of adjoining suites on the top floor and you fear for the mini-bars, you really do.

That meal at which John Huston persuaded Werner Roth to take on the Baumann part, rather than portraying Jean-Paul Remy, must have happened on this night, because everyone remembers getting straight down to work the following morning with a 6am start. The players were collected and driven out to the PoW camp set, where they were given a uniform and a haircut, as well as a script. From the look of things on screen, I'm not sure Bobby Moore let anybody touch his hair but, once the players were kitted out, they were all very quickly confronted with the new world they were stepping into.

Mike Summerbee and the others went into the cafeteria, housed in one of the PoW huts, and found a scene straight out of Hollywood. 'Michael Caine was there. He already knew Bobby. The German [sic] actor, Max von Sydow, was there, and Stallone and Pelé. They had no idea who I was at the start and I wondered if I would be out of my depth.'

If the older and more experienced Summerbee was overawed by what he was walking into, it's fair to say that the younger players from Ipswich were even further out of their comfort zone.

John Wark says: 'I didn't know what I was letting myself in for. We didn't realise until we got to Hungary what a big deal it was and what big characters were in it.' When I asked Kevin O'Callaghan what he was told about the film before he flew out, he said: 'Nothing. I didn't have a clue.' He was clearly not so daunted that he didn't get involved with his more famous co-stars, though. He told me: 'I got a picture the first day there, sat by one of the sheds, with Bobby Moore one side and Pelé the other side.' He also says that any nerves were put aside on that first day by the ultimate ice-breaker: 'We had a little game of football. Pelé was brilliant. All he wanted to do was play football.'

The lack of a detailed briefing about what the film was going to entail was a recurring theme with anybody I spoke to. Hallvar Thoresen said he was told 'not very much, only the broad base, of course, but no details at all, so every day was a new experience'. And Søren Lindsted said: 'I didn't know anything.' Although he did concede that what he needed to know was limited: 'I have a six-second sequence where I'm eating goulash, which took about an hour. I say "yes" when Michael Caine asks me something and that was my part in the entire movie.' That may be true until the match kicks off and Bobby Moore also said that his part mostly involved 'just lurking about in the background', but this wasn't the case for everyone. For some of the newly arrived players, things went up a notch rather quickly. Russell Osman recalls that the production staff started handing out scripts and somebody told him: 'You have dialogue tomorrow morning with Michael Caine.' Osman chuckled at the memory of this bolt from the blue. 'I said, "I'm sorry, you must have got me mixed up with someone else, because we're just here to do the football scenes." Then Kevin O'Callaghan got a script and Warky got given a script and they said "No, you've actually got a role to play in the film".' Wark also remembers simply being told 'this is your part, these are your lines' and having to cope with that quickly.

I suppose it is possible that keeping the inexperienced members of the cast in the dark was all part of a master plan to stop them getting nervous about needing to act but I can't believe how lucky the film-makers got. I'm not quite suggesting that Osman, Summerbee and O'Callaghan, who are called upon to do the most acting among the footballers, are BAFTA winners but, for three sportsmen with no acting experience between them outside of Summerbee's panto appearances, to cope with the dialogue they were given in the way that they do is remarkable. I can think of countless films where even a short line or two by a famous person making a cameo appearance takes you out of the film a bit.

To take two completely random examples, for no particular reason, consider Elon Musk in *Iron Man 2* or Donald Trump in *Home Alone 2: Lost In New York*. Summerbee says that 'there were no acting lessons, you just had to look and learn' and, apart from the voice tests that decided that Kevin O'Callaghan and not Laurie Sivell got the Tony Lewis part, there doesn't seem to have been any auditioning for parts. And, yet, Russell Osman says that: 'Most of the dialogue I did was used, which is fortunate.' As I say, I think it was Freddie Fields and John Huston who were fortunate.

Summerbee does suggest that Michael Caine did his best to get them involved and then to help them out from behind the camera, giving pointers and helping them to concentrate. Anyone who remembers Michael Caine's screen acting masterclass, *Michael Caine on Acting in Film*, has seen that he knows exactly what he is doing for the cameras and is full of expert advice for those who are less experienced. I highly recommend watching both that and the Peter Serafinowicz parody of it but you will learn much more from one than the other. Summerbee described his time with Caine as 'a bloody privilege to work with someone like that'. Russell Osman also remembers Caine being supportive as they opened their acting account with the meal scene upon arrival at the camp, in which Osman's Doug Clure and the others eat stew. 'It was quite daunting, really, because you're sat there, never been in that situation before and Michael Caine's there. He relaxed everyone by telling a few stories, though, then he said "Right then, a couple of minutes and we're out of there." So, he was brilliant.'

When I asked Russell how it came to be that he and Mike got the most lines, in particular when pleading the case in the tunnel to go back and play, he said: 'I don't think there was any discussion about anyone else doing it. Maybe because me and Mike had been a bit gobby about one or two other things. I think I was lucky. I put myself out there a bit more. I've never got nervous about things. In for a penny in for a pound and I was the same with that. Just get on with what I've been asked to do. It's only now you realise how lucky we were to be involved.' Despite having never acted before, Osman impressed his director so much that the possibility of further work was suggested. 'John Huston did say to me one day, "Why don't you come back to Hollywood with us?" but I was in my early 20s, so obviously I wasn't going to do that. But it was nice to hear and he was great – a proper gentleman.' Had Osman taken him up on his offer and left Ipswich Town for Tinsel Town, you would imagine Bobby Robson might have thought his summer plan for his players had backfired but, with most of his football career stretching out in front of him, Russell decided that his movie career was one and done.

Kevin O'Callaghan's big scene with Michael Caine was, of course, the moment that Tony Lewis needs to have his arm broken by Colby and Kevin was, understandably, nervous. 'Shitting myself. I've never acted in my life. I didn't even act in school. I was rubbish. I didn't even get in the school plays.' However, once again, he credits his esteemed co-star with calming him down a little. 'I also had a bit of an affinity with Michael Caine, because he was from the Elephant and Castle and he found out I'd played for Millwall.' He says that a bit of South London solidarity really helped him out, that Caine was brilliant with him and that they nailed it in one take.

Bobby Moore joked to *Thames News* about his co-stars, saying 'I think one or two might be disappointed if we don't get Oscars now' but, while the sudden surge in dialogue might not have had them thinking about awards, it certainly had some of them thinking about rewards.

Bobby Robson had negotiated the fees of his Ipswich players but when they arrived, they realised that all the other players were on twice as much as they were. The speaking parts also felt like more work than they initially signed up for, so Osman, Wark and O'Callaghan got a delegation together to go and see Freddie Fields about getting some more money. How they got on is still up for debate, because the versions of how things played out differ between the three men. John Wark recalls that, 'I was the spokesman. I went to his hotel and chapped his door, said I was representing Ipswich Town – this was after about two or three weeks – and I said, "I think we should get more money or royalties or we're seriously thinking about leaving." And do you know what his exact words were? "Eff off." And I had to go back to the lads and say "Oh. We're just staying with the money we've got." Imagine if we had got royalties, though. I'm not much of a negotiator.'

However, Russell Osman says: 'It was Lorimar, who made *Dallas*, and you're negotiating for a few extra hundred quid with them.' He says that Fields did offer them royalties, which makes sense, given that he is the agent credited with such deals, but the players preferred the cash up front and Osman recalls that they did come to an agreement. Kevin O'Callaghan tips the balance of probability in favour of them successfully getting a raise, as he says that Fields was 'pretty tough' but that they managed to treble their money or close enough. 'Although me, Russell and Johnny Wark had the speaking parts, we got the same money for everybody. I don't think they ever thanked us, to be fair,' he chuckled.

Wage discrepancies aside, the players bonded over their kickabouts and the fact that they were all experiencing, together, this odd new existence as film stars. O'Callaghan says it was only his Ipswich team-mates that he knew before filming began but some of the other players knew one another already, either personally or by reputation. Moore and Summerbee came as a pair, as did Thoresen and Lindsted from FC Twente. Paul van Himst and Co Prins were already firm friends. Ossie Ardiles had played against some of the Ipswich boys and had already met Mike Summerbee. Kazimierz Deyna had a similar frame of reference to Ardiles and they all knew one another by reputation, at least. Of course, Pelé was indisputably the biggest star among them but his relationship with Bobby Moore was a good bridge for the rest of the team. In fact, everybody was on such good terms that they came to call Pelé by the informal name he prefers – Eddie. Because, as every football fan knows, Pelé's real name was Edson Arantes do Nascimento. And I'm sitting here with John Smith on my passport. Life's not fair, is it?

The players that I spoke to could not say enough wonderful things about Pelé and the experience of working with him, which is all very heart-warming. Hallvar Thoresen said: 'He was fantastic and he socialised a lot with us. He was a really nice person, not only one of the greatest ever, of course, on the field.' Mike Summerbee said: 'He had no airs and graces at all about him. We just got on very well. We would all have breakfast together.'

John Wark remembers that Pelé still had 'it' when it came to the football, too. 'Pelé must have been 41 at that time and some of the things he did ... We did piggy in the middle, keep the ball and he was putting it through everyone's legs. What a player!' Russell Osman also remembers those games and says that, given the talent there was in the circle, you 'did not want to get stuck in the middle or you would be there a while'. It always seems to come back to the love of the ball. Osman, again, says: 'There just seemed to be a good camaraderie between everyone, because the common denominator was football. Michael Caine liked his football, we're having a kickabout with Ossie and Pelé every lunchtime and we're all getting on like a house on fire because of that silly leather football that we all like kicking about.'

Unfortunately, of course, due to the inconvenience of making a movie, some of that kicking about needed to be filmed for the training sequences. Hallvar Thoresen seemed to resent it slightly, saying 'the training was fun but it was a bit like "stop, do it again" and footballers don't like that very much', as if it were a case of their mums interrupting their game to call them in for their dinner rather than them being involved in a multi-million-dollar movie production. Everybody also had to contend with using the 1940s-style equipment. 'The old boots were awful and so was the ball,' said Ossie Ardiles and the usually unflappable Bobby Moore was also concerned about the ball, with its protruding leather lacing that could easily cut an eyebrow. They obviously got used to them, though, because the old boots and balls didn't stop Ossie flicking one over his head or Bobby's Terry Brady getting a goal and an assist in the big match. Moore even manages to look good in the film when he's playing in the army boots we first see him wearing.

We already know that Bobby was one of the dissenting voices who brought a stop to the plans for Hatch's match-winning goal but it seems that he had broader concerns about what some of the football might look like. In a report from the set, over shots of him on the camp training ground, he told BBC's *Film '81* that acting could be 'actually detailed right down so that everything is inch perfect' but that could never be the case in making the football look good, no matter what modern set-piece coaches might tell you. Moore worried that simulating the football scenes was one of the difficulties they faced in making the film and it seems that he took steps to fix that. It is far more pronounced when we get to the match, where Robert Riger, the sports director, was slightly sidelined but the training sequences also came in for some attention by Moore and one or two of the others.

Ossie Ardiles told me that: 'What they wanted to do was terrible. Some of the exercises they wanted us to do were really for kind of amateur people. In fact, they showed a little bit of that in the film. And we're supposed to be the best players in the world and it was too elementary.' Although Pelé gets the official credit as the football co-ordinator for the film, Ossie was at pains to tell me that Bobby Moore and Mike Summerbee did more to shape what the football looked like, although it feels like several players added weight to any argument they had. Ardiles says that, eventually, they just said, 'Don't worry, we'll just do it. You put the cameras where you want and then choose the best.' Russell Osman agrees that, eventually, the players were able to take charge of the football side of things, having convinced everybody important of the sense of it, including their director. 'John Huston would ask us what we would normally do and we just got on with it.' All of which led to much more content footballers, as Ossie Ardiles told me that once everything was ironed out, 'Basically, we just played football and trained. Sometimes we knew the camera was there and sometimes we didn't. They were just filming and filming and filming. I was so happy.'

Of course, to varying degrees, the professional players were joined in their training sessions by Sylvester Stallone as Hatch, Benoît Ferreux as Jean-Paul Remy and Michael Caine as Colby. Caine told one of the visiting crews that, although he was portraying a once great player, he was definitely no more than an enthusiastic amateur: 'I grew up in south London. I mean, I played football any time I could. Two coats in the park and all that. The thing that struck me from having watched so much football, say on the television or from the stands, is the difference when you actually get down there on that ground.' Caine spoke with awe at the pleasure and the difficulty of trying to play with the talent he had to play with, although Russell Osman suggests that Caine might not have been as involved as he claimed. 'I know he came out for one session and he stubbed his big fat cigar out and we were only doing a little run up and down but he pulled his calf. So, he wasn't doing much on that front.'

Lack of footballing ability or effort aside, Michael Caine was incredibly popular among his co-stars. Søren Lindsted said that Caine was one of the friendliest people he had met and Hallvar Thoresen recalled that Caine spent a lot of time chatting with him and the other players. The word 'gentleman' came up more than once among the others. Ossie Ardiles said he was brilliant and wanted to talk about football all the time: 'We all wanted to talk about his films, how he had worked with this girl or that girl, but he only wanted to talk about football.' Although, perhaps, Ossie simply wasn't there at the right times, because John Wark says: 'Michael Caine was lovely. He couldn't play football but he was really down to earth and funny. He used to tell stories about his other movies.' Either way, kicking a ball around with Pelé and chatting to Michael Caine about either football or his films seems a wonderful way to spend a summer.

Caine was a helpful presence on set and apparently revelled in his roles as leader of the pack, raconteur and mentor to the footballers dipping a toe into show business. Mike Summerbee said that: 'The tricks of the trade were wonderful to see. We used to go and watch him when he was filming and see how easily he did it, stepping the right way as the camera rolled past and not looking at the camera.' But it wasn't only the inexperienced cast members who looked up to Caine.

In his entertaining autobiography, *Do You Know Who I Am?*, Tim Pigott-Smith shows that even experienced actors could swoon a bit with admiration for Michael

Caine's acting ability and general conduct around the set. He says: 'He knew everyone on the unit within days and he would still know them today.' This is all very well and it is good to be nice but it's also nice to be good and Caine was. Pigott-Smith waxes lyrical about Caine's 'effortless control' of scenes and, just as I will never tire of great footballers talking about other great footballers, the same applies to actors. The admiration for Caine drips from the pages of *Do You Know Who I Am?*, with Pigott-Smith recognising that, although *Escape to Victory* may be a bit slight, what heft and weight it has comes largely from Caine filling one of the two central roles.

Of his part as Colby, Caine was quoted as saying that his character 'is uncomfortable with himself' but shares a 'streak of determination' with the actor himself. 'I tried to play him with great watchfulness, tremendous stillness. Very, very quiet, so that the tiniest movement was a violent act.' That, right there, is some of that gravitas Freddie Fields needed alongside Stallone's star power for his film.

It wasn't all hard work for Caine, though. In his more recent autobiography, *Blowing the Bloody Doors Off*, he talked about the fun he had making the film and said that working with the footballers was 'a dream come true'. You see, like me, Michael Caine was clearly someone to get giddy around footballers. The man has worked with anyone you would care to mention but he was weak at the knees at rubbing shoulders with some of the lads he had on his Allies team.

It wasn't all sunshine and light on set, however, and Michael Caine's diplomacy was called upon once or twice to deal with his main co-star. Tim Pigott-Smith alludes to a bit of temperamental lateness on the part of Sylvester Stallone and says that Caine remained entirely professional in the face of it. Indeed, it does seem that Stallone not being on set when he was supposed to be became a problem at certain points during filming. Michael Caine tells a thinly veiled story in his second autobiography about an actor who objected to being kept waiting around on set one day and sent a message the next morning to say that, because he had been kept waiting for four hours the previous day, he would be in four hours late that day.

In this account, Caine is discreet to the point of being annoying, because we all want the juice. Caine goes on to say that the production was held up because nothing could be filmed without this unnamed co-star and, when he did turn up, he felt the weight of the cast and crew staring at him, hoping he would take him to task about it. Caine says that he was, indeed, furious about it but, rather than tear the late star off a strip, he took the gentle approach of taking him to one side and telling him that he had done him a favour. He pretended that he had been out the previous night and failed to learn his dialogue but that, because of the star-imposed delay, 'I've had a fabulous nap. I've learnt my lines and I'm feeling great.' He even asked his opposite number if he could do the same again the next day to cover for another night out and a possible hangover and Caine reports that, as a result, the star was never late again. Now, Caine is intentionally coy about the identity of this co-star and perhaps I'm being unfair in speculating on Stallone's candidacy but from other reports of slightly diva behaviour, including that testimony from Tim Pigott-Smith, it could reasonably lead you to think that it may very well have been him. Although Caine and Stallone must have got on well together besides this, because, many years later, they came together to work on an ill-advised remake of *Get Carter* and, having seen that version, I would conclude that you would only work on that film if you loved somebody involved very much.

Of course, all of the above detective work and skirting around the issue of whether Stallone was the diva in question, is rendered unnecessary by the fact that Michael Caine tells exactly the same story in his first autobiography but includes all the names and details, so we know that it *was* Sylvester Stallone and *Escape to Victory* all along. Mystery solved.

Sly catches a bit of flak for his behaviour on set from some quarters; some, but not all, of it justified. Bobby Moore diplomatically said that his American co-star kept himself to himself but said that he was fine when they were together and intimated that the problem might have been that he was simply not as forthcoming and welcoming as Michael Caine. I can completely see how the players and much of the cast would gravitate towards Caine before Stallone. Sly was the only American on set and football was alien to him; Pelé was probably the only one of the players he was aware of before filming began. In contrast, Michael Caine knew his football and would have known something of most of the players he was thrown together with. He would also have been a British success story that much of the cast might have looked up to. He had also been doing this for much longer. He would have just seemed more approachable to those on set. Obviously, he must take great credit for that for his own outgoing personality and inclusive, nurturing attitude to the young cast but it's easy to see how Stallone might have been a little bit sidelined even before filming began. Ossie Ardiles supports this view, saying: 'It was a bit more difficult for him, because he didn't know anything about football. He maybe knew Pelé but not anybody else. Michael Caine knew everybody.'

Some of the players were certainly more reserved about the *Rocky* star when we spoke. John Wark said: 'The only one who didn't mingle was Sylvester Stallone. He thought he was slightly bigger than everybody else.' Søren Lindsted spoke about the entourage Stallone always had around him and others said that he didn't really mix with the group. Kevin O'Callaghan said, 'He might have come in the canteen once or twice. But out of everyone, it was him giving it the "I'm the big star".' Even Bobby Moore's first wife, Tina, who visited her husband in Budapest, felt compelled to criticise Stallone in her own account. She claims that Sly wanted a trampoline in his goal to make him look good while catching the ball and had his uniforms tailor-made to be tighter than everyone else's to accentuate his muscles, with Tina saying: 'One night, we were smuggled into Sly's apartment by his PA. It was full of weights.' You might put this book down when you have finished and consider me something of a Stallone apologist but that last one is just someone exercising, isn't it?

It is true that the man who would be Rambo spent plenty of time – every spare minute, in fact – working out but it feels like we can forgive him that. You will recall Clive Merrison talking about Stallone doing pull-ups halfway through their big scene together and Michael

Caine says that, 'Every time we finished a scene, we all slumped in our chairs and watched Sly run continuously round the nearest open space or, if there was no open space, he would do push-ups and sit-ups.' Caine joked more than once that he lost weight himself, just watching him.

In his first autobiography, the one in which he names and shames Stallone for holding everything up on set, he says that the American was fine to work with and easy to get along with but he does concede that he had 'developed one or two "Hollywood star" idiosyncrasies', which certainly chimes with the ego problems he had suffered in the preceding years since his breakout success. One of those 'idiosyncrasies' is keeping everyone on the film set waiting, which is unforgiveable, but if the other on display on *Escape to Victory* was his fitness regime, then that one seems more easily forgivable, to me. The self-improvement would have been another thing to set him apart from the rest of the gang on set, particularly in front of a whole host of accomplished athletes, but Stallone would have felt it was necessary.

With modern cinema awash with superhero movies, most leading men are ripped and toned beyond belief – think about the likes of Chris Hemsworth or Henry Cavill with their shirts off. It's difficult not to, isn't it? Back in 1980, however, Stallone was starting to break the mould as a leading man who looked like that. Compare his slightly doughy body shape in *Rocky* in 1976 to the condition he is in by *Rocky IV* in 1985 and the transformation is incredible. By the time of the latter film, Stallone was involved in a literal arms race with Arnold Schwarzenegger at the box office as their biceps grew with their profits but in 1980, he was only on the journey to that shape he became known for and he can be regarded as a trailblazer for that. With that in mind, I think I would be able to forgive him a few squat-thrusts here and there.

Stallone's biggest critic among the footballers on set was Kevin Beattie. Signed on to be Michael Caine's body double, he saw any attempts by Stallone to work on his own body as showing off. Beattie is quoted as calling him 'an arrogant little sod' and 'really full of himself' and the footballer brought him down a peg or two by arm wrestling him. Beattie says that the other players goaded Stallone by saying that the Ipswich defender was every bit as strong as he was and, eventually, the actor took the bait and challenged Beattie to an arm wrestle for £100. Stallone later went on to make the preposterous *Over the Top*, in which he plays Lincoln Hawk, a truck driver who wins a Las Vegas arm wrestling championship and a convenient new truck for doing so, all the while bonding with his estranged son in trying circumstances. I only hope that the film took its inspiration from this moment on set when Sly aggressively held hands with the Ipswich defender.

The set-up was the best of three; one with each arm and then, if it was a draw, a coin would be tossed to decide which arm was used for the decider. Beattie described the scene in his book, with him winning with his left arm, then Stallone equalising with his right. Then the deciding coin went up. 'I shouted tails and tails it was and, of course, I picked my left,' recalled Beattie. 'He was not a happy man, as, although it was harder that time, The Beat came shining through and Stallone was really pissed off, as I got my £100 and he never spoke to me for the rest of the filming.'

In 1982, Stallone was quoted as saying of *Escape to Victory* that he had felt that it might even be his last film. 'The fame game had gotten to me. I had lost. I had hit, basically, emotional rock bottom.' And I don't think this was solely to do with losing the arm wrestling challenge and £100 to Kevin Beattie. The man was clearly struggling a bit as he tried to cope with his fame and all that it brought with it, so maybe we should cut him a bit of slack.

And it isn't all bad reviews from among his team-mates. Mike Summerbee simply said that 'Sly was superb', Ossie Ardiles says that Stallone was, like Caine, happy to help with any acting tips he could give and Søren Lindsted said that they spoke a lot. On top of that, Stallone had a very good reason for extricating himself from the group and spending a lot of time in his trailer or hotel room. Caine said: 'I wondered whether he had a woman in there – or perhaps a personal trainer – and, finally, I asked him what was so attractive about his trailer. "I'm writing *Rocky III*", he said.' Here is the nub of it. Tim Pigott-Smith is a little dismissive of Stallone's endeavours, saying he was in there 'writing Rocky 17', but I am firmly of the opinion that if the man has shut himself away in his trailer to write *Rocky III,* then let the man stay in his trailer and write *Rocky III*. Given the option of coming out and feeling inadequate in a game of piggy in the middle with some of the best football players in the world or staying at the typewriter and giving Clubber Lang to the world, I would very much rather he did the latter. Let the man write.

There was one gripe that Stallone had on set, which Caine resolved to help him out with. That was that he felt there was a lack of direction from John Huston. Sly would compare Huston's notes with Michael and often there were none. As a director himself, Stallone felt that they needed more, so Caine resolved to show a little solidarity, agreeing they would take the problem to Huston together. Huston fended them both off by claiming that if you've cast the right people you don't have to say much to them. 'Only directors who don't know how to cast actors have to talk to them all the time.'

Caine says that, 'A suitably chastened Sly backed off and left it at that but, as he departed, he whispered to me, "I still think a director should say something to the fucking actors!" and the subject never came up again.' I guess this is similar to the argument between those who think football is all about tactics and those in the Harry Redknapp school of thought, who believe in just putting good players on the pitch and letting them play. In that regard, John Huston is very much like Harry Redknapp and this is surely the only book in which you're likely to read that sentiment being expressed.

Michael Caine says that he did receive a more technical note directly from Huston. The veteran director was prone to filming tracking shots and putting his tracks down through the middle of the scene to do so; the actors would then need to step across the tracks without looking down mid-scene at where they were going. Finding this awkward, Caine asked why Huston stuck to this technique and was told that stepping over the tracks meant that they weren't really there, which also meant that the camera wasn't there, 'which is the first principle of directing a movie; you make the camera disappear'. Caine thanked him for the lesson.

Huston and Caine had already worked together, very successfully, on *The Man Who Would Be King* but Stallone was thrilled to be working with Huston for the first time and it seems he was only too happy to accept his well-earned authority and did as he was told. Aside from the query about Huston's economy of direction, Stallone was able to keep in check any other issues he may have had. Huston was moved to say of his star: 'I'd heard about Sly's reputation for throwing his weight around but his behaviour here has been as modest as one could hope for. He couldn't be more disciplined.'

Stallone said of his director, 'Sometimes you're not aware Huston is even around. Then he'll come on like a thunderclap.' Although, to be fair, it does seem like Huston sometimes really wasn't around. Stallone had endured directorial problems on *Nighthawks*, finding himself having to step in and direct a scene himself after the original director, Gary Nelson, was fired and his replacement, Bruce Malmuth, was yet to come on board. Given this and his previous problems with Norman Jewison and John G. Avildsen, it's possible that Stallone would have been looking forward to working under a firm hand from Huston so that he could concentrate on being a jobbing actor on this one.

A visit to the set by *The Guardian* found the 74-year-old director 'sitting alone off to one side. He appears somnolent in the Hungarian sunshine. Perched on an elevated director's chair, he browses through Pelé's autobiography while Pelé and Co. are being directed by an American TV sports expert.'

The 'TV sports expert' was Robert Riger, the veteran of ABC's *Wide World of Sports*, who was brought in to lighten the loadm for Huston when it came to the actual football and we'll meet him again later as his way of shooting the match comes under scrutiny. But at this point, Huston seemed grateful for anybody to be taking some of the strain – or even all of it – off his hands. 'Action is not my strongest suit,' Huston happily admitted to *The Guardian*. He felt that a director's time was better spent on character work 'when the cast of thousands is elsewhere and he has the stars in front of him and he tells them "Give me the show."' Which is nice work if you can get it.

Ossie Ardiles says that there was a clear division of labour on set and that division was predominantly Huston keeping himself away from the football side of things. 'John was not too much involved with us. He didn't meet with us; he was always eating on his own. In a lot of ways, he put his name to the film but he was never watching the game, for instance. Maybe he did a lot more in the cutting of the final film but we didn't see a lot of him. The assistant director and the producer did a lot.' Mike Summerbee thinks that Huston, initially at least, might have had some reservations about working with the football stars, expecting them to be temperamental and difficult to control, but any fears of such behaviour were quickly dispelled. Applying the same dedication that had given each of them their football careers, Summerbee says: 'We always turned up on time and we threw ourselves into the film-making process.' Alluding to a better working relationship than Ossie Ardiles outlined, he writes in his book: 'We enjoyed John's company and he enjoyed ours.' Russell Osman echoes that, saying he was a great guy, 'very chilled out, very relaxed' and John Wark says: 'Everybody had so much respect for him.'

If the footballers' respect for the director was new-found, it's fair to say that there was already plenty in the bank among the more traditional actors. Maurice Roeves certainly signed on to work with the great man, perhaps aware that Huston was in ill health and possibly running out of films to make. Even when the two of them disagreed about whether Roeves's character, Pirie, should have a cigarette in his mouth in one shot – with Huston pulling it out of the actor's mouth and ripping it in half in front of him – Roeves 'loved working with him'. Similarly, Clive Merrison adored being directed by Huston and not just because he did those reversals with him when Stallone wasn't around. Of that summer in Budapest, he said: 'Oh, a marvellous time. He's a hero of mine. And I think he enjoyed working with me. I've got a Polaroid of me standing there in soldier's garb and he's sitting in a wheelchair attached to an oxygen tank for his emphysema. And he's looking at me adoringly. He used to say to me, "I like you, boy. You've got humour."' Clive did concede, however, that 'John Huston didn't give a shit about football.' Well, you can't have everything, I suppose.

Tim Pigott-Smith describes Huston as 'a mighty impressive man' with 'charisma in spades'. However, it was clear to everyone that his best days were behind him and that his health was deteriorating. Pigott-Smith talks of him struggling with 'a Vesuvian cough' and the oxygen tank referred to by Clive Merrison was ever-present on set. It meant that Huston was, perhaps, not at the top of his game at this late stage of his career and made him a little erratic on set. Aside from Huston taking a step back from the football sequences, Pigott-Smith says that, unfortunately, directing films seemed a chore for the veteran at this stage and he even recalls one occasion when he dozed off in his chair during a take. Thankfully, with daughter Allegra on hand to assist him and production manager Tom Shaw earning a lot of credit, Huston had the support network around him to get him through the shoot.

Werner Roth certainly enjoyed the time he got to spend with Huston. 'It was very interesting for my part. I had a chance to get to know John. I drove with him to the set every day and he was nice and sociable. We got to know each other quite well. He was on set every day and I would try to watch him work and learn as much as I could about the business.'

One unexpected issue that Huston – and Freddie Fields – faced towards the end of filming was a Screen Actors Guild strike. The production shut down on 29 July, with only five days left of principal photography. Just as similar disputes in recent years have been prompted by changes in streaming services, the 1980 strike was triggered by arguments over residuals from the burgeoning video cassette market. The deal that Fields had originally struck with the Hungarian government was for consecutive weeks of filming and there was a danger that, if the strike couldn't be resolved in time, they would need to move to another European location to finish off the one or two remaining scenes they needed. Michael Caine flew home to Los Angeles for a few days but, ever the negotiator, Freddie Fields was able to put together an interim deal with SAG to complete the movie. Caine returned, Stallone was able to work once again and the remaining filming resumed on 31 August and finished within five days.

Finding a film that you love is a wonderful thing but realising that everyone had a lovely time making it is heart-warming and adds to the joy of it. You don't want to go too far and make a film where everybody making it clearly had a better time than anybody watching it (I'm looking at you, *Ocean's Twelve*) but if you can have a lovely summer in Budapest and make a much-loved film while you're doing it, then well done everyone.

Forty-five years on from that summer, everybody I spoke to – and everything I've read about it as research for this book – indicates that, apart from Sylvester Stallone battling with the fame monster a little bit, the set was a harmonious one. We've already heard that the players enjoyed themselves as their own gang, kicking the ball around together on camera and off it but it seems that there was a lot of cross-pollination between them and the more traditional cast of acting talent. Mike Summerbee best summed up the mood when he told me: 'Well, the actors wanted to be footballers and the footballers wanted to be actors.' And there is probably a lot of truth in that. Pelé certainly agreed, telling visiting *Daily Express* reporter Victor Davis: 'I've always had a fantasy that I'd like to be a film star. I've now discovered there are film stars who have fantasies about being sports stars. So, we are all happy.' Indeed, it's a sentiment that I came across again and again.

Making a film was an exciting, slightly alien experience for the footballers but they were made to feel welcome by actors who enjoyed having this band of athletes close at hand. The football fans among the actors would have been thrilled and even those who preferred cricket or, shudder, didn't like sport at all would surely have felt a frisson of excitement at having some of these guys around. Russell Osman told me that 'the mutual respect between everyone was great', John Wark says he enjoyed a chat, particularly with the Scottish actors (Maurice Roeves said that they stayed in touch) and Michael Caine said: 'I help them with the dialogue and they help me with the football. So far, their acting has improved a lot more than my football.' Søren Lindsted remembers that Pelé, in particular, would help Caine and Stallone with the limited amount of football they had to perform, while Stallone said of Pelé's acting: 'He gets better every day. He gets looser and more natural. The man's a natural. What can I tell you?' If Pelé is to be believed, Stallone really was a fan of his acting chops. In 1985, he told Brazilian reporters that Sly had offered him a part in *Rambo: First Blood Part 2*, with $250,000 on the table. However, it is so difficult to see where Pelé would have fitted in that film that I've decided to take these reports with a pinch of salt.

They were long days at the camp, with that regular early start and filming until seven or eight in the evening, but there were, inevitably, breaks between shooting and Tim Pigott-Smith's account makes it sound better than Center Parcs. 'You can play chess, backgammon, read, kick a football about with a legend, have some decent food in the middle of the day, courtesy of good caterers, meet fascinating people, chat with stars.' Pigott-Smith seems to have been a big hit throughout the cast. Russell Osman, Mike Summerbee and Laurie Sivell all speak of him as a lovely guy with whom they stayed in touch after filming and Ossie Ardiles fondly remembers playing cards and a lot of chess with him. 'The camaraderie was brilliant,' says Ossie. Indeed, it sounds like Ossie was never out of that board games cupboard, because Clive Merrison also recalls that: 'He was learning English furiously at the time and he played Scrabble in the back of the catering truck and I played with him to expand his vocabulary.'

The love-in wasn't confined to the Allies side, as Max von Sydow was allowed to join in and he was only too happy about it. He told *Clapperboard*: 'It has been a great experience for me to meet all the soccer players from so many countries.' But it does seem that he had his favourites. Søren Lindsted told me: 'He came down to say hello to Hallvar and I. He knew there were other Scandinavian guys.' Von Sydow was another with whom Tim Pigott-Smith struck up a lasting friendship. He said they would pass the time coming up with limericks about the cast and crew – which, unfortunately, we don't have access to.

Despite the lovely time he clearly had while making a great impression on so many people, Tim Pigott-Smith couldn't wait to get home. A recurring theme of his book is the homesickness he constantly felt if he was away from his family when filming anything and it certainly curtailed his big screen career. On *Escape to Victory*, ironically, it meant that he did a bit of a runner.

He was due to finish in Hungary on a Tuesday, checked his rushes on the Wednesday to make sure he was good to go and asked the production office to get him on a Thursday flight home, where his wife, Pam, was waiting with theatre tickets for the weekend. Daniel Massey still had one more scene to film, watching through the window as Hatch escapes, and, to Julian Curry's dismay, he, too, was added to the scene. Hearing rumours that he might also be thrown into a scene that all three already felt was ridiculous and unnecessary, Tim took the radical step ('my master stroke') of shaving off his moustache – making him Rosey no more. In the middle of the night, his hotel room phone blinked to tell him he had a message from Freddie Fields telling him to stay in Budapest to shoot this final scene, which led to an uneasy night's sleep as he felt 'the cool night air on my top lip'. He sent a message in the morning, explaining that there would be a continuity problem because of the absent moustache and off he went to the airport and back into the loving arms of his family.

For the next couple of weeks, he was expecting a phone call from an irate Fields to give him a dressing-down for his unprofessionalism but all that came was a call from Julian Curry, chiding him for running off and leaving them in it. In best Jeeves and Wooster fashion, he told him: 'Frankly, Piggers old stick, your behaviour was less than collegiate.' Curry and Massey had been left hanging around on set on Friday and Saturday and, by the early hours of Sunday morning, were beginning to get to the end of their tethers when an overly cheerful Freddie Fields came into the canteen. They let the producer, who was no doubt thrilled to almost have the entire film in the bag, know that they were unhappy. His reply was:

'Aah! You should have done what Tim did. He shaved his moustache off and fucked off home.' On big American movies, he explained, it's not until you behave badly that they treat you with respect.

11.
OFF SET

ALTHOUGH FILMING days were long, John Huston's health dictated that the core of the production worked a five-day week, so there was still plenty of time for the players and the rest of the cast to fill away from the set. What on earth could they do to pass the time? Perhaps a drink or two. Mike Summerbee says that the experience was 'like one long booze-up, one long football team tour'. That's not to say that there was any misbehaviour. It just seems that the growing sense of camaraderie and the convivial atmosphere on set spilled over into the streets, bars and hotels of the Hungarian capital in the evenings and at weekends.

Sylvester Stallone, Michael Caine and Pelé all stayed in the Hilton Hotel in Buda; I've never been but, from what I can gather, it's the nice part of the city, with more highlights to enjoy than Pest. I like to think that the same thing is the case in Bucharest, where Bucha is the good bit and the Rest is not so good but I can't confirm this, as I haven't been there, either. At one time, back in the 15th and 16th centuries, Budapest was a cultural hotspot in Renaissance Europe and currently it is a very popular stag-do destination. Our heroes arrived somewhere in between, when it was neither. In 1980, it was still behind the Iron Curtain and under heavy Soviet influence.

Michael Caine found the outward signs of communism to be depressing and claimed that it lent a strange atmosphere to some of the places they visited, with a sadness pervading the air and a distinct lack of smiling groups of patrons in the restaurants they frequented. When he did come across a group of people seemingly having a nice time, he discovered from the restaurant staff that they were Communist Party officials and some younger female companions, which jaded him even further. Sylvester Stallone also found it 'a very lonely place' and harboured a natural distrust of the authorities in charge of the country, saying: 'The police have keys to everyone's house. They can turn off all the electricity in a city if they don't like what's going on.' He was also convinced that his hotel room was being bugged by somebody, based on the reactions of hotel staff when he would see them in the morning. The oppressive regime notwithstanding, most of the local people they met were only too pleased to see them and there was still plenty of opportunity for fun and entertainment amongst themselves.

Paul Cooper, who, let's remember, wasn't terribly busy during his working days anyway, told me: 'You chucked together a load of footballers and actors, foreign footballers as well, and it was just a great big old melting pot and it did work. And Michael Caine was brilliant. All he was interested in was "What bar are we going in tonight?" He loved the craic with the lads.' The regular routine seems to have been to get transported at the end of each day from the Gensdorf set outside the city, back to the hotels, have a quick wash and change into something clean and tidy – or very smart in Bobby Moore's case – and reconvene soon after, usually for a meal out. It seems that, sometimes, these dinners would be big all-encompassing affairs including everybody and, on other occasions, smaller groups would head off together but there were no rules to it and the possibility for cliques to form seems to have been kept to a minimum. Werner Roth recalls that everybody, including Caine, Max von Sydow and the players 'socialised quite a bit off-set' and Hallvar Thoresen remembers that they 'went out eating and had some beers', adding with a laugh: 'But we were up early every morning – too early for a vacation.' So, things never really got out of hand, it seems.

Ossie Ardiles points out that one of the reasons that everybody was almost duty bound to eat, drink and be merry was that they were being given daily expenses or per diems in Hungarian money and, due to the regime's rules, they would not have been able to save any of it and take it home with them. 'So, everybody was spending money like confetti there, mainly in restaurants.' The philosophy of 'you can't take it with you' is a well-worn one when it comes to attitudes towards money and, with this group, it seems that it was literally the case.

The *Escape* cast's stay in Hungary coincided with an election and bars and restaurants were forbidden to sell alcohol on voting day. To circumvent this, Michael Caine wore combat trousers with several pockets, each full of booze for sharing. Having managed to make it to a restaurant table without alerting the waiters to his subterfuge by clinking as he walked, Caine proceeded to pass the grog around, under the table, to his fellow diners. Mike Summerbee remembers that the waiters were baffled by them slowly getting 'absolutely legless', despite never buying a drink. Thank goodness for Michael Caine's drinking trousers. There's your next pub team quiz name sorted for you.

Kevin O'Callaghan – just 18 at the time, remember – says that the drinking didn't stop when they got back to the hotel, either. 'We'd go up to bed and come back down to the hotel bar and Bobby Moore and Mike Summerbee used to still be there. Pelé would get his guitar out and we'd have a sing-song. It was beautiful. It was a special time. We had the best time ever.' I asked Russell Osman if he thought that Bobby Robson might have questioned his decision to send his brave boys off to Budapest for the summer if he had seen the amount of drink they were putting away. He agreed that Robson may have been a bit concerned about his players developing bad habits in the company of some legendary drinkers but that, for the most part, his thinking would have been along the lines of 'out of sight out of mind; go and have a good summer and we'll see you in August'. That said, there really were some impressive drinkers in the group. As Osman says, with a sense of pride in his voice: 'I've never seen anybody drink gin and tonics like Bobby Moore.'

Feeding into that idea that the actors were thrilled to be around the footballers and vice versa, Maurice Roeves told the *Daily Record* in a 2012 interview that 'one of the highlights of my career was having dinner with two legends ... Pelé and Bobby Moore' and it seems that Moore and Pelé were pretty much joined at the hip in Budapest, enjoying one another's company and frequently being the centre of attention in football-mad Hungary. Universally popular among his colleagues, even before he entertained

The team in their classic kit, trying to ignore the swastikas. (Back Row L-R) Russell Osman (Doug Clure), Paul van Himst (Michel Fileu), Mike Summerbee (Sid Harmer), Sylvester Stallone (Robert Hatch), John Wark (Arthur Hayes), Kazimierz Deyna (Paul Wolchek), Søren Lindsted (Erik Borge). (Front Row L-R) Hallvar Thoresen (Gunnar Nilsson), Osvaldo Ardiles (Carlos Rey), Michael Caine (John Colby – Captain), Pelé (Luis Fernandez), Bobby Moore (Terry Brady), Co Prins (Pieter van Beck)

World Cup Memories 1 – Pelé and Bobby Moore's friendship captured in an iconic image. Brazil 1-0 England, 7 June 1970, Guadalajara

World Cup Memories 2 – Ossie Ardiles, starring in the final for Argentina v Netherlands, 1978.

Tormentors of England 1 – Captain of Poland, Kazimierz Deyna, shakes hands with Martin Peters of England before their memorable Wembley draw, 17 October 1973.

Tormentors of England 2 – Hallvar Thoresen celebrates after scoring the winning goal, and captaining Norway as they gave England 'a hell of a beating', Oslo, 9 September 1981.

Ipswich Town 1981/82, including Escape to Victory *alumni Russell Osman (back row centre), Kevin Beattie (back row fourth from left), John Wark (middle row fourth from left), Paul Cooper (middle row fifth from left), Robin Turner (middle row seventh from left), Kevin O'Callaghan (front row third from left), UEFA Cup (front and centre).*

New York Cosmos captain, Werner Roth. He was sold the role of dastardly German skipper Baumann by John Huston and his finger framing.

Pelé on set with Sylvester Stallone.

Stallone throwing himself around as heroic goalkeeper Hatch.

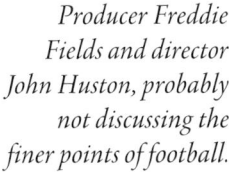

Producer Freddie Fields and director John Huston, probably not discussing the finer points of football.

The 'Cardinals of Gensdorf' relax in their red training gear. Benoît Ferreux can be seen at the far end.

Moore, Stallone and Caine look despairingly through the train window. Our best evidence that Jean-Paul's escape scene was filmed.

Major von Steiner (Max von Sydow) and Captain John Colby of West Ham United and England (Michael Caine). Officers and Gentlemen.

Michael Caine perches in his chair alongside Pelé, Bobby Moore and Paul Cooper during the filming of the match.

Sylvester Stallone, Bobby Moore and Michael Caine scrub up well for the London premiere

Top: A slight difference of opinion in the Allies' goalmouth.

Bottom: Luis and his team-mates celebrate his bit of magic.

them all with his guitar, Pelé would often become the focal point within the group and with those outside of it. Søren Lindsted told me that 'the girls on the film set loved him' and that he, himself, had several photos taken with Pelé and has kept them, along with an autograph from the great man, in a scrapbook. When Pelé was out and about among the adoring public, Clive Merrison remembers that he had a member of his entourage walking behind him with an ice cream trolley full of Pelé memorabilia, which he would just hand out 'to crowds of people wherever he went'. This is a truly lovely thing, although I do pity the occasional Budapest resident who might have had no idea who Pelé was and just stopped them in the hope of buying a Raspberry Ripple. Merrison also wonders if Pelé's astronomical fame was one of the reasons that Sylvester Stallone withdrew into himself a little on and off set. Here was this huge Hollywood star, used to attention wherever he went, but in Hungary, the land of Puskás and the 'Mighty Magyars', interest in Stallone was dwarfed by the interest in the world's greatest footballer. Merrison says that the place went crazy and 'once Pelé arrived at the hotel, Stallone made himself scarce'.

Certainly, the players remember that Stallone didn't mingle as much as the other actors and he would often leave the city on weekends, heading for Paris or London, with his entourage, or St Tropez with John Huston. Michael Caine was also known to take the odd trip to Paris but was very much a part of the social scene when he was around. While in Budapest, Stallone needed to be coaxed out of his room, if he came at all, and often it was Caine who sought to include him. Perhaps he felt a keen responsibility to bring these two worlds together and make sure that his American co-star was involved? Caine remembers Stallone mostly insisting that he had to go to his room and continue writing his script for *Rocky III* but, occasionally, he would relent and say: 'Sod it, I'll come to dinner, anyway.' I can't help thinking that the 'sod it' here is Caine's turn of phrase, rather than Stallone's own. Mike Summerbee remembers one night when they successfully involved Sly in their plans. Several of the wives had flown in to visit and, while Tina Moore and Tina Summerbee were enjoying a meal with their husbands and Michael Caine, they spotted Stallone sitting in a corner with his agent. Summerbee recalls that: 'Michael called him over and he sat next to Tina and, suddenly, Stallone was part of the group.'

Just as working on his next *Rocky* script was one valid excuse for not joining the group as much as he might have done, Stallone had a second, equally justifiable, reason. He was trying to patch up his marriage to his first wife, Sasha, whom he made a contrite call to, inviting her to spend time with him in the Hungarian capital. Sasha was clearly on his mind as he wrote that script for *Rocky III*, because, in the opening montage when Rocky is bashing up some weaker contenders and being protected from Clubber Lang, one of his opponents is called Joe Czak – and Czack is Sasha's maiden name. Sasha Czack is a very cool name to have but it does sound like cartoon dog Muttley trying to say 'crackerjack'.

It is also worth noting, given the circumstances in which he was writing, that the third instalment of *Rocky* is about Balboa riding too high on fame and hubris, getting cut down to size by Clubber and having to get humble once more to find his inner strength and 'Eye of the Tiger'. It feels like Stallone was leaning on his own experience as he typed away.

According to his biographers, Stallone was, indeed, undergoing a period of reflection in Budapest, having felt himself going off the rails a little in recent years. He was studying a book he had been given, *The Keys to Reality* by Allan Martin Osman, which gave him a new spiritual outlook. It led him to return to two major elements of his life. The first was *Rocky* and the second was Sasha. Contrite about previous misdemeanours, he called Sasha and invited her to Hungary where, according to Marsha Daley, 'they spent long, loving evenings in cosy after-hours restaurants, dancing and dining by candlelight. It was a second honeymoon and put them in a romantic mood'. Understandable, then, that Stallone wasn't always at the dinner table with the football lads, drinking Michael Caine's thigh-temperature pocket booze.

Stallone and Sasha weren't the only ones with marital concerns whilst in Budapest. Filming came at a difficult time for Bobby and Tina Moore. The couple were already struggling and 'soldiering on', according to Tina, when, right before filming began, Bobby told Mike Summerbee that he had just fallen in love with somebody else. Moore had just met Stephanie, who would later become his second wife, on a flight from South Africa to London and, according to Summerbee, he had fallen hard. Despite the looming split in their marriage, Tina came out to Budapest to spend time with Bobby and there were good times and laughs to be had with Michael Caine and his wife, Shakira, who also made a flying visit, but Tina says that: 'Back in England after filming had finished, our problems hadn't gone away.'

Bobby Moore's own marriage problems didn't stop him trying to spread the love and look after a much younger couple while in Budapest. Kevin O'Callaghan spoke fondly of Moore as he told me the story of his own girlfriend's visit during filming. He recalled that Bobby asked what time she was arriving. 'When I was just about getting ready to go and meet her at the station, he said "Come with me" and he had a chauffeur-driven car to take me to the airport to pick my missus up. When she came out, she couldn't believe it. Bobby Moore was standing there and he took us to dinner. She had to ring her dad up and say "You ain't gonna believe me, I'm sitting down having dinner with Bobby Moore!" He was a hero. He was brilliant. He was such a nice bloke. I became quite close with him.' This is the power of *Escape to Victory*, bringing heroes together with those that admire them and coming out the other side of it as friends – whether that's Max von Sydow and Tim Pigott-Smith or Bobby Moore and Kevin O'Callaghan.

Aside from the eating and drinking and sing-songs with Pelé, other pursuits were available in Budapest. Tim Pigott-Smith and Daniel Massey would tour the museums and art galleries on offer, mastering the public transport system as they did so. Massey also took the opportunity to introduce his co-star to opera while they were there, thanks to the subsidised Hungarian National Opera and its 'ludicrously cheap seats'. Clive Merrison says that, when he arrived, Pigott-Smith met him at the airport and took him for a massage at the old baths. Indeed, the famous old medicinal spa baths were also popular with the rest of the cast – and, presumably, the crew – getting several recommendations across the interviews I carried out. Merrison was also glad to spend some time with Max von Sydow. He told me he was a proper actor, that *The Exorcist* was one of his favourite films and that the Swede was something of a hero to him, too. 'He didn't have anything to do with the Hollywood shenanigans. His passion was trying to find suppressed impressionist painters around Budapest. So, I went off with him one day. He was also a bit of a gourmet and we had wonderful variations of roast deer. That was fun.'

The beautiful city, which takes inspiration from Paris in its layout and architecture, seems to have been a hit with everyone who spent time there. Werner Roth spoke about cycling around Budapest and along the Danube with colleagues. It truly was the best of times.

For those whose tastes weren't already catered for by the eating, drinking, singing, museums, opera, cycling and impressionist painters on hand, John Huston also ran a poker game on Thursdays, where presumably some of those Hungarian allowances changed hands. And once his defences had thawed somewhat, Sylvester Stallone even invited people to his own suite for a viewing of *Paradise Alley*, which Clive Merrison remembers going along to.

For all the alternatives available as entertainment for the players, there was only ever going to be one way to wrap things up. On the last night of filming for the footballers, Bobby Moore and Mike Summerbee threw a party in their hotel suites. Ossie Ardiles remembers that they all had to leave very early the next morning but it didn't stop everyone taking part and enjoying bottles of wine and beer, left to chill in a bath packed with ice, as well as a case of Chivas Regal, supplied by Michael Caine. John Huston arrived with his secretary and his daughter, Allegra, and rounded things off by presenting every footballer with the gift of a director's chair, so that they would never forget their brush with Hollywood.

As if they ever could.

12.

THE MATCH

NOW IT'S time for the match and let's not kid ourselves, it's what we've all been waiting for. I have watched the film many times since I was a kid but I've watched the match sequence many times more in isolation. And why not? It's got everything.

Escape to Victory was shot largely in sequence, so the players had spent weeks genuinely bonding as a team in the prisoner of war camp before they pulled on their iconic white kit, featuring one red and one blue stripe, and took to the field in front of thousands of extras to film the end result of Von Steiner's initial thought about a friendly between his camp's PoWs and a local barracks team. Things have, of course, escalated into a showpiece match between the cream of the available Allied forces and the best that Germany can offer at Stade de Colombes, with the eyes of the world watching. The sense of something special happening wasn't just within the film. Paul van Himst spoke of a real sense of an occasion being created within the stadium, telling me it was 'like a final of a World Cup'.

Those Budapest extras who poured into the MTK Stadium must have had mixed feelings about their local ground doubling for Stade de Colombes. The Paris stadium had been the venue for the 1938 World Cup Final, which Hungary had lost to Italy in a game with heavy fascist overtones. Throughout the tournament, the Italian team made fascist salutes before their matches and, when required to wear a change strip, wore black in a nod to the fascist Blackshirts at home. Appearing in the crowd for the movie would have been a nice day or two out for the locals but I'm sure seeing their home ground draped in so many swastikas would have felt odd. Paul Cooper described the setting as: 'Eerie. Quite unreal. You've got all these swastikas hanging there and it makes you wonder "God, what was it like?"' And there are so many swastikas.

The stage is set, the marching band plays and a whole raft of commentators begin relaying the scene in French, German and Italian. Then the teams emerge from the tunnel, though not before a prank was pulled by Bobby Moore, according to Tina. In an old classic, Bobby's ex-wife claims that Caine delivered some rousing words which didn't make the final cut, then marched out: 'Bobby, of course, had whispered to the lads to hold back. So, when Michael finished his call to arms and turned round, he discovered he had been giving this rousing team talk to himself.' It's a bit of fun and it might have been something they did at half-time, rather than the more formal start, but we'll have more important things to discuss come half-time.

The band strike up the German anthem and the assembled officers snap to attention and show off their different levels of badness. The toadying lickspittles among them throw up an arm in the Nazi 'Heil Hitler' salute and we judge them as harshly as they deserve to be judged – it's wrong, what they did. Others, naturally including Von

Steiner, prefer to salute and show themselves as slightly better eggs in the grand scheme of things. As the anthem plays, we get a pan along the German team, with Werner Roth, Laurie Sivell and Robin Turner all present and correct. Laurie Sivell says that he and his 'German' teammates weren't given any time to train together or even kick a ball around and many of them met for the first time on the day the game was filmed. He did say that both teams got changed together in one big dressing room, which must have been odd to observe, though I hope that people in there were debating who had the smarter kit.

We are spared all of the Allied anthems – there would have been seven or eight different ones and we haven't got all day – and the German propaganda commentator, played by Anton Diffring but oddly dubbed by someone else, begins his broadcast to British listeners and we're almost ready to go.

For completists among you who want to know the Allies starting XI, it is as follows:

1. Robert Hatch (USA) – Sylvester Stallone
2. Michel Fileu (Belgium) – Paul van Himst
3. John Colby (West Ham United and England) (Captain) – Michael Caine
4. Pieter van Beck (Netherlands) – Co Prins
5. Doug Clure (England) – Russell Osman
6. Terry Brady (England) – Bobby Moore
7. Arthur Hayes (Scotland) – John Wark
8. Carlos Rey (Venezuela) – Osvaldo Ardiles
9. Sid Harmer (England) – Mike Summerbee
10. Luis Fernandez (Trinidad) – Pelé
11. Erik Borge (Denmark) – Søren Lindsted

Kazimierz Deyna's Paul Wolchek (Poland) and Hallvar Thoresen's Gunnar Nilsson (Norway) take their places on the bench, along with the nameless other Eastern European players, and both come on to play their part, even if, whisper it, substitutes weren't really allowed in the 1940s. Let's chalk it up to Von Steiner trying to play fair.

I did ask some of the players if they could remember whether they decided this starting XI amongst themselves or if somebody in production told them how to line up but, with the passing of time, nobody was sure.

The numbers which the players wear are interesting. Nobody I asked seemed to think there was much of a premeditated plan for who wore what and certainly not too much is made of who is playing in which position but surely No.10 was always earmarked for Pelé and Bobby Moore was deliberately put in his iconic No.6 shirt? So closely associated with the number is Bobby that West Ham have retired the number, never to be worn again. Such is the respect the club gave him that they retired the shirt a mere 15 years after his death and a mere eight years after Hayden Foxe wore it. Well done everybody. On the German side, Werner Roth was given the No.4 shirt that he always wore with the Cosmos and says: 'I assume that they did their research and knew that I wore 4, so I think they did that as a nod to careers.'

Roth then gets his first head-to-head shot on screen, this time with Michael Caine's Colby as he wins the toss and decides that the Allies can kick off. There is then just time for Renée's lad to run on to the pitch, past the armed guards, hand over a bunch of flowers to Hatch and deliver the iconic line 'Hatch! Hatch! Half-time!' to indicate that the escape is on for the interval. Given the number of jittery German guards with rifles in the stadium, his burst through the cordon carries the risk of seeing him gunned down but a film that has disappeared one of its players rather than show his doomed escape attempt isn't about to start riddling kids with bullets in the six-yard box. Not when there's a game to be played.

We finally kick off and an early ball forward leads to an almost immediate shot on goal from Erik Borge, an opening salvo that Søren Lindsted is proud to put his name to, but it proves to be just a range-finder, as goalkeeper Schmidt gathers it comfortably.

Before we settle into the game completely, however, it is worth looking at the series of events which led to the match looking the way it does.

John Huston undoubtedly brought a lot to the film and people were delighted to be working with him but, having made it clear that action sequences and, more specifically, football action sequences, were not going to be his strong point, he needed help. Consequently, Freddie Fields took alternative measures by hiring the famed sporting director Robert Riger, from *Wide World of Sports*, as the second unit director. Respected though Riger was, he knew his own limitations and it seems that his world of sports wasn't quite wide enough to include football, so he had never directed a match. He had the self-awareness to know he needed help, though, and he ensured that the very best football film crew was hired to shoot the match footage. I was lucky enough to speak to one of the cameramen he hired – Harvey Harrison.

Harvey told me: 'There was a group of us that were taken out there, basically to make the football match work. We were camera assistants and then became cameramen. We became regarded as the No.1 team for making sports films. It wasn't just football; we did the Olympics and winter sports and motor racing, golf, tennis, everything really.' It was an expert crew that had been put together by Michael Sanderson, of the Sanderson family that created the first camera equipment hire company. Sanderson hand-picked his crew and they became known as 'Dad's Army'. Not because they were old and decrepit and ran around shouting 'Don't panic!', you understand, but 'because we all called Michael "Dad".' This crew were the people that shot the official World Cup films for FIFA and Harvey had been working on them since 1966. By 1980, however, when the call came to work on *Escape*, Harrison was making his way in the more conventional movie industry and 'slowly getting into feature films'.

Tim Pigott-Smith was sufficiently impressed with the new arrivals to call them 'the hottest sports photographers in the world' and went on to say in his memoirs: 'It was exciting and, because the success of the film was entirely dependent on the game, the tension increased tangibly.' Harvey says that he felt that tension and that, for him at least, it wasn't a particularly happy shoot. 'A lot of the people on the main filming didn't like us youngsters coming in and taking over the football and the escape sequence in many ways. It was strange for us, because we were on a film where, for many years, we'd been on live sport. Maybe we were a bit brash. I think they were just a bit put out by us.'

Harrison went on to shoot one final World Cup film, in 1982, which was narrated by Sean Connery. The 1986 one, *Hero*, was voiced by Michael Caine, perhaps invited to do the job because of his post-*Victory* association with the game. By then, Harvey Harrison had moved on to work full-time in the movies, later becoming a second unit director and working on late-period Sylvester Stallone works *Rambo* (the later sequel) and *The Expendables 2* but he fondly remembers some aspects of shooting *Escape to Victory*. 'We had great help from Pelé and Bobby Moore and we just got on and did it. The director from ABC got involved but we had to tell him how a football match went.' With the right crew now in place to capture any football magic there was likely to be, everyone could start to work on what the football might look like and there was something of a difference of opinion in the approaches.

Robert Riger produced what Don Revie might have called a dossier – a huge document full of diagrams and shot descriptions, mapping out detailed sequences he wanted the footballers to recreate on camera as close to his design as they possibly could, and he produced some footage to support his approach. However, the feeling quickly grew that such a plan would not work for football, as it might have done for the likes of baseball or American football. Werner Roth felt that Riger's plan was doomed to fail because 'in soccer, you don't kind of have that control with your hands like the other sports that he had experience with. It really didn't come off well. And, collectively, we suggested that they just let us play.' Who takes the credit for pushing the case for this change is debatable. Some players talked about them pushing back on it as a whole group but most agreed that Pelé and Bobby Moore were the main voices of reason, with Werner Roth and Mike Summerbee also adding their weight to the mini-mutiny.

Russell Osman says that the senior players convinced Riger and, crucially, John Huston and Freddie Fields of the sense of letting the footballers control the flow of the game in a more natural way. 'Instead of choreographing the way the game is going to go, they were saying that the German side were all professional footballers, anyway, so they thought that, between us, we should be able to let them dominate the first half and score a few goals without it looking too set up, then be able to turn it around second half.' Ossie Ardiles says that it boiled down to a case of: 'Look, it's better if we just play. Let us play, you film and then, afterwards, you just use the best bits.'

Naturally, there were some sequences that had to remain choreographed, because they were a part of the storyline – such as the penalties and Pelé's overhead kick goal – and time was found to film flourishes like the Ossie Ardiles 'Rainbow Flick' but, overall, a more naturalistic approach was adopted by everyone. Some would be quick to dismiss Robert Riger as someone who was found out in this situation and sidelined; however, I think he should take some credit. He was hired, naively, by Freddie Fields as a general sports expert and, when Riger realised that he needed help with that, he brought in 'Dad's Army', the best football crew on the planet. Furthermore, when his meticulous homework on designing action sequences was dismissed as being entirely the wrong approach, he seems able to have taken the criticism on board, put the ring binder down and gone with the flow of things – allowing the footballers to teach him about their sport, of which he had extremely limited knowledge. Werner Roth agrees, saying that Riger 'picked up on it really quickly and made adjustments to his approach and his camera positions and I think it came off quite well in the final analysis'. Fittingly, it was a team effort and Riger can still take credit for much of the slow motion work, which the *Telegraph* described as having 'a balletic quality'.

The new approach saw the players allowed to play for short bursts of around ten minutes at a time, with the cameras rolling and picking up the action. The directors were able to call from the sidelines if they wanted a German attack or an advance from the Allies and they would then occasionally step in to grab close-ups. When *Clapperboard* visited the set, they filmed some of the match being shot, including capturing glimpses of the footballers ready for action and playing piggy in the middle, with Kevin Beattie clearly on show in Colby's No.3 shirt. They caught up with Bobby Moore, who was a little worried about what the football scenes might look like at that stage, pointing out that football in 1943 was very different to that of 1980. He spoke of his desire to get it right and make it look authentic. Bobby was relaxed enough to declare that everyone felt that the footage shot so far was 'very effective' and said he was pleased. In total, the crew shot 17 hours of footage to give us the game we know and love in the finished film.

It's a game that, despite Borge's early shot, does not start well for the Allies. The Germans break quickly down the left and look good doing it. When the cross comes in, it's the first thing Hatch has to deal with and he nervously fumbles it behind for a corner to nods of approval from the onlooking German top brass in the stands. The corner goes too deep but is crossed back in once more and, with Hatch flapping, one of many Germans crowding the box rises to head it in.

GERMANY 1-0 ALLIES

Hatch is too wet behind the ears to know that if you're going to come for those as a keeper, you've got to get them and Colby has a quick word to try to calm him down. In the commentary box, the villain switches on some recorded applause to pretend that the watching French are all for a German victory. And then we're back under way.

Here, we get our first glimpse of Luis Fernandez turning on the skill as he weaves between defenders before being unceremoniously stopped in his tracks by a heavy challenge, which goes unpunished. One or two more heavy tackles fly in and, before we know it, Germany have scored again when their falling No.10 sends a daisy cutter past Hatch, low and to his left.

GERMANY 2-0 ALLIES

If we didn't know Hatch's backstory here, we would simply be saying we want a bit more from a goalkeeper who goes down in instalments to a shot he could have thrown his hat on. Escape or no escape, Colby must be regretting his decision to smash Tony Lewis's arm up back at the camp, because he would surely have stopped both goals.

As the Resistance continue to dig beneath the stadium, the Allies are digging themselves into more trouble as they inevitably get drawn into a bit of a battle. Given that everyone on the pitch is, you know, at war, it is, perhaps, understandable that a little bit of niggle creeps in. Both sides are guilty of going in too strong and there is a scramble in the penalty area during which boots and insults fly. Co Prins, as Pieter van Beck, gets a nice moment when a decision goes against the Allies. Behind the referee's back, he uses one arm to throw up the Nazi salute and his other hand to create a Hitler moustache. It's the kind of thing that was once thought of as a harmless bit of fun but would be an instant red card these days. Pieter isn't long for the pitch, anyway, as the tackling goes too far. He is scythed down by a two-footed challenge from behind by Werner Roth's chief baddie, Baumann, and is stretchered off. With another referee, this would also be a straight dismissal for Baumann.

Experiments have been run in which modern referees have been invited to view old games and give their verdict. One such experiment involved the 1970 FA Cup Final between Chelsea and Leeds, which is often considered one of the most brutal games ever captured in full by the cameras. In 1997, referee David Elleray watched a re-run of that final and deemed that he would have dismissed six players had he been in charge. Watching it in 2025, Michael Oliver reckoned he could easily have sent off 11 players. On the night, there was just one booking dished out by Eric Jennings. When I think of today's referees watching the match in *Escape to Victory*, which they possibly do whilst cowering behind the sofa, they must be thinking that only two or three players would stay on the pitch.

Was there ever a danger, with so many rough challenges flying in during filming of the match, that one or two people might go too far? Werner Roth thinks not because 'we were all cognisant of the fact that we didn't want to hurt anybody but we all played honestly and some of the interactions had to be exaggerated, like the injured players. We had to make it look real.' That's easy for him to say – it's him who has just taken poor Pieter out of the game. Russell Osman told me: 'You see that some of the tackles going in on Ardiles are proper good tackles. There wasn't any holding back but, as long as everybody knows, that's fine. It's when somebody is going in half-heartedly and you don't expect it that somebody can get hurt.' He also felt, quite rightly, that insurance issues today would mean there would be 'absolutely no chance' of filming the match as they did in 1980.

Despite the code that everyone knew they were playing rough, there were some injuries. Michael Caine pulled a ligament, which restricted his already limited ability to look like a player when required. He also told *Thames News* that: 'I could never explain to the Hungarian professional footballers who were playing us that I was an actor and not a real footballer. So, all they did was they looked at the opposing team, which consisted of all these great players, and they found the weakest link – which was me. So, I would run on to the field to do my bit and straight up into the air I'd go!' There is a suggestion, however, that when Caine's treatment got too rough, his body double and minder, Kevin Beattie, would be called upon to exact retribution at the first opportunity.

Ossie Ardiles suggested to me that Co Prins was selected as the victim of this crunching tackle because, as the oldest player besides Caine, 'he couldn't really move too much' and was all too happy to leave the field. Two German soldiers carry Pieter to the dressing room, while Von Steiner looks on, concerned at the turn the game has taken, and the Allies presumably hope that the French Resistance haven't arrived early. Gunnar Nilsson (Hallvar Thoresen) heads to the dressing room with the stricken Pieter, seemingly to take care of him, but actually to rip the No.4 shirt from his back and take his place on the field. As discussed, substitutes seem to be allowed in this game; let's not dwell on that.

Things go from bad to worse for the Allies as Terry Brady concedes a penalty with a lazy challenge that is most unlike Bobby Moore. In fact, when it comes to the great acting performances, you can keep your De Niros and your McDormands and your Day Lewises, because, for Bobby Moore to put in a last-ditch tackle that is anything other than perfectly timed and immaculately clean, it shows that he was fully immersed in his role. This is a Terry Brady mistake, not a Bobby Moore one.

Amid the protests, Robin Turner gets a fleeting nice moment as he throws a remonstrating Sid to the ground and then gives him the tapping-the-head gesture, which used to be the universal signal of 'you're crazy, pal'. But Sid can protest all he wants. Terry did not get anything on the ball and the referee may be bent but he's correct in awarding a penalty here.

As Colby fills in Hatch on the basics of what a penalty is, which you feel a better coach may have covered before now, it's worth noting that, as the referee looks to place the ball, the player in the No.7 shirt for the Allies is now Kazimierz Deyna, instead of John Wark. This is because

John Wark was genuinely injured. He explained: 'I just hurt something during the game. There were a few tackles flying in and I hurt myself.' The injury to Wark was bad enough to hamper his pre-season once he was back at Ipswich. He missed the first two or three weeks and 'Bobby Robson wasn't happy. But I was back for the start of the season.' He certainly was. He scored on the opening day away at Leicester and went on to score 35 more in a vintage, UEFA Cup-winning season for the club. 'I was on fire that season,' he gleefully told me. Perhaps dressing up as a prisoner of war, getting kicked by Hungarians pretending to be Nazis and having your voice dubbed in a Hollywood movie is the pre-season preparation that every player needs. Well, has anyone else tried it?

As I have said previously, I can't help thinking that more should be made of Deyna's Paul Wolchek making it on to the pitch to replace Wark's Arthur Hayes. Surely him getting on to the field – and later scoring – is a strike to the heart of the Third Reich, every bit as much as the Caribbean Luis Fernandez is a blow to the Nazi 'master race' idea. At the very least, you might think that shots would have been included to show Wark down injured and also having to come off, as it would increase the feeling of the plucky Allies being kicked out of the game by their dirty opposition.

As it stands, it just looks like a continuity error, with Wark there one minute and Deyna the next. It's possible that such things just weren't deemed essential when John Huston came to edit the film together or we can't rule out that the substitutions and coming and going of players were rules that the American director simply wasn't familiar with. Tim Pigott-Smith remembers there being one point during filming of the match when Huston staged a foul on the halfway line, thinking that the referee could award a penalty for it. When somebody put him straight and said the foul needed to be inside the penalty area for a penalty to be awarded, he was livid and was heard to swear and call it a 'stupid game!' One of the TV crews visiting the set captured the moment an assistant says to Huston 'we have the penalty shot now but we don't have what the penalty was for' and Huston responds 'that's right, we've got to show that'. So, it's possible that Huston, Riger and one or two others were hanging on to the rules by their fingernails. Harvey Harrison remembers: 'Huston, by that time, bless him, was a bit old and he was sort of out of it, really. He didn't understand what football was about at all, so he just sort of sat in his chair and let us get on with it.'

Back at the penalty spot, Baumann dispatches the kick past Hatch and things are going from bad to worse for the Allies.

GERMANY 3-0 ALLIES

Briefly, after play resumes, we get a lovely example of the players being allowed to get on with it as Ardiles brings the ball forward but allows it to run away from him and Roth tackles him. It looks like a proper football match. But we don't have much time to dwell on this, because, in the blink of an eye, the Germans have a fourth goal after Hatch ill-advisedly comes out to claim a ball he is never going to get. The ball is swept home, despite the best efforts of Brady and Colby on the line. For those of you watching along as you read, Colby, in this moment, is very definitely being played by Kevin Beattie.

GERMANY 4-0 ALLIES

According to Paul Cooper, who was only used for a few of the widest shots as Stallone's stand-in, it is surprising that we don't see more of Beattie. He fondly recalled that: 'Michael Caine was very insistent on sitting some of his scenes out and letting Kevin Beattie run up and down while he sat there with a fat cigar.' The cigar also got a mention from Harvey Harrison, who told me: 'Michael was great. Great humour. He took the piss out of Sylvester Stallone and he used to wander around the field smoking a big cigar, then come over to film the odd close-up.' Although, in his defence, Caine obviously felt like he was doing enough at his age as he felt 'so bloody weary, with a bad back, swollen ankles, pulled tendons. I suddenly realised I was nearly 50, on the field with people 15 years younger than me and already retired.' Even with two Colbys on the pitch here, the Allies might be struggling but, at this point, the Michael Caine version dispenses a bit of advice to his beleaguered keeper, which has always seemed a little unfair to me.

As he berates a subdued Hatch, he tells him 'stay on the line and narrow the angle', which is impossible to do isn't it? Either you stay on the line or come out and narrow the angle. Between withholding corner advice, leaving the explanation of what a penalty is until one is conceded and issuing confusing instructions, it feels like Colby needs to take some of the blame for the mess that Hatch has got his team into here.

THE MATCH

Hatch is then briefly seen to redeem himself by getting away with a two-footed lunge to clear the ball in his own six-yard box; for a man keen to use his hands at every opportunity, it's an odd decision but it's effective. And then it's over to Luis Fernandez. He skilfully beats Baumann, which must have been fun for Pelé and Roth to film, then he goes past another German before being taken out by two defenders, acting in unison, and is left in a heap, with a broken rib. The foul goes unpunished, which brings Von Steiner to his feet, has Rose looking as peeved as his stiff upper lip will allow and even has the highest-ranking Nazis in attendance thinking it is a bit much. It's a bad foul. Luis has to leave the field and Colby says they will play with ten men, which is a slap in the face for the other Eastern European lads on the bench. Maybe Colby is hoping that Luis can return or maybe he just knows that it's almost half-time and they will be escaping soon, anyway. When a bit of dialogue is called for here, with two Allies players required to react, of course it's again Russell Osman they go to, as he says 'this ain't going to be easy' to a concerned-looking Mike Summerbee.

Down to ten men, four goals down and with Nazi Germany rampant across Europe, the plucky Allies team decide that enough is enough, take a stand and begin to fight back. The next high ball that comes into the box is taken well by an improving Hatch, who receives a kick in the face for his trouble. Assuming there will be no whistle coming, Osman's Doug Clure clears up and brings the ball out, setting up a counter-attack. As the French fans sense that something is in the air, Rey eventually works the ball out to Erik Borge on the left and his cross from the byline is met with a cushioned volley at the far post by a criminally unmarked Terry Brady, the shot going in as goalkeeper Schmidt tries to scramble back across the goal.

GERMANY 4-1 ALLIES

The stadium erupts, properly this time, not just on the commentator's tape machine. When I pointed out to Søren Lindsted that it was a great cross and that the volley couldn't really be missed, he just laughed and said: 'Of course!' If the hairs on the back of your neck aren't standing up as the crowd rises, the players celebrate and the music swells, then perhaps this isn't the film for you. It's stirring stuff.

And then it's half-time and the Allies head down the tunnel. Well, one tunnel but not all of the available tunnels, of course. The Allies burst into the away dressing room with renewed hope. We hear pundits frequently say that just before half-time is a good time to score. That may never be more apt than here, unless you're Hatch. He has got the escape all set for the interval and if he and the other lads had traipsed in four down, then he may well have won the popular vote and led his beaten teammates down the hole so diligently and expertly dug by his Resistance contacts. I've played in matches where we've been 4-0 down at half-time and if I'd been offered a way out to avoid playing the second half, I would surely have taken it. And I wasn't even a prisoner of war. And, yet, these boys are made of stronger stuff. Terry's goal from Erik's cross has given them all a little something – hope. In 'proper football man' terms, they fancy the job.

Before we get to the tunnel, however, we have a bit of business in the changing room, as the lads trip over themselves to tell Pieter about the goal. I love Michael Caine in this scene. His enthusiasm is palpable as he tells his fallen comrade about Terry's goal. You see, for Colby at this point, the escape is on. He thinks they've played as much football as they're going to and, for him, the consolation goal is victory enough. It's made the game worthwhile.

Amid the general hubbub of the excitable players, Colby and Hatch move across to peer into the bath, waiting for the Resistance to come bursting through and ruin some perfectly good tile work. The American explains to the players that their escape has been arranged all the way to the Seine, where a boat awaits to take them into the country. When the ground is broken, it's Claude who emerges with a cheery 'salut' and some encouragement for the players to get a move on. He's oblivious at this point to the fact that his hard work is wasted on them. The dissent begins immediately, led by Doug Clure urging his team-mates to reconsider. He insists he doesn't want to go, because they can win the game, despite all the evidence to the contrary.

When he spoke to *Newsnight* on the film's release, Sylvester Stallone was full of praise for the players in this scene. 'Oh, they're great. It seems like every soccer star is a natural actor. There's a scene in the tunnel where they all decide they want to go back and not run away. They just all made up their own dialogue and they were rambling on and we just had to tell them "Stop! You're completely overshadowing the actors."'

This is a crucial moment in the film, as the enthusiasm for continuing takes hold among the majority of the team. So much so that they even convince Colby, with Sid telling him: 'It's not as if we're being slaughtered, skipper.' With Colby successfully won round, it is only Hatch who needs to be convinced and you have to say that, whatever else you think of the brash American, the man is a saint here. He's nursing a bleeding mouth and a concussion from a kick in the head and he's been exposed as a poor goalkeeper in front of thousands of fans. On top of that, let's remember that this is the second escape attempt that he has been forced to abandon for the sake of the team – the first one being brought to an end precisely because he needed to arrange this very escape for the whole, ungrateful team. And he is probably on a promise with Renée. And yet, for all that, Hatch is convinced to go back and fight the good fight against the seemingly unassailable Germans. He doesn't respond when Colby berates him and says that they can't possibly go back without him but then Luis steps in to play good cop to Colby's bad cop. His gentler approach, telling Hatch how much the game means to them, pays dividends. He gets philosophical, arguing that 'if we run now, we lose more than a game' and, incredibly, it works.

John Huston's jump cut to the flags outside in the arena is very effective, as it gives us a moment's pause to wonder, before the team triumphantly re-emerges for the second half. There is consternation from Renée in the stand, because she knew that the escape was planned for half-time. If nothing else, she is probably furious that all the work her friends have done underground, when they could have been watching the game, has gone to waste. In the posh seats, there is also bafflement from Rose and Waldron, who can't believe their eyes.

The team are all genuine smiles as they trot back out, resolved to give it their best shot, and we see a track-suited Arthur helping the still-injured Luis back to his seat on the bench. I did point out to John Wark that, given that his character had come off injured, perhaps they could have let him escape down the tunnel with the French, who had otherwise come all that way for nothing. He chuckled at the suggestion and ruminated: 'Aye, I probably should have. I wish I did.' We can only hope that they took the injured Pieter, rather than leaving him lying next to a great big hole that he might have to take the blame for like a guilty puppy.

If Hatch was reluctant to rejoin the fray, then at least the actor playing him was having a lovely time. Stallone told *Film '81*: 'It's incredible to be out there on this field. When they really get out there and play, it's incredible. I stand there in awe.' And while the actors were getting used to the footballers in full flight, the footballers were still adjusting to having their natural environment swamped by a film crew. Mike Summerbee said of the multitude of cameras that surrounded them: 'If you were picking your nose, it would be caught on film somewhere.' In which case Mike can be grateful that if he did pick his nose, the shot got left on the cutting room floor.

The reinvigorated Allies start the second half well and, just as in the first period, the opening chance falls to Erik Borge, who shoots straight at the keeper. Soon after, however, they get things right. Carlos Rey gets his chance to shine, as Ossie Ardiles goes on a mazy run, plays a sharp one-two with Paul Wolchek (Deyna), dribbles around the flailing keeper and scores.

GERMANY 4-2 ALLIES

In the stands, the French supporters are galvanised by the prospect of a comeback and even Waldron pulls a face that suggests that he might finally be able to see the morale-boosting benefits of a good showing in the match.

It's a goal that is clearly cut together from a few different sequences but the final action of it does have the sense of a real goal from Rey. Indeed, this is a section where the more natural-looking football really comes to the fore and has room to breathe. It did get me wondering about the goals that appear in the film, though. I asked everyone if the scorers of the three goals, besides Pelé's obviously pre-determined one still to come, were set in stone or just occurred naturally as they played. Søren Lindsted said that they 'just let us play for five or ten minutes at a time, just playing free football, and we scored all the goals. And they took the best ones. I remember I scored some goals and Hallvar scored.' Obviously, none of those were considered right for the final cut. Ossie Ardiles thinks he may even have scored a better goal than the one that was included but says, in his book, that he was told it hadn't been caught properly on camera. He did, however, confirm that the goals came from 'just play'. He went on to say: 'Russell and me and Deyna, we got to play a bigger part, because we were in our prime and a bit younger than Mike Summerbee or Bobby or Pelé. They couldn't do as much as we could. I wasn't even 30 years old. There was a huge, huge difference. So, my goal – it happened. The Deyna goal – it happened.'

The montage of action continues, with tackles continuing to fly in, saves at both ends and more skill from Carlos Rey. It is Rey again who dribbles his way through and has a shot saved by keeper Schmidt, only for Wolcheck to guide the rebound home for a third Allies goal.

GERMANY 4-3 ALLIES

It is the most genuine-looking goal in the game and the celebrations and recriminations among both teams look authentic. You've heard enough from me about wanting the film to make more of Wolchek's triumphant return from near death in a labour camp but perhaps it wasn't considered because this goal took the film crew by surprise. Curiously, the shot they use to show the players celebrating the goal has Deyna on the outside of the group while somebody else, possibly Russell Osman, is heartily congratulated. It is certainly the most difficult Allies goal to determine the scorer of until you've watched it a few times.

The tide is definitely turning now. Laurie Sivell gets a moment to look incredibly frustrated in the German goal, while Werner Roth barks orders as the rattled Baumann tries to keep his team together in the face of the unexpected onslaught. It's here that the beauty of the game is allowed to shine through, with a couple of slow motion shots, one of a group of players rising to contest a header and a second for Ossie to enthral a watching cinema audience with his trademark 'Rainbow Flick'. Werner Roth sells it well as a bemused Baumann underneath its beautiful arc, too.

A German attack is stopped as Hatch claims a ball under pressure from Baumann, with whom he grapples, and then the Allies are off again. Clure, Brady, Rey and Clure, again, string passes together in the German half before Wolchek pounces on an under-hit backpass and goes around the keeper. His shot from a tight angle hits the post but Doug Clure hasn't stopped running and he meets the rebound and slams it home for what should be the equaliser. Unfortunately, in amongst the flowing move, an ominous shot of the linesman – or referee's assistant in modern parlance – is slipped in, which points to bad news for the Allies. Sure enough, the celebrations all around the stadium are short-lived as the flag goes up and the goal is disallowed for some unknown reason. Wolchek is denied a second assist to go with his goal in what is turning out to be a sensational substitute appearance from the Pole and Clure is denied a perfectly good goal. More than four decades after it was filmed, sitting across a table from me in Suffolk, Russell Osman was still maintaining 'nothing wrong with it at all' but the laugh as he did so suggested that he's over it, really, so don't worry for him.

In the heat of the match, though, it is very raw, as there is nothing the goal can possibly be ruled out for. It cannot be offside, despite what the flag suggests, and if it's a foul on the goalkeeper, then it is the softest example ever seen of such a foul being given. It is plain and simple corruption. Not the type that Arsenal fans regularly grumble about but genuine, Nazi-infused corruption. And, yet, Von Steiner's superior officer only told him that the referee was bent, not the linesman. Perhaps it's like *The Departed*, with the lino saying to the startled ref: 'What, you thought you were the only one on the inside?'

The protests are led in broadest Cockney by Colby and Brady but they are in vain as the referee brazens it out and the goal remains disallowed. Shameful. In the stands, Waldron and Rose exchange a glance which shows that there is no way the Allies will be allowed to prevail in this game, while Von Steiner swallows something hard and jagged and even his superiors once more shift uncomfortably in their seats at the bare-faced cheek of such a rank bad decision.

And so, at 4-3 down and with a legitimate equaliser disallowed, all seems pretty much lost here, I'm sure you'll agree. The lads have given it their best shot but come up short in the face of unchecked fouling and corrupt officials. It seems that the Allies denied themselves a perfectly good escape for no good reason, after all. Perhaps they made the wrong choice? It's enough to get you down. Let's draw a discreet veil over things for now to look at something else to cheer ourselves up for a moment, shall we?

13.

FOOTBALL ON FILM

WITH THE game in Paris pretty much up and the lads looking for all the world like they will be denied their fairy-tale ending by some dodgy officiating, let's take a moment to catch our breath. We're not leaving early, though, because people who leave football matches early are not to be trusted, as we know. Instead, we're just pausing to briefly consider something else.

By this point, you must be convinced about my love for *Escape to Victory* but the last thing I want to be is a party bore, cornering you in the kitchen and chewing your ear off about the only football film I like. There are others out there, you see. And if *Escape to Victory* isn't the greatest football film of all time, then what is? It's time to examine some alternatives.

In spite of quite rightly being the most popular sport in the world, there are proportionally not that many films about football. Hollywood ignored the sport for a long time, until the conditions were right for *Escape to Victory* to spring to life, and other sports have been far more fertile ground for the movie business.

Boxing is probably the leading sport in terms of screen time and there are countless examples of the genre, from the sublime to the ridiculous. It is a sport that lends itself to drama and human stories and it is also easier to choreograph than most sports. Hollywood successfully stages fight scenes all the time; what's the difference if it's in a ring with gloves? Baseball is probably not far behind boxing in terms of the number of films and I can see the appeal. I have never been to a baseball game and, if I'm honest, nor do I fully understand the rules but it doesn't stop me loving the likes of *Moneyball*, *Eight Men Out* and *Bull Durham*.

In a 2020 article, *Rolling Stone* magazine listed *Escape to Victory* – or simply *Victory*, as it was released in America – at No.21 in their list of all-time greatest sports films but this was a list that covered all sports and also incorporated documentaries, with *Hoop Dreams* dunking its way to the top spot. It's a great showing in some esteemed company but documentary and drama are, in my own opinion, uneasy bedfellows on any list. It feels wrong to be comparing *Senna* and *Happy Gilmore* – they aren't the same thing.

The list also had Sylvester Stallone's *Rocky* at two on the list and John Huston's 1972 boxing drama, *Fat City*, at 15. It isn't a list I entirely agree with but it is still a strong showing from *Victory*, given that this is a US magazine in a country that hasn't always seen football in the same exalted light as much of the rest of the world does.

When considering other examples of football on film, we have to think about how much football is required to qualify a movie as a football film. Does it need to be the driving force of the story or can it just provide a backdrop? Is the unforgettable use of Archie Gemmill's goal against the Dutch in *Trainspotting* enough to make it a football film? Surely not? Personally, I would also rule out the entire overcrowded hooligan genre, as these films are far more about the associated violence than they are about football. Since you ask, though, within that sub-genre, Alan Clarke's 1989 film *The Firm*, starring Gary Oldman, is the leading light for me, with *I.D.* trailing behind it and many others further back.

It isn't an exact science but let's take a look at some of the other 'football films' and see how they compare to *Escape to Victory*, shall we? I will try to be as fair and balanced as I can but let's face facts – I haven't written a book about *Goal II: Living the Dream*, have I?

GOAL (2005) / *GOAL II: LIVING THE DREAM* (2007) / *GOAL III: TAKING ON THE WORLD* (2009)

We may as well start here. The fictional tale of young Mexican footballer Santiago Muñez (Kuno Becker), as he rises to global superstardom. The selling point of these films was that, as he moved through Newcastle United and Real Madrid, he rubbed shoulders with real footballers, who made cameo appearances. The close-up footage is inter-cut with actual footage and a Laurent Robert free kick is even used at a vital moment.

The first two films are just a bit po-faced for me, though. They aren't much fun. And the third one completely disregards Santiago's story after a car crash and, instead, focuses on England at the World Cup, with different characters leading the action, a needlessly tragic storyline and a much smaller VFX budget.

PORRIDGE (1979)

The movie version of the great sitcom centres around a football match and an escape, so bears a passing similarity to *Escape to Victory*. Except this one has Gorden Kaye from *'Allo 'Allo!* in it as the coach driver.

A match between Slade Prison inmates and a visiting showbiz XI, which contains none of The Goodies, is used as cover for a daring escape which Fletch (Ronnie Barker) and Godber (Richard Beckinsale) get roped into against their will. The football sequences are good fun and there are enough of them to include the film in this list. But while *Porridge* might be the very best of another, overcrowded genre – the 1970s sitcom big-screen outing (deal with the truth, *Mutiny on the Buses* fans) – it falls just short of being the best football film there is.

THE DIVINE PONYTAIL: BAGGIO (2021)

Harder than making a convincing film about football is making a convincing football film about a story we know, with recreations of incidents that inevitably looked far better IRL, as the kids say.

This film is more of a melodrama than anything else and leaves you with no idea whether Roberto Baggio was any good or not (he very much was). No impression can be gained from the little action that's on display; for instance, his goal for Italy against Nigeria in the 1994 World Cup is not served well. No action sequence features a challenge, as players waltz by one another, which is certainly not an accusation that can be levelled at *Escape to Victory*. Luckily for the film, the dramatic moments on which it focuses are static – his controversial substitution against Norway and his penalty miss in the 1994 final shoot-out. Although, to be fair, the 1994 World Cup Final is one of the dullest football matches of all time and would be very difficult to turn into a good film.

The drama here, such as it is, concerns whether or not Baggio will be accepted once more after his penalty miss. Spoiler alert – he is.

THE KEEPER (2018)

Having said that it's difficult to tell a true football story, it can be done, even if *The Keeper* does take a few liberties with the story of Bert Trautmann's journey from German prisoner of war to broken-necked FA Cup Final hero.

It's an extraordinary story told well in a charming film. The football looks okay but benefits from being post-war, lower league (when he is playing for St Helens Town) and centred around a goalkeeper. Each of these factors makes it easier to render authentically. A decent film, though, with a lovely turn from John Henshaw as Trautmann's coach, boss and father-in-law. Well worth your time one afternoon.

THE MIRACLE OF BERN (2003)

More German action here as we see West Germany's World Cup win in 1954 in Switzerland from their perspective. I grew up thinking of it in similar terms to the 1974 win, with a coldly efficient West German team beating the darlings of the day in Hungary (1954) and the Netherlands (1974) and spoiling everyone's fun. This puts a different slant on it, with the plucky German side overcoming the odds against the dominant Hungary team containing the likes of Hidegkuti, Kocsis and Puskás.

The film is more of a portrait of post-war Germany and folds in several plot threads. There is Richard, trying to bond with his son after years away as a Soviet prisoner, we have adidas making a name for themselves by providing boots that make a crucial difference in the rain-strewn second half of the final and there's the story of winning goalscorer Helmut Rahn.

There are faithful recreations of some of the goals that look okay but the football on display is very slow.

THE GAME OF THEIR LIVES (2005)

Another tale from the early World Cup years as plucky USA caused a massive shock by beating England in the first tournament they felt worthy of their presence, in 1950. Can that be right? It all seems a bit far-fetched, doesn't it?

FEVER PITCH (1997)

It's about football and one man's obsession with it but is it a football film? Nick Hornby adapted his own book and grafted on a romantic comedy plot to go alongside Arsenal's 1989 title win and it is okay but it's nobody's best work.

Ultimately, I think it suffers because no film is ever going to be as dramatic as what actually happened in the last game of that season. Michael Thomas and Brian Moore are what we remember from 1989, not Colin Firth and his leather jacket.

THE DAMNED UNITED (2009)

Now then, young man, when it comes to football films that do tell a true story, albeit with a bit of artistic licence, then I'm prepared to stick my neck out and say that *The Damned United* is the best among them. Michael Sheen is brilliant as Brian Clough in this adaptation of David Peace's novel about Clough's 44 turbulent days in charge of Leeds United.

There isn't lots of actual football in the film, outside of the famous training ground scenes, but what there is has an authentic feel to it. Stephen Graham may not look much like Billy Bremner but he gives him the right amount of belligerence and menace.

The Damned United is a film that I've often stumbled across while flicking through the channels and it always proves almost impossible to turn off. A great film and a contender.

UNITED (2011)

Michael Sheen and David Tennant seem inextricably linked these days, so it's no surprise that if one has one of the great football films on his CV, then so does the other.

Tennant's entry sees him play Jimmy Murphy, the man who kept Manchester United going in the aftermath of the Munich air disaster. It was made for TV but it is feature length and it is too good to leave off this list on a technicality. It is up there with the best.

The film wisely avoids showing any actual football but accurately creates an impression of a great team senselessly wasted. The recreation of the crash itself, or at least the moments either side of it, is harrowing and all too real. Jack O'Connell as Bobby Charlton, Dougray Scott as Matt Busby and Sam Claflin as the tragic Duncan Edwards all do excellent work and the only grumble is that the Jimmy

Murphy statue outside Old Trafford looks nothing like David Tennant.

THE ARSENAL STADIUM MYSTERY (1939)

Possibly the first of the genre, *The Arsenal Stadium Mystery*, you won't be surprised to learn, concerns itself with a mystery at Highbury. It's a comedy caper as police investigations take place around a game between Arsenal and The Trojans, who were actually Brentford players of the time. Genuine Arsenal faces like Eddie Hapgood, Cliff Bastin and boss George Allison take part in what is an interesting curio but definitely not the best football film.

NEXT GOAL WINS (2023)

Taika Waititi's comedy is based on the 2014 documentary of the same name about coach Thomas Rongen guiding his hapless American Samoa team to their first-ever win and, indeed, their first-ever goal.

The football doesn't need to be good, as American Samoa are not good, and it is suitably cartoonish in a film with a lot to love about it. Michael Fassbender proves he is not just there for the nasty things in life but the show is stolen by Oscar Kightley as the head of the football association which brings him in. If *Cool Runnings* wasn't mentioned at the pitch meeting, I would be astonished and *Next Goal Wins* can live with the comparison. And what higher praise is there than that?

THE BEAUTIFUL GAME (2024)

Another film that places its main character as a former West Ham player, *The Beautiful Game* is a decent, modern entry into the football film canon. Following the travails of Micheal Ward's Vinny and with a lovely performance (what other kind is there?) from Bill Nighy as scout-turned-coach Mal, the film is essentially promotion for the Homeless World Cup.

The football content looks pretty good but benefits from being small-sided games and of a lower standard. Like *Escape to Victory*, it carries the message that football is transcendent and can offer freedom from your circumstances. A lovely film with two great leads carrying it.

MEAN MACHINE (2001)

After making a splash in the Guy Ritchie films *Lock, Stock and Two Smoking Barrels* and *Snatch*, it was perhaps inevitable that former player Vinnie Jones would front a football-themed film to make best use of his new-found talents and his name.

Look no further than this sort of remake of 1974's *The Longest Yard*, which, you'll remember, shared some DNA with *Escape to Victory*, with its prisoners against guards premise.

This transposes the action from the US to the UK and the sport from American football to soccer and places Vinnie Jones in the Burt Reynolds lead role as the imprisoned former pro. Vinnie can't match the leading man charisma of Burt Reynolds but not many can. The film packs any number of recognisable British actors around Jones to help, including Danny Dyer, Jason Statham and Robbie Gee.

The result is quite good fun.

BEND IT LIKE BECKHAM (2002)

You can tell that football had been through its post-*Fever Pitch*, post-Gazza's tears, Premier League-inspired gentrification by the turn of the century, because, by then, the movie business had caught up with it and there were a rash of football films. *Bend It Like Beckham*, starring Parminder Nagra and Keira Knightley as footballers Jess and Juliette, is arguably the most famous among them.

The start of the film is unpromising, with Jess cut into some real Manchester United v Anderlecht footage, which looks pretty bad, but it gets significantly better from there on. The football sequences aren't quite good enough to give you the idea that Jess and Jules are the special players with a golden future they are supposed to be and it may crowbar in a couple too many references to David Beckham but there is a lot to enjoy.

The central characters are both likeable and both have their problems with overbearing mothers. Jess has the expectations of her as a woman in Indian culture as an added barrier between her and her football and it's a battle we want her to win. The film deals with the British immigrant experience, as well as attitudes to women's football, and successfully wraps it all up in a feelgood film.

The film also has Shaznay Lewis in it, which makes it the best film to star anyone from All Saints – fighting off not-so-stiff competition from *Honest*.

A SHOT AT GLORY (2001)

Ally McCoist is not only the best co-commentator available, spreading joy wherever he goes, he might also be the football player who is best at acting. Just don't tell Russell Osman I said that.

McCoist leads the line in *A Shot at Glory*, as Jackie McQuillan, a veteran striker with fictional Kilnockie, offered one more, well, shot at glory, as the team advance towards the Scottish Cup Final.

It's not a good film as such but it has a bit of charm and, like *Victory*, has an eclectic cast list, with McCoist, Ally Maxwell and former Bolton manager Owen Coyle rubbing shoulders with Robert Duvall out of the two good *Godfather* films and Michael 'Batman' Keaton. Yes, you read that right.

The football sequences look good and fair play to everyone concerned for letting McCoist cross the forbidden divide and portray McQuillan as a Celtic, rather than a Rangers, legend. However, that does lead to a bizarre extended McCoist montage which has been badly coloured to make all of his Rangers shirts look green but, obviously, not hooped. It might make a point about the religious divide in Glasgow but it's distracting and the sequence is way longer than it needs to be, to the point where you are questioning your sanity.

Between Robert Duvall's shaky accent and Michael Keaton obviously filming his scenes somewhere other than Scotland, McCoist's might be the best performance in it.

A CAPTAIN'S TALE (1982)

When I first discovered that this film existed, sometime in the 80s, it would have induced in me a similar level of excitement to that which I felt about *Escape to Victory*. Here was a film about football that brought together Terry from *Minder* (Dennis Waterman) and Dennis from *Auf Wiedersehen, Pet* (Tim Healy) and my head must have almost fallen off with excitement at the prospect of it.

However, in the event, this story of West Auckland travelling to Turin to win the Sir Thomas Lipton Trophy, a kind of inaugural Club World Cup, doesn't live up to the billing. It's okay but the football all looks a bit modern, the pace of the story is pretty pedestrian and Waterman's north-east accent is about as good as mine, I'm afraid.

WHEN SATURDAY COMES (1996)

Sean Bean's brewery worker, Jimmy Muir, dreams of playing for Sheffield United but his appetite for booze and women and a self-destructive streak get in his way – until they don't and he gets his chance. From that description, you could probably successfully imagine almost everything that happens in this film, apart from the fact that Sheffield Wednesday legend Mel Sterland turns up in it playing for the Blades. Sterland did say, in his autobiography, that he wore a Wednesday shirt beneath his red United stripes but he honestly says so much in his autobiography that I can't stop thinking about it.

When Saturday Comes is not great, I'm afraid. I'm sure it meant a lot to Sean Bean to pull on the shirt and play for his beloved Blades and I'm pleased for him but it doesn't make for a good film. Even the always excellent Pete Postlethwaite can't save it.

It does share cinematographer Gerry Fisher with *Escape to Victory* but not much else.

MIKE BASSETT: ENGLAND MANAGER (2001)

I find *Mike Bassett: England Manager* to be a real divider of opinion. There are those who regard it as comedy genius and those who dismiss it as no good. I find myself somewhere in between but it's good fun, with a lot of lovely moments, such as the infamous accidental naming of Tony Hedges and Ron Benson in his England squad after he scribbles names down on the back of his fag packet. The only trouble with the film is that, as funny as it is, it will never be as good as the Graham Taylor documentary that inspired it.

The Impossible Job had followed Taylor's England through the disastrous qualifying campaign for the 1994 World Cup and *Mike Bassett* took the lead from it. However, the film had the disadvantage of being fictional and, therefore, not as jaw-dropping and memorable as what might be my favourite piece of television of all time.

Bassett is played by a very sweary and frequently bleeped Ricky Tomlinson and he is ably assisted by Bradley Walsh as a Phil Neal clone nodding along as they career towards brave but inevitable failure.

There's even time for a small cameo from our man Pelé, as himself this time, stumbling in as Bassett dances in his pants on the bar. I'm sure it's nothing he didn't see in Budapest all those years ago.

YESTERDAY'S HERO (1979)

Yesterday's Hero stars Ian 'Lovejoy' McShane as Rod Turner, a once great, now washed-up striker with a drink in his hand, relationship problems and more than a hint of George Best about him. Turner gets one last shot at the big time due to the eccentric chairman of 'The Saints', who drafts him in to boost their cup run.

The football in this looks pretty good, due in part to Ian McShane looking like he could play a bit and some successful editing between the fake action and the real footage of the 1979 League Cup Final between Nottingham Forest and Southampton. The Saints kit is deliberately the same as Southampton's classic Admiral away kit, you see. Clever stuff.

The film has a lot going on. Written by Jackie Collins, it is inevitably a bit saucy, as Rod is torn between his regular girlfriend, played by a pre-*Dempsey and Makepeace* Glynis Barber, and his old flame, singer Cloudy (Suzanne Somers), who is stepping out with the flash chairman, played by Paul *Just Good Friends* Nicholas. On top of that, we've got Adam Faith as the manager who catches Rod swigging booze at half-time, Kelvin from *EastEnders* as a lovable orphan (because you've got to have orphans) and Sue from *EastEnders* behind the bar.

GREGORY'S GIRL (1981)

Now then. The question here is whether *Gregory's Girl* counts as a football film. Because if it does, it might just be the best football film. Certainly, it's the best film on this list. It's *Gregory's Girl*, for goodness sake.

Awkward teenager Gregory is our hero and the football element comes from his lust for Dorothy, who happens to be the best player at school. Not only is it breaking ground by putting a woman footballer on screen more than 20 years before *Bend It Like Beckham*, it's packed with memorable lines and moments, like Chic Murray as the headmaster, playing piano for his own pleasure and saying 'Off you go, you small boys!', and window cleaner Billy saying: 'If I don't see you through the week, I'll see you through a window.'

From Gregory's relationship with his sister, Madeline, to his clumsy chatting-up of Dee Hepburn's Dorothy, to his date with Susan (Clare Grogan), there is a lot more charm than football in the film.

Remember that Alan Rough and his team-mates did some coaching with Hepburn, so perhaps it does count as a football film, but the best thing we see on a football pitch is the gag when Dorothy scores and every player on the pitch, bar Gregory, seizes their chance to kiss and hug her in celebration.

***

As a bit of fun, I asked everybody I interviewed about other football films they might have seen. Were there any which they thought got the football right and, heaven forbid, were there any they might consider to be better than *Escape to Victory*. Luckily, most of the footballers I spoke to were far more cine-literate than Michael Owen, who famously claims that he has only ever seen eight films – *Rocky, Heat, Ghost, Jurassic Park, Cool Runnings, Seabiscuit, The Karate Kid* and *Forrest Gump*, since you ask. Three of these films have sequels but not as far as incurious Michael is concerned.

It will not surprise you to learn that the *Escape to Victory* boys were fiercely loyal to their own work and overwhelmingly felt that it was the best representation of football in the movies. John Wark said: 'When I've watched our film, I think that looks like a proper football game.' And Werner Roth reasoned that: 'Having been on set and seeing the thinking process that went into filming that, I think it's one of the best soccer films ever made.' Hallvar Thoresen was equally enthusiastic, saying: 'For me, of course, this is the greatest football film. The line-up, great footballers and great actors. A great story.' When I asked Ossie Ardiles if there was another film which recreated football well, he emphatically said 'not a single one', while Russell Osman was a little more circumspect in his response.

He told me: 'There aren't many others that stand out, because the football often looks a bit Mickey Mouse. Whereas, in what we did, our acting might be a bit rough around the edges but the football looks good.' I think he's right and it will always come back to this. The decision to cast real footballers and let them do the acting required of them pays dividends in making the film the firm favourite it is today. If you think it's easy for footballers to convincingly deliver a line of script, let me point you in the direction of Steven Gerrard in 2011's *Will*. You may think again.

Russell did give *Mean Machine* credit as a film he liked and said, slightly wistfully, of Vinnie Jones: 'He's a good lad. He went on and did really well, so it can be done.' What could have been, Russell. Hollywood was there for the taking. Laurie Sivell praised the football in *Yesterday's Hero* and pointed out that Ian McShane's dad had been a player for Manchester United and Bolton in the 50s, while *The Damned United* justifiably came up a couple of times, with Paul Cooper and Kevin O'Callaghan, although Kevin was quick to qualify it with: 'It's not as good as *Escape to Victory* though, is it?'

Those approaching the match at the end of *Escape to Victory* and worrying about the authenticity of the football and finding it wanting aren't really comparing it to other dramatic representations of football matches, they are comparing it to actual football matches. And on that basis, it does and always will fall short, because a real football match is always going to be better, more exciting, more unpredictable than even the finest-crafted match action on film.

However, as far as football on screen goes, it might just beat all of the opposition. Unless *Gregory's Girl* counts, in which case *Gregory's Girl* is the best one. Or maybe it's still *Escape to Victory*. It's definitely one of the two, anyway. Or one of the others. Whatever you like, really.

14.

VICTOIRE

GERMANY 4-3 ALLIES (continued …)

With an air of despondency we just can't shake, we return to the match. The fightback has been spectacular, with those second-half goals from Rey and Wolchek adding to Terry Brady's strike just before half-time to drag the Allies back into what appeared to be a lost cause. As in war, momentum is kind of a big deal in football and the Allies had it here until poor old Doug Clure had a perfectly good equaliser ruled out for absolutely nothing. I'm confident that VAR officials could have watched it for five or six minutes and not found anything wrong with it – yet the linesman and the referee have chalked it off between them. Now it seems clear that, no matter what they do, there is no way that the Germans are going to let them get a result here today.

But wait. What's this?

With just four minutes remaining on the clock, Luis Fernandez feels that his time is now and he beckons Colby to the bench. He tells him that he feels better and that he wants to play and he trots back on to approving applause from the crowd and concern among the German team. His bravery is there for all to see as he puts his body on the line in the face of insurmountable odds to return to the fray. If

I were his coach, I might wonder if he could possibly have managed ten minutes rather than a measly four, bearing in mind they have been battling away with ten men for the entire second half. But that's me.

The Allies immediately get the ball to their talisman and, right away, Luis comes in for some unwanted attention from Baumann, who adds to his villainy by repeatedly punching Luis in his already broken ribs. Obviously, this is a scene that needed to be specially shot and Werner Roth has fond memories of tussling with his old pal. 'I remember Riger tried to do that scene with a cameraman and an assistant on a vintage motorcycle. The cameraman is in the sidecar and we're running behind the motorcycle and trying to stay in frame while I punched him mercilessly. But when we looked back at it, you could actually see the exhaust fumes in the shot.'

Despite having to do a few takes, with and without a motorbike and sidecar on the pitch that must have given the MTK groundsman nightmares, Roth says it was fun to film. He has joked that the punches were payback for Pelé never picking up the bill when they were Cosmos team-mates.

Wriggling free from Baumann, Luis gets the call from Terry to play it out wide and he does so, even though Kevin O'Callaghan insists it was him pinging the ball out to Bobby Moore during filming. Terry has been given the freedom of the right flank yet again by an errant left-back, who is nowhere to be seen, and has the time on the ball to find a pinpoint cross, which is so good that it sends the whole film into slow motion and has its own theme music. A more wistful tune accompanies this moment, giving it the feel of a nature documentary about birds in flight and letting us know that something beautiful is about to happen. As the cross arcs in, it sails over the heads of Sid and two defenders, before being met in mid-air by Fernandez, who executes a perfect bicycle kick to rocket the ball past Schmidt for an Allies equaliser.

GERMANY 4-4 ALLIES

This is the stuff of schoolboy fantasy and the bit you told your mates about when you first watched it as a kid. An overhead kick simply became 'a Pelé' for a good while after seeing it. As in: 'Did you see Danny Wallace score that Pelé last night?'

There are several things to note here in the aftermath of the goal. Firstly, the guards on the roof behind the goal get a tremendous view of it. Secondly, Fernandez's Allies team-mates don't give much thought to his broken rib as they pile on to celebrate with him. And thirdly, some wags will say that Pelé probably counted this goal – and the multiple replays of it – in his end-of-career goal statistics. Not me, you understand, just some wags. I am amazed that, after disallowing Doug Clure's goal, the referee hasn't ruled this one out for high feet but it's possible he was too dazzled by the skill of it to think of doing that in time.

We see Von Steiner watching and admiring the moment from the stand. I worry that there is an officer a few rows behind him who looks like he's talking and has probably missed the goal. You do get these people who chat instead of watching the game at football matches and they can be annoying but I think we can all agree that, Nazi or not, it would be a shame if anyone missed this particular goal. Von Steiner, who has attempted to play fair all along, is in awe of the breathtaking moment, regardless of which side scored it – he just really loves football. He ill-advisedly rises to his feet in admiration to applaud the goal. He gets disapproving and disbelieving looks from his superior officers for doing so and his smile back at them surely won't save him. Let's face facts, he's going to be shot for this, isn't he? Even if it's the mass escape and accompanying riot at the end of the game he has arranged that will ultimately seal his fate, this clapping cannot be helping his cause. I have twice applauded opposition players at West Ham games. One time it was Sergio Agüero for Manchester City and the other was Dimitar Berbatov for Fulham – both just for a bit of brilliance. Neither time did it go down well among some of my fellow supporters. I got the impression that if they had the weight of the German war machine in their hands, then one or two of them might have happily seen me up against the wall for doing such a thing, so I can't imagine these guys showing any leniency in these circumstances. Not to spoil too many war films but we've seen Robert Duvall and Robert Vaughan shot by firing squads for less in *The Eagle Has Landed* and *The Bridge at Remagen*, respectively, and I do not fancy Von Steiner's chances here.

Luis is carried shoulder-high back to the restart by his jubilant team-mates and the crowd understandably go crazy for it, beginning their synchronised chant of 'Victoire!' all around the ground, which stirs the souls of the British officers and makes the nerves jangle among the German ones. Presumably they are chanting victory to urge the team on to a possible winning goal but maybe the victory has already been achieved, with the remarkable show of defiance that the comeback to 4-4 represents. To get an equalising goal is one thing. To do it upside down with a broken rib is quite another. 'Victoire', indeed.

With Pelé's name above the title, it is only fair that he gets to perform this defining moment. If you have it in your locker, then a Hollywood movie, with slow motion cameras rolling, is certainly the time to pull it out. Sylvester Stallone was suitably impressed by it, saying: 'You don't really realise the genius of Pelé until you see it slowed down. How can anyone have 800 muscles co-ordinated at the same time?' But how many takes were required to achieve this magnificent feat? That depends on who you ask.

Mike Summerbee is adamant that it was 'one … one take' and John Wark agrees with him, telling me: 'First time he put it in the corner. Everybody was in awe of him.' Paul Cooper was watching on and agrees that it was 'first time … first take'. He elaborated and told me that the crew told them: 'We need to get this overhead kick and we need to get it done in as little takes as possible. If we can do it in four or five, that will be fantastic.' Cooper explained: 'So, anyway, they set it up. Laurie's in goal for the German side, Pelé goes up, Mike Summerbee threw the ball up for him and he did an overhead kick, first time, straight in the top corner. So, I said to Laurie "That looked good, the way you did that" and he said "I didn't even see it!" And the whole set of players applauded Pelé when he did it. It was just one of those moments in time when you're just like "Bloody hell!" It was extra special. He was past his sell-by date as a player but he was still playing exhibitions. What a player he was.'

So, we can remove a little of the magic from the goal with the revelation that, in real life, the ball was thrown up for him rather than crossed but only the hopeless romantics among us thought it was a clean strike from that beautiful cross, all captured perfectly. However, there is also some question about how many takes it might have needed to nail it.

Kevin O'Callaghan introduces an element of doubt by saying: 'They were saying that we only had three takes, because of the cost of the slo-mo cameras. I always thought that Pelé did it the first time but the lads reckon it was the second time.' Laurie Sivell says: 'Pelé's overhead kick … they had to do that a couple of times.' He should know, as he was in goal facing it; and, yet, he is being modest here, because there is a very good reason that they couldn't use the first take. Russell Osman takes up the story: 'It could have been even better. In general play, he did it first time and shot it towards the bottom left-hand corner but Laurie pulled off an amazing save. So, they knocked it back out and I think that one went over the bar, then I think the third one he put in the top corner. It could have been done the first time if Laurie hadn't saved it.' I guess if you're a goalkeeper it's hard to fight those instincts. It is heartbreaking to me that Laurie Sivell saved a Pelé overhead kick and nobody ever got to see the footage. Russell agreed, saying: 'I know. It's probably locked away in the vaults somewhere. It's probably the best save Laurie ever made.'

Ossie Ardiles also agreed with this version of events, saying: 'He did it first take. Only one problem, though

– the goalkeeper stopped the ball. The problem was, it wasn't very far from him, so he didn't want to let it in. So, they said "Oh, Pelé, it was beautiful but can you do it again because the goalkeeper stopped the goal?" So, he said "Okay" but the second time he could not do it. At his age, it wasn't easy at all.'

Clive Merrison remembers that: 'Tim Pigott-Smith gave me the nod that this was going to happen and we went down and we saw him do it. One take. And then Huston asked for two more. Each time, it was perfect.' Clive did admit that 'time may have elaborated the detail on my stories', so this may be a romanticised version of the tale, but I do love that he was in the stadium for it and that it was Tim Pigott-Smith who got him there. Pigott-Smith really was the glue that held together this production. Everyone's friend, everyone's confidant. Until he did his runner, of course.

The truth around the kick is probably somewhere in between. I don't doubt that the first one filmed saw Pelé execute the overhead kick and make the right connection and I don't doubt that Sivell saved it but the practical truth of it is that it wasn't important. Harvey Harrison was filming it and said: 'In my memory, we would have done it three or four times, anyway, to get the various angles. When you're filming it, you can do it as many times as you like and get all the good angles. It wouldn't have mattered if he did it the first time, he didn't have to get it in.'

So, what we see in the film isn't one moment captured by many cameras, it is an amalgam of different takes, but we can agree that the first take was caught well by Pelé, whether it went in or not. As Ossie Ardiles says: 'They wanted to do it in one big shot but they couldn't do it. But you don't notice at all. It was very, very nicely done.' All of which seems fair enough, because, as Laurie Sivell quite rightly points out: 'It's really hard to score an overhead kick, isn't it, to be honest.' Amen.

The dreamers among you should look away now, though, because other accounts serve only to strip away the stardust a little more. Hallvar Thoresen says: 'I remember when we were practising this and it didn't go well. I know that he was supposed to hit the bar but he never hit the bar.' Goals do look better when they clatter in off the bar, on that we can all agree. Paul van Himst thinks: 'It was very difficult and took many attempts – six or seven.' The always positive Werner Roth says that it came off well because Pelé had done it so many times in his career but, even so, he concedes that 'we did about ten or 12 takes of that' and Søren Lindsted remembers spending half a day on the sequence.

And so, based on several eyewitness accounts from the day, we still don't quite know how many times the ball was crossed, or thrown up, or Pelé connected, or didn't, or scored, or didn't. But we do know that we see at least one overhead kick genuinely go in. So, Luis Fernandez has his hero moment, this goal counts and the Allies are level.

Do we spare a thought for the dejected Germans at this point, kicking off knowing that they had a four-goal lead but that they have now effed it right up? Probably not. It could get worse for them, as there is still time for Luis Fernandez to invent the 'Rabona' pass to set up Nilsson for a shot at goal, which keeper Schmidt copes well with. The keeper then gets it launched, booting it downfield for a flick-on for Baumann to race into the box – and then disaster strikes. Carlos Rey comes flying in with a tackle, Baumann goes down and the referee awards a penalty.

Here's the thing. Given the disallowed Allies goal and some of the fouls by Germans which the referee has let go, they could definitely have created an incident here where a penalty was awarded for no good reason and there was a whiff of cheating and injustice about the decision but I will be honest with you – this is a stonewall penalty, all day long. Baumann is going wide and the Allies just need an impassioned Sunday League coach to continuously shout 'Stand him up! Just stand him up! Stay on your feet!' to help them see out time until the final whistle for a very respectable draw. Instead of that, a giddy Carlos loses his head, dives in rashly and gets precisely none of the ball. It really is a shame about Rey.

I asked Ossie Ardiles how this sequence came about and if it was always the plan for him to concede the penalty. He said that people often bring it up and 'take the mickey' out of him for it.

'It was in the script that there had to be a penalty there but I was not the only one who did it. I think my one was chosen because it was maybe a penalty, maybe not, benefit of the doubt, do you know what I mean? It was not 100 per cent a penalty.' Oh, it is Ossie. It is. When I asked him if he thought VAR would give the penalty, he laughed and said: 'That's a good question.' He knows the game's up.

'We were just playing but some of the others were not good and my one looked pretty good. Pelé and Bobby Moore didn't want something where I was half a yard away from the other guy. They didn't want something so obvious. They wanted something more credible.'

The production notes issued to the press allude to the fact that there is cheating going on, saying: 'The Germans are given many penalty goals on questionable calls.' I don't want to be *that* guy but there really are only two penalty decisions given by the referee in the game and, corrupt or not, for my money he gets them both right. There, I've said it.

The Allies surround the referee and the commentator says it's a sad state of affairs that they have resorted to fouling, which is a bit rum considering what has been going on in the game – and across much of mainland Europe, if we want to get into it. But the protests are in vain and the penalty kick stands. The sense of injustice among the crowd is enough to provoke a rousing rendition of 'La Marseillaise' around the ground. As a national anthem, it's a cracker, and, in my opinion, perhaps only rivalled by Italy's and it sounds good here as it gets another defiantly sung Hollywood rendition to rank alongside the one in *Casablanca*. Patriotism and defiance are swelling inside the stadium and it has the German soldiers worried and possibly even the Alsatians twitching. Surely at least the game will be won, though, with Baumann stepping up to take it against the decidedly average Hatch. Surely the American doesn't stand a chance.

Hatch walks out to the penalty spot and John Huston, who arrived to ensure that he filmed these final set pieces, frames that dream shot that he sold to Werner Roth in the restaurant some weeks before. There is Stallone and there is Roth. Stallone and Roth. Head-to-head in an echo of

Rocky and so many of his opponents. Despite bringing his own acting skills to the fore here, Roth was full of praise for his co-stars, saying of the players who get close-ups as they nervously wait on the edge of the box: 'They are so believable and so emotionally invested that it really worked well.'

Silence falls, then the whistle blows and Baumann strides up and strikes the ball to Hatch's left. The rookie goalkeeper goes the right way and strains every sinew to get to the last kick of the match. In the event, he doesn't just get there and keep it out – he catches it and the game stays level!

FINAL SCORE: GERMANY 4-4 ALLIES

I do worry slightly about what happens next, because we don't actually hear a final whistle being blown and Hatch blindly boots the ball back into open play while everyone celebrates with him. There is an outside chance that the ball could be gathered by Germany and sent back into a dangerous area but, with Baumann on his knees in despair and the Allies celebrating wildly in front of him, maybe all chance of a winning goal has gone. The crowd certainly thinks so, as we see a jubilant man with a moustache that wouldn't look out of place in Asterix's village get a celebratory peck on the cheek and they all start up again with the 'Victoire!' chant. It's that kind of day.

In amongst these manic player celebrations, Russell Osman copped an unfortunate one from Sylvester Stallone. He told me: 'He's waving his arms around when we're celebrating with him and he punched me in the face. I thought he'd broken my cheekbone. Jesus Christ, you don't want to get a punch in the face off of Rocky, do you?'

If we forensically pulled apart Pelé's overhead kick to see how much the daylight faded the magic, it seems only fair that we do the same with the penalty save. It's worth a reminder at this point that, of course, this was originally supposed to be Hatch running downfield and scoring the winner, so, before we get too critical of the save, let's be thankful that the original ending to the match ended up in the bin.

Søren Lindsted reckons that the penalty save also took half a day to film, while the footballers stood around watching, increasingly reluctantly. Ossie Ardiles's memories are similar, suggesting that the whole thing took 34 takes. 'For some of the takes, we were not even watching, we were talking about what we were going to do tonight. On some takes, he saved the penalty but the camera was filming from behind and they wanted everyone to celebrate with him.' The man taking the penalty, Werner Roth, reckons it was around 18 takes, while Sylvester Stallone self-deprecatingly joked that it was close to 200. It certainly seems that there were quite a few attempts to film a sequence that Roth diplomatically described as 'challenging'. Stallone was game enough to throw himself around between the posts but all the coaching that Gordon Banks and then Paul Cooper had done with him were not enough to get him into a position where he could convincingly save a well-taken penalty. Roth had to readjust. He said that he told John Huston that there was no way the German captain would take a bad penalty, so, although he started out putting them high and in the corner, he gradually needed to recalibrate and bring his shots lower and closer to Stallone, until he could actually save one. By this stage of filming, Stallone's body had taken a battering to match any he had endured on his *Rocky* films but he was still happy to throw himself around and try to make the penalty look as good as he could. He told *Newsnight*: 'I was trying to get the man kicking the ball to do it harder. He was afraid he was going to damage me or something. It took a while for him to get up his nerve and for me to get the timing, because, of course, I doubt very seriously that I could stop many penalty kicks.' It seems that Stallone may have learned his lesson from his earlier finger-breaking challenge to Pelé on the camp set.

Perhaps not all of the takes were the fault of Stallone's imperfections or Roth's hesitancy. This was pretty much the only football action that John Huston shot personally and, given that the static penalty was an environment he could control, it's entirely possible that he went overboard with shots to ensure they had what he wanted in the can. Satisfied that he did, Huston moved on to the final moments of the film – the crowd breaking down the barriers, attacking the guards and rushing the gates, dragging the Allied players along with them.

There is a glimpse of one of the Eastern European players from the bench being smuggled out and it's good to know that they, too, are seizing their chance. Hatch is reunited with Renée in the throng, as coats are put on his back, along with those of Luis, Colby and Terry Brady. Terry even gets a lovely hat that presumably Bobby Moore had to formally approve before agreeing to be seen in it.

So, we know that the main four stars of the team are getting out. Von Steiner watches on from the stand, sees what is going on but doesn't seem to mind at all. There is frantic activity all around him but he provides a moment of stillness, as he watches the spectacle but does nothing to stop it. Perhaps he feels that the performance on the pitch was deserving of their freedom away from it? And, after all, he can worry about that firing squad later.

Speaking of shooting, what are the guards doing at this point? We see one or two of them get overwhelmed as the crowd storm over the barriers but there are hundreds of German soldiers in and around that ground. And yet, not one of them raises a weapon and starts firing. Please don't mistake me for somebody that wants to see players and fans dropping like flies as they are mercilessly gunned down but it feels like a little more could be done to stop what's happening. They can't all be struck motionless with awe at what they've seen from Luis Fernandez and Hatch in the last few minutes.

As the players are swept away, I have so many questions. Did Rose and Waldron get out, too? Do any of the German players get attacked by passing fans or did they all make it to the tunnel okay? And speaking of tunnels, at which point is the work of the Resistance discovered? And just how confused are the soldiers that found it, knowing that the team chose to go back out and fight back for a plucky 4-4 draw, instead of using the tunnel? We should spare a thought for Tony Lewis, whose arm was broken so that others may prosper; spare another for Jean-Paul Remy, who never got off the train in Paris; and if you have another, then please spare one more for

Pieter van Beck, who lies injured in the dressing room while all this is going on.

The crowd reach the gates and burst through them, scattering into the side streets around the ground and taking the players with them to an uncertain future but one with hope of getting home. The screen fades to blue and, as Bill Conti's score builds to a climax, it's all over.

I did ask each of the players what they thought might have happened to their characters at the end of the film. Søren Lindsted said 'I hope I escaped and lived happily ever after' and Russell Osman said: 'I think he got out and got home safely.' Let's hope so. As we don't see Doug Clure escaping, it is, of course, possible that he was still there, trying to grab his team-mates and hang around to see if there was going to be any extra time, because 'we can still win this'. Hallvar Thoresen joked and said 'maybe a beer first and then back home', while John Wark, still smarting a little from being dubbed, said: 'He probably went to some school or college to study every day, to get the language right.' And then Mike Summerbee gave me the best answer of all: 'Yeah, we got away. I'm here now, aren't I?'

The players did remember the filming of this sequence being 'a bit hairy', as people came rushing on to the pitch. 'I actually thought that, for me, that was quite dangerous, because you could fall over and injure yourself. You had to watch yourself, because there were a lot of people on the pitch running and you don't know where they're coming from,' said John Wark, while Mike Summerbee was a little concerned about 'the type of people coming on the field. They could've been people with knives or whatever. It wasn't easy. A lot of people came on the field and you rely on the crew as to what sort of person was there.' Fortunately, there were no major incidents, so the crew did their job in that regard. In another area, however, they perhaps didn't. As the crowd rush on, there are one or two anachronistic clothing choices among the crowd and it feels like it might have been somebody's role to ensure that sort of thing didn't happen. There are lots of jeans and jackets that don't seem very 1940s and, as they head out of the gate, there is at least one adidas tracksuit.

Hallvar Thoresen remembered the moment like this: 'I think it came a little bit out of control, because the people that were trained to sit there and to run out on the pitch, they didn't exactly know what to do and they started to do their own things. Well, grabbing our shirts and things like that, trying to get some souvenirs. But it was not frightening. They were all friendly but it was a little out of control.' So, who were these people and what kept them there, other than the thrill of seeing Pelé and the rest play football?

Thoresen says that there were around 5,000 people in the stadium and that the crew kept having to move them around the ground to be in the background of every shot. He also says they were likely paid something. Russell Osman thinks that was likely 'jeans or a few dollars' but Werner Roth has much bigger-ticket items in mind when he says: 'They would give away refrigerators and mopeds and appliances to get people into the crowd.'

Whatever their motivation, Werner Roth says there was an air of confusion around the shot. 'John would give the direction in English and the Hungarian translator would give the direction to the crowd in Hungarian over big loudspeakers. John had given a weekend to shoot this final scene but when we first tried it with everything set up and prepared, there was a gunshot to indicate when the fans were supposed to charge on to the pitch and they charged on over the barriers but they stopped on the running track, because they weren't really sure they were allowed.' Paul Cooper, however, claims that this initial reluctance was linked to what was on offer for the fans and, whether it's quite true or not, all good stories warrant telling.

Cooper's version has the crew telling the crowd that 'the first 200 people through the arch would get tickets to Disneyworld, Florida. They said, "When the gun goes off, everybody run for the arch," so the gun went off and nobody moved. The director was confused and asked the interpreter why they hadn't moved and he said, "Well, they can't leave the country. They can't get a visa to America, so that's no good to them".'

'So, he said, "Well, what is good to them, then?" and was told "Denim jeans, tape recorders, all kinds of electrical goods." So, they reshot it the next day and came back with a lorry full of televisions and things like that. And that time, it was a proper riot. They just jumped on the lorry and got as much as they wanted.'

Whatever the motivation, the crowd members did their job. They storm from the stands and carry our heroes out of the ground and back to their humdrum, regular lives as top-level footballers. Could their worlds ever be the same again?

15.

RELEASE

WITH FILMING wrapped, prisoners escaped and the restaurateurs and bar owners of Budapest no doubt left in tears at the dip in their takings, the cast and crew of *Escape to Victory* scattered to the far winds and returned to their lives. The footballers who were still in the cut and thrust of their careers went back to their clubs with tales of stars and stardom to make their team-mates jealous, while the actors moved on to their next roles.

Pelé and Sylvester Stallone were soon back together, appearing alongside one another in September 1980 at half-time during the Soccer Bowl – the NASL championship match – between Fort Lauderdale Strikers and New York Cosmos. The legacy of Pelé's time playing in America can be seen in the line-ups that day, with international stars Franz Beckenbauer and Giorgio Chinaglia playing for the Cosmos and Gerd Müller and Peruvian legend Teófilo Cubillas playing for the Strikers.

The game was goalless at half-time but finished 3-0 to Cosmos, which no doubt put a smile on Pelé's face. But we're far more interested in the Pelé and Stallone double act in the interval, brought to you by Rolaids Antacid Tablets, as they feverishly sell the movie to the watching public. Stallone was happy to concede that he was 'so ignorant about this game until I met Pelé about 18 weeks ago'. He recounted the story of facing shots from Pelé on set and says that he did so because he had previously been asked about how many pitches a baseball pitcher like Steve Carlton of the Phillies would have to throw for you to hit one. Stallone had said he could throw a thousand and you wouldn't hit one, so he was keen to put an equivalent football scenario to the test.

Stallone, as the more experienced chat show guest, naturally takes the lead of the two of them and is self-deprecating and humble throughout, praising Pelé as 'a genius of the sport', as well as discussing the presenter Jim McKay's ABC colleague, Robert Riger, 'covering the balletic qualities of soccer'. Throughout, Stallone talks of his new-found respect for the game of football. Quite right, too.

Over in Europe, in the football season that followed filming, the Ipswich players swept to UEFA Cup glory and Ossie Ardiles won the FA Cup with Tottenham, so maybe there was something in the water in Budapest. John Huston, meanwhile, was ensconced with editor Roberto Silvi to cut the film into shape. It was at this point, too, that Bill Conti came on board to add his memorable, eminently hummable soundtrack to the film. Huston's line to sell the film was: 'It is a kind of morality play in which a simple brown ball replaces the guns and bombs of warfare.' If only, John, if only.

In May 1981, a subtle title change was announced. The film would continue to be called *Escape to Victory* around most of the rest of the world but in America, it would simply be called *Victory*. It's possible they felt that the original title gave away the ending somewhat but, given that the game ends in a 4-4 draw, the new one could have been accused of false advertising. Triumphs of the spirit are all well and good but where is this winning goal we were promised on the poster?

When the trailer was released, Clive Merrison found himself right at the top of it with his 'escape in the good weather line', before the classic gravel-toned voiceover kicks in and delivers a series of corny lines like: 'The Allied high command called them crazy – and maybe they were.' It also gave away Ossie Ardiles's goal and had the cheek to announce that the film was 'introducing Pelé'. Who exactly did they think they were introducing him to? Pelé was already the most famous player of the world's biggest game. Does his movie debut count as introducing him? If it was meant to herald the dawn of a great acting career, unfortunately he didn't go on to live up to it. I guess he'll just have to settle for all the football stuff but that's okay, because people seem to like that.

The film was released in America at the end of July 1981 and that summer it went up against *Raiders of the Lost Ark*, *Superman II* and a re-released *The Empire Strikes Back*, so it had its work cut out to find an audience. Also big at the box office were Dudley Moore comedy *Arthur*, with its lovely Christopher Cross theme tune, and the truly terrible (but popular for Bo Derek reasons) *Tarzan the Ape Man*. On its first weekend, *Victory* grossed a respectable but not spectacular $2.4m but, in the following weeks, it faded badly, with takings falling and the number of screens it could be seen on shrinking. It seemed that America was still not ready for a film about soccer, regardless of the talent involved. The film would go on to do much better internationally, because of the global appeal of the game, but it would still get beaten in the worldwide box office list by the big guns already listed and plenty of other films, including our old friend *On Golden Pond*.

In the UK, the film was released in early September 1981 with a Variety Club charity premiere at the Odeon Leicester Square. Soft Cell were No.1 in the pop charts with *Tainted Love* and the other big film release that week was John Boorman's *Excalibur*. Michael Caine and Sylvester Stallone were there, of course, along with Bobby Moore. Not all of the football players could make it along, because most of the active ones had games that weekend, but Tottenham obviously felt relaxed enough about their Saturday game at home to Aston Villa to let Ossie Ardiles and some team-mates go along to central London for it. Spurs had won the FA Cup in May of that year and been all over *Top of the Pops* with their cup final song, so, by now, Ossie was a triple threat on the field, in the charts and at the box office. He told me: 'We hadn't seen the film at that point, so we didn't even know the result of the game. We knew that Pelé's overhead kick was going to be in the film and Stallone's penalty save but we didn't know which goals of theirs or goals of ours would be in the film. So, the film was a surprise for us.' Ossie says that it was a good night. 'After the film, there was a party. We all had dinner with Michael Caine and Stallone and Bobby Moore and we ended up dancing the night away in Tramp.'

This party in Tramp caused a little consternation in the press because, evidently, it wasn't the official party for the film – that took place in Covent Garden, where the expectant reporters were forced to write about TV star Anthea Redfern and her car dealer boyfriend Laurence Matz for their showbiz columns, instead of Stallone and Caine and the rest. An irate Lorimar executive was quoted in the *Sunday People* as saying: 'It's a bloody disgrace. They should have come. If only for a while. But that's typical of superstars. They do what they want.' It seems that they had all become quite good at escaping.

The circumstances in which the other players saw the film varied, mostly due to their football commitments. Werner Roth says he got to see it 'at the screening before the film was released' but Paul van Himst says he didn't see the film until it appeared on television in Belgium, presumably a few years later. He did say he was excited to see it when it came on but it seems incurious of him not to seek it out before then. Both Søren Lindsted and Hallvar Thoresen said they were invited to premieres – in Tokyo, in Søren's case – but they could not get time off from FC Twente to attend. Instead, Lindsted saw it sometime later when he was back in Denmark on holiday and was invited to the local cinema in Holbaek to watch it. Thoresen had to watch it on video, like all the best people did.

In Ipswich, there was understandable civic pride in a bunch of Town players taking to the screen, so the Gaumont hosted a special Ipswich premiere of the film, which all the Ipswich players involved attended. The public was there, too, and a good time was had by all. Apart from John Wark, of course; for it was there that he discovered that his voice was dubbed and he knew, deep down, that he would never hear the end of it. Sylvester Stallone, meanwhile, had a very special screening of the film, with president Ronald Reagan at the White House.

If the box office for *Escape to Victory* wasn't everything that Freddie Fields dreamed it would be, the reviews by critics were the definitive mixed bag. In America, everyone looked to Siskel and Ebert for their reviews in 1981 and even the two of them couldn't find consensus on what would become a divisive movie. Roger Ebert thought the film was a bit predictable and derivative of other hits like *The Great Escape* and *The Longest Yard*, which are legitimate criticisms. Gene Siskel liked it a lot more, however, calling it an 'audience picture' which plays to the crowd. Siskel said: 'I thought this was a very pleasing picture. I got caught up in the most fundamental way that movies work on people. I was rooting for the good guys.' And even the much harder to please Roger Ebert had to concede that people in his screening were cheering during the match.

In the UK, Barry Norman was always considered the authoritative voice of film criticism, on television anyway, and he came down on Ebert's side when it came to *Escape to Victory*. He called it a 'melodrama, directed in, I can only assume, a fit of absent-mindedness by John Huston' and he also had a dig at 'portly PoW Michael Caine', which seems a bit unnecessary. But if there's one thing we know about Barry Norman, it's that he could be a bit sneery at times. If there are two things we know then it's that he made pickled onions and that he could be a bit sneery. But if there's one, it's the sneery thing. I must confess a slight vested interest here, because Barry Norman was also once a bit rude to my dad when he was delivering to the BBC, so maybe I'm not keen to listen to his judgement on this film that I love. And there was that time he reckoned he nearly had a fight with Robert De Niro. Imagine how that would have gone. Still, nice pickled onions. Norman also found time in the same episode to give a bad review to *Escape From New York*, so maybe he just doesn't like films with 'Escape' in the title. In the interests of balance, he did run a competition on the same show to win copies of *Alien* on VHS and a *Film '81* T-shirt that I would gladly pay good money for now, so maybe it wasn't all bad news.

Further poor reviews for the film were easy enough to come by. Alan Brien, in the *Sunday Times*, called it 'eminently missable', expressed disappointment in this addition to John Huston's patchy record and was another one to pick on 'paunchy' Michael Caine. However, he did draw attention to the fact that the Nazis were naïve in not foreseeing the potential humiliation in being beaten by a team containing a black player and Eastern European concentration camp survivors, which does lend weight to my feeling that more could have been done with Wolchek/Deyna's magnificent personal comeback. Garth Pearce, in the *Daily Express*, had nothing nice to say, either. He referred to Michael Caine as 'lumbering' and looking 'as if he's carrying a couple of footballs stuffed under his shirt', said Stallone was 'like a punch-drunk boxer for the umpteenth time' and, when he wasn't being personal, said the whole thing was 'complete with limp dialogue, laughable plot and almost lunatic miscasting'.

Films and Filming magazine had Adrian Turner review *Escape to Victory* and he compared it unfavourably to *The Great Escape* and sniffily said that: 'One is just grateful that the film and the match don't go into extra time.' Not to be outdone in the stuffy film magazine stakes, Tom Milne, in *Monthly Film Bulletin*, bemoaned 'the blatant wish fulfilment jingoism of this slice of nonsense' and described the climactic match as 'ludicrous beyond belief'. Philip French, in *The Observer*, didn't like it and nor did Alexander Walker of the *Standard*, Andrew Sarris of *The Voice* or Nigel Andrews of *The Financial Times*, as critics practically queued up to give the film a kicking. Andrew Hislop, in the *Times Literary Supplement Review*, was needlessly mean, particularly about Michael Caine's waistline, suggesting that 'he has been putting in extra training in Langan's Brasserie for a De Niro grow-with-your-part role'. His only words of praise were for Clive Merrison and Werner Roth.

My favourite bad review of all, though, if it's possible to have such a thing, is that of professional firebrand Christopher Hitchens, in the *New Statesman*. He complained of 'a mass of clichés' and a preposterous plot, wrote unfairly about the 'piggy sockets of Bobby Moore' and said of Hatch's escape sub-plot: 'There's a girl somewhere in this bit but the film's certificate prevents us from finding out if he screws her or not.' All a bit much. I enjoy it, though, because his talk of 'the Berlin World Cup in 1938' shows that he doesn't really know about football, his dismissal of the music as 'pathetic' is well wide of the mark and because I can't really imagine what films the Hitchens household would ever have enjoyed. It's tough to imagine the childhood Christopher or brother Peter enjoying so much as a cartoon at the Saturday morning flicks without angrily pulling it apart. And he's so wrong about the music. Whatever else you think of the film, you cannot knock Bill Conti's music.

There were some glimmers of light, however, and even in some of the bad reviews, some good points were raised. Madeleine Harrisworth, in the *Sunday Mirror*, said: 'It's all just an excuse to show off the abilities of bought-in soccer stars like Bobby Moore, Pelé & Ossie Ardiles.' And I would have to ask if that is such a bad thing? David Castell, in the *Sunday Telegraph*, said: 'If you doubt for one second that the team will not come out for the second half, then *Escape to Victory* is not for you.' And there, I would have to agree with him. Nobody is saying that *Escape to Victory* is a challenging film. Nobody is saying it raises questions that stay with you for hours after it has finished. But it is good fun and it's difficult to see why anyone would take against that quite as vociferously as some of these critics did. Derek Malcolm, in *The Guardian*, was commendably even-handed when he said: 'If you expect nothing very much, you'll probably go away happy enough. If you think of what Huston is capable, you may be a little disappointed.' Now we're starting to find some common ground.

Ian Penman was never likely to go overboard with praise for a film such as *Escape to Victory* when he was writing for the cool kids that read the *NME* in 1981. Indeed, he opened by calling it a 'horrendous yarn' but couldn't help letting a little praise slip in here and there. He conceded that the match action is nail-biting and that he was 'quite carried along with the clichés', before absolutely nailing the legacy of the film by saying: 'Wait for it to turn up some Sunday afternoon in the 21st century.' Very prescient words, given how frequently the film *does* crop up on British television on Sundays and Bank Holidays to this day.

It certainly wasn't all bad news when the reviews came in. The film also garnered praise from uneasy bedfellows like the *Daily Telegraph* and the *Morning Star,* which both agreed that it was a film that could move you to cheers. *Time* magazine praised the 'funny, smart script', along with Pelé's 'wondrous skills' and Bill Conti's 'huge score', as Richard Schicker was clearly taken along for the ride. Richard Barkley, in the *Sunday Express*, delightedly called it 'an exhilarating splash of hokum' and the *News of the World* called it: 'Pure boy's own stuff. Fabulous fun.'

Obviously, I'm biased as a fan of the film, but I think it is these types of reviews that hit the bullseye. There are good films and there are bad films and then there are a lot of films that are perfect if you're in the right mood or of the right frame of mind. I would argue that *Escape to Victory* sits in the latter category. I can see why it isn't universally loved but I also think it's churlish to find too much fault with it. It's a film to watch with a smile on your face and what could possibly be wrong with that?

There are two reviewers who, by their own admission, were not fans of football but who, nevertheless, found themselves won over by the film. Molly Plowright, in the *Glasgow Herald*, said that she found her 'attention glued to the screen', despite her general lack of enthusiasm for football, and had particular praise for Bobby Moore 'revealing a most likeable screen personality'. Margaret Hinxman, of the *Daily Mail*, went into it as someone who 'groans when *Match of the Day* strikes up its idiot signature tune and Jimmy Hill fanatically assures me it's been a great day for soccer (is there ever any other kind?)' but said that she found herself on the edge of her seat and talked of 'spell-binding, roof-raising excitement'. Always nice to find room for a dig at Jimmy Hill in any football-related article.

Several articles published at around the time of the film's release focused not on whether it was any good or not but rather on the story that the BBC had already paid a whopping $1m for the TV rights, despite not being able to show the film for three years. Charlie Catchpole, in *The Sun*, was particularly upset about this, displaying the sort of pearl-clutching about the licence fee that you might have thought was a modern phenomenon, but is probably as old as the licence fee itself. In the event, the BBC added the film to its Christmas schedule in 1984 and showed it at prime time on Boxing Day. I suspect that, by that point, we had our own blank tapes to record on to in our homes – in plastic cases designed to look like leather-bound books, of course – because I definitely remember that we had our own copy of the film for a while, recorded off the telly, and it may well have been that premiere that we grabbed.

In the final analysis of 1981 then, the fortunes of *Escape to Victory* were a mixed bag. Released to great fanfare, the film went up against some stiff opposition and disappointed at the American box office, while doing much better worldwide. The reviews, as you've seen, we're also mixed, provoking pleasant surprise and vitriol in equal measure. It was the sort of reception that can be moulded to fit whichever narrative you care to push. It was, by no means, a disaster but it's fair to say it didn't shake up the world as the makers might have hoped.

Certainly, Sylvester Stallone had hoped for more and was hurt by the fact the film took less money in America than *Paradise Alley* and received some of the same bad reviews that *Nighthawks* had. It seemed to him that the public were rejecting him as any character other than Rocky Balboa. Fortunately for him, he had the third instalment of the Italian Stallion's story just around the corner, as well as *First Blood*, in which traumatised double-hard veteran John Rambo would finally give him a second character and franchise that the viewing public wanted to watch him in.

Among our film's other stars, Michael Caine regarded it as a success but Tim Pigott-Smith dismissed it as 'a turkey', despite having a lovely time making it. Mike Summerbee, meanwhile, confesses to being apprehensive about the reviews, saying he was very keen for them to be good. In the event, he was able to dismiss the bad ones as coming from those who didn't like football and said, in his book, that 'it did brilliantly at the box office and the general public loved it'.

You can see what I mean about being able to bend the reception to fit your own version of events. The film had done badly in America but had performed much better in the UK, including being the highest-grossing film at the Odeon Leicester Square, where it ran for seven weeks. It had extended runs all over the country and across Europe, where a more football-orientated audience lapped it up. The ploy of having stars from a variety of countries seems to have worked in those territories and the film also did well in Germany, despite obvious barriers for the audience. Remarkably, the film was also a success in Japan, where it was the sixth-biggest-grossing film of the year.

As time went on, that initial box office and critical reception would matter less and less, as the film slowly developed the cult status it enjoys today.

16.

LEGACY

OVER THE course of writing – and, hopefully, reading – the book, a kind of familiarity creeps in with regards to *Escape to Victory* and the people involved, to the point where it doesn't seem so strange anymore that this confluence of the football and movie worlds happened. But stepping back to take in the full picture once more reminds us how truly remarkable it is that this collection of people rubbed shoulders for a month in Hungary and produced what has become, in the fullness of time, such a well-loved film.

Rumours of remakes persist, particularly since the turn of the century, as football has grown in popularity in the United States. Among Michael Caine films, *Alfie*, *Sleuth*, *The Italian Job* and *Get Carter* have all had the remake treatment, none for the better – but, so far, not *Victory*. Sylvester Stallone was responsible for the second *Get Carter* and regretted it, saying in 2022: 'I learned the hard way that the nostalgia and the identification with a certain period is very close to people's hearts and they're not giving that up.' Any number of directors, players and actors have been linked with attempts to revive *Victory* and, in an age of Soccer Aid and similar high-profile celebrity matches, it seems that we have a better idea which actors might be able to convince as players if called upon but, at the time of writing at least, all efforts have come to nothing. Because it isn't easy.

The idea of securing a soccer star of Pelé's level of fame to headline a remake may still seem plausible but finding active players to bolster the cast – and players for whom a few weeks' extra money means enough for them to commit – seems more difficult. One or two, for sure, but the chances of a kindly manager actively encouraging his players to head off for a summer into the unknown seems unlikely, even if insurance would allow it. Current players have contract clauses preventing them driving certain cars or playing certain other sports, so it seems unlikely that many of them would be allowed to get kicked with army boots for a month over a summer. We can all put fantasy casts together in our heads – and many of us have at any given point since the original – but it's undeniably tough to pull off the real thing.

Once we are on the outside of the film and consider what everyone did next, the disparate nature of the cast and their day jobs comes to the fore again. Michael Caine moved on to make *Deathtrap* with Christopher 'Superman' Reeve, while the Ipswich lads kicked off the next football season away at Leicester City's Filbert Street, with John Wark scoring the only goal.

Remember, Wark had missed pre-season due to the injury he sustained while filming the match in Budapest, but he showed no ill-effects of it by the time things kicked off in earnest. And if Bobby Robson was unhappy about the knock to Wark – or, indeed, the drinking done by his players while they were away – then he didn't show it. Laurie Sivell says that he doesn't think Robson minded about the drinking and was probably quite pleased. 'We had a few beverages out there but we'd have only done that on holiday or at home that summer.' The only difference was that some of these drinks came from Michael Caine's trousers.

If Robson was happy when his new film star charges returned to him, something happened soon enough to one of them to remove the manager's smile. Kevin O'Callaghan was mostly on the bench at the start of the 1980/81 season, so insisted on playing in a reserve match to stay sharp. Bobby initially wasn't keen but was eventually persuaded of the value of the plan. Unfortunately, during the reserve game, O'Callaghan 'ran through from the halfway line and had a 50-50 challenge with the goalkeeper and heard a crack. I thought it was just a clash of shin pads but, when I looked down, the arm that I had broken in the film was really broken. Bobby went mad, because I couldn't play the following night. How's that for a coincidence? Right in the same spot. Completely snapped in half.' Robson resisted the temptation to get Sylvester Stallone to take his place.

For his part, Stallone moved directly on to that new Rocky script he had been so diligently working on between takes in Hungary and *Rocky III* went into production in spring 1981. After finding it challenging working under the direction of John Huston, Sly was keen to direct himself, once more, and he duly did. A few years later, when he came to write the fourth instalment of the franchise, it's easy to see how the Cold War paranoia he felt in Budapest, with bugged rooms and surveillance, fed into the script for *Rocky IV*, as our hero fights against the might of the communist Soviet Union and wins.

Rocky and Rambo movies alone were enough to keep Stallone near the top of the box office charts throughout the 80s but rumours of ego problems still occasionally dogged him. More action films, some ill-advised comedy attempts and co-starring again with Max von Sydow in an ill-judged *Judge Dredd* failed to really earn Stallone the respect he craved. It wasn't, perhaps, until the brilliant *Copland* in 1997 that he received plaudits for his acting. In more recent years, critics have seen the value in the heart and soul he brought to the screen but, even then, it was again his portrayal of Rocky Balboa that did that, in the eponymous sequel and then the revitalised *Creed* in a supporting role. He was Oscar-nominated for the latter.

Michael Caine continued to follow the Michael Caine pattern after *Escape to Victory*. Frequently in good films, often in bad films, but always charming. His 1980s included a BAFTA for *Educating Rita* and an Oscar for *Hannah and Her Sisters* and films such as *Blame it on Rio*, *Water* and *Jaws: The Revenge*, that were almost certainly chosen purely for their sun-drenched locations and their pay packets. And why not? Loved by filmgoers and sometimes undervalued by critics, he also attracted fulsome praise from directors such as John Frankenheimer, who directed him on *The Holcroft Covenant* and called him 'the best movie actor I've ever worked with' – and that man has worked with some great actors.

Sir Michael Caine is a national treasure and a gifted raconteur with a million stories. His tale of visiting John Huston on his death bed – along with his *The Man Who Would Be King* co-star, Sean Connery – is a cracker.

The pair visited Huston in hospital and found him barely conscious and babbling. They made their peace with the situation and said their tearful goodbyes, only for Huston to recover and direct a film six weeks later. He went on to make two more after his brush with death, *Prizzi's Honor* and his long-cherished project, *The Dead*, before dying for real in 1987. When Caine had seen Huston in the intervening years, he told the director: 'The next time I come to say farewell to you, you'd better bloody die or I'll bloody kill you. Do you know how upset we were?' Huston replied: 'Well, Michael, you know people get upset. And people die.' Before Caine fired back with: 'Yes, but not twice.' Caine described Huston as one of his idols and one of the great talents of his era. It was an era that lasted a very long time.

Freddie Fields, who had brought Huston, Caine, Stallone and the rest together for *Victory*, went on to his own further successes. He became a president and chief executive officer at MGM Film Co. and went on to produce *The Year of Living Dangerously* and, most significantly for me, he produced the Oscar-winning *Glory* in 1989. Now, that's a film.

The legacy of *Escape to Victory* lies not in the moderate box office or the immediate critical reception but in the way it has grown in stature over the ensuing years and seeped into popular culture, to the point where it has become a welcome and regular fixture on our TV screens.

We're not talking about ITV2 levels of showing *Hot Fuzz* but the frequent appearances in the schedules suggest that it picks up an audience each time it airs.

Ten years after its release, the film was unavailable to buy on video but during the 90s, it underwent something of a reassessment, due in part to the 'new lad' culture that permeated the mainstream. This new cultural phenomenon was typified by *Fantasy Football League*, the comedy show about football, hosted by Frank Skinner and David Baddiel. The set was strewn with football memorabilia, such as a Subbuteo tablecloth, and, right there on the wall, was a poster for *Escape to Victory*.

Russell Osman has certainly felt a cultural shift in attitudes to the film: 'When it first came out, people were pooh-poohing it but then it developed a cult following and got shown every Christmas. And now people are putting out T-shirts and merchandise. But nothing like that happened for about 15 years after it. We never did interviews about it or anything until then.'

Retrospective articles about the film began to appear in magazines around the same time as *Fantasy Football* and even the broadsheets took another look. In a 1996 piece for *The Observer*, Will Buckley wrote a bullish defence of *Escape to Victory*: 'This film is routinely panned by the critics, who snidely damn it with that faintest of praise "It's so bad, it's almost good." Codswallop. The movie is a classic. It contains a fast-paced plot, some crisp dialogue and a football match that the commentator rightly describes as "a sizzler".' The public were starting to agree with him, if they didn't already. Calls for the film to be released on DVD (yes, it had been that long) were eventually heeded. Often, the film gets a retail push around the time of a World Cup and viewers presumably rise along with hopes of something equally stirring at the tournament to come.

John Ramsden, writing in the *Historical Journal of Film, Radio and Television* in 2006, observed that the packaging of the film gradually became more red and covered in George Crosses to align it with Bobby Moore, 1966 and all that. Odd to think of it in that way, given the deliberately international flavour of the Allies team that we're rooting for, but Ramsden insists that *Escape to Victory*'s 'message has been absorbed, reinvented and repackaged and, hence, continues to play its part in the contemporary British – but especially English – obsession with the Second World War'. It's a sentiment that Clive Merrison concurs with: 'They have their own momentum, films like that. War and football is a winning combination in this country.'

Since this reappraisal, movie magazine *Empire* has also been kind to the film, running a 'where are they now?' piece on the team and telling of the 'cult adoration' it enjoys. In 2006, when reviewing one of those World Cup releases, Nick de Semlyen, who went on to become editor of the much-loved magazine, called it 'irresistibly silly and thoroughly feelgood'. I'll take both.

A measure of the place which the film holds in the firmament occurred in planet-eating football behemoth *Ted Lasso*. When the show needed some music to form the backdrop of an inspiring Coach Beard presentation on 'Total Football' to his AFC Richmond players, what did they choose? You guessed it; it's Bill Conti's *Victory* work that you can hear. What else could it be?

Nobody believes that *Escape to Victory* is high art but who wants high art on their television after a big Sunday lunch? In time, the film has found its place in the hearts of so many people. Russell Osman says of the film's current status: 'The way it's received now, it's quite an achievement. Good fortune does shine on you and maybe I've had good fortune, because people think I did a not bad job in it.'

However, even if the film had been locked away and never seen again beyond 1981, those who made it would have been happy with their own legacy. Firm, lasting friendships were made among the cast. It's clear that, Sylvester Stallone issues notwithstanding, everyone on set got on and had fun.

John Wark describes filming as: 'The best five weeks. That summer was fantastic.' Laurie Sivell told me: 'It's something you can look back on with pride. It was great. We had a good time.' And that's a winning combination. Sivell told me that he still had his kit from the film, plus a script and a signed football, and it seems that most of the players have kept memorabilia from the shoot, to go along with their treasured memories. Søren Lindsted still has his shirt and had the boots until they went so bad that he had to throw them out. Mike Summerbee gave his shirt to a charity auction but he was looking at pictures from the film on the wall of his study while we spoke on the phone. Paul Cooper, of course, keeps his special signed photograph from Sylvester Stallone in the toilet.

Søren Lindsted will never forget the time he spent with Pelé and the rest but it seems that not everybody is quite ready to embrace his movie career just yet. He told me: 'I showed it to my grandchildren about five or six years ago but they lost interest after five or six minutes. Maybe when they are older?'

Outside of his own family, however, neither he nor the other players are short of attention. He says that there are often enthusiasts who want to meet him and he receives letters and requests for autographs from all over the world. A few years ago, he went to a showing of the film and a Q&A session in Jutland in his native Denmark. That is the legacy of players being chosen from across Europe. Interest in the film is retained in each of their countries.

Somewhat inevitably, the least interest seems to be in Werner Roth's homeland of the USA, where football has grown in popularity but is still dwarfed by the traditional US sports of baseball, basketball and American football. Roth says: 'There might have been one or two interviews over the years but not a lot of interest in it from the media. It gets played here at least once a year, so the old soccer group is always interested in it but it hasn't really found a new audience.' It seems a shame but it perhaps also explains why none of the remake plans have yet to come to fruition.

Among the other players, the story was far more similar to Søren Lindsted's than Werner Roth's. Ossie Ardiles says that people often want to talk to him about it, particularly in Japan, where it remains very popular. *Escape to Victory* is so frequently what people want to talk to him about that he has started saying to people: 'Yes, by the way, I won the World Cup as well but forget about that.' I wonder if they pick up on the sarcasm everywhere.

John Wark says: 'It's amazing that, for all I've done in my football career, people still always say, "You were in that movie."' It's a situation exacerbated by his current role in hospitality at both Ipswich and Liverpool. Fortunately, he has the stories to entertain them all on demand.

Several of the players say that, whenever it appears on television, they get calls and messages telling them it's on and Kevin O'Callaghan constantly gets people asking him 'how's your arm?', particularly at his golf club, while Clive Merrison says he gets asked about the film 'every time I go in a pub'. Clive also told me that when he was doing a play on the London Fringe: 'This bloke turned up wearing a T-shirt that was signed by all the members of the *Escape to Victory* cast, including Bobby Moore. So, he started it a long time ago. And I was the last person he got. Then I heard that, five days later, he sold it for about £8,000 on eBay.' The *Escape to Victory* business is still booming, it seems.

Russell Osman was also able to confirm a lovely story that I first read in the autobiography of Leroy Rosenior, who played under Osman's management at Bristol City. Rosenior remembers a game where 'we were losing 2-0 and came in for half-time. Russell went nuts at us and read us all the riot act. From the corner of the room came a small voice … "Come on lads, we can still win this."' Rosenior says that the gag from the brave, but anonymous, player 'brought the house down' and when I mentioned it to Russell, he smiled and said: 'That sounds about right.'

Forty-five years on from the making of this extraordinary film in the heat of a Budapest summer, the legacy lives on, with every one of those involved still being reminded on a regular basis of their part in it. I am delighted to have been one of a lengthy line of people to ask them about it and to jog their happy memories. Long may that continue. I'd like to thank them for their time and you, for yours. Now if you'll excuse me, I've got a film to watch … again.

Victoire.

BIBLIOGRAPHY

BOOKS

Ardiles, Ossie, *Ossie's Dream: My Autobiography* (Transworld Digital, 2010).

Beattie, Kevin, *The Beat* (Skript Design & Publishing, 1998).

Caine, Michael, *Blowing the Bloody Doors Off – And Other Lessons in Life* (Hodder & Stoughton, 2018).

Caine, Michael, *What's It All About?* (Century / Random House / Stoke Films, 1992).

Clay, Catrine, *Trautmann's Journey – From Hitler Youth to FA Cup Legend* (Yellow Jersey Press, 2010).

Daley, Marsha, *Sylvester Stallone: An Illustrated Life* (Zomba Books, 1984).

De Semlyen, Nick, *The Last Action Heroes – The Triumphs, Flops, and Feuds of Hollywood's Kings of Carnage* (Picador, 2023).

Gallagher, Elaine, *Candidly Caine* (Robson Books, 1990).

Huston, Allegra, *Love Child – A Memoir of Family Lost and Found* (Bloomsbury, 2009).

Lucas, George *Star Wars* (Sphere Books, 1977).

Marsh, Rodney with Brian Woolnough, *I Was Born a Loose Cannon* (Optimum Publishing Solutions, 2010).

Matthews, Stanley, *The Way it Was: My Autobiography* (Headline, 2001).

Matthews, Stanley & Mila with a helping hand from Don Taylor, *Back in Touch* (Arthur Barker Limited, 1980).
Milne, Larry, *Ghostbusters (A novel based on the screenplay by Dan Aykroyd and Harold Ramis)* (Coronet, 1984).
Moore, Roger with Gareth Owen, *A bientot* (Michael O'Mara Books Limited, 2017).
Moore, Tina, *Bobby Moore by the Person Who Knew Him Best* (CollinsWillow, 2005).
Pelé, *Pelé: The Autobiography* (Simon & Schuster, 2007).
Pigott-Smith, Tim, *Do You Know Who I Am? A Memoir* (Bloomsbury Continuum, 2017).
Rosenior, Leroy with Leo Moynihan, *"It's Only Banter": The Autobiography of Leroy Rosenior* (Pitch Publishing, 2017).
Rovin, Jeff *Stallone! A Hero's Story* (Pocket Books, 1985).
Sanello, *Frank Stallone: A Rocky Life* (Mainstream Publishing Company, 1998).
Sellers, Robert, *Hellraisers: The Life and Inebriated Times of Richard Burton, Richard Harris, Peter O'Toole and Oliver Reed* (Preface Publishing, 2009).
Sterland, Mel with Nick Johnson, *Boozing, Betting and Brawling: The Autobiography of Mel Sterland* (Green Umbrella Publishing, 2008).
Stewart, Rod, *Rod: The Autobiography* (Century, 2012).
Summerbee, Mike, *The Autobiography* (Optimum Publishing Solutions, 2010).
Jonathan Wilson *The Outsider – A History of the Goalkeeper* (Orion, 2012).
Yablonsky, Yabo, *Victory* (Bantam Books, 1981).

ARTICLES

Andrews, Nigel *Review* (Financial Times 4 September 1981)
Baker, Barry *Deadliest Game of All* (Daily Mail, 23 June 1980)

Barkley, Richard *Review* (Sunday Express, 4 September 1981)

Barnes, Mike *Casting Director Rose Tobias Shaw Dies at 96* (Hollywood Reporter, 12 November 2015)

Brien, Alan *Review* (Sunday Times, 4 September 1981)

Britt, Ryan *How the First Star Wars Novel Almost Spoiled the First Star Wars Movie* (Esquire, 11 November 2022)

Buckley, Will *Review* (The Observer, 10 March 1996)

Castell, David, *Review* (Sunday Telegraph 6 September 1981)

Catchpole, Charlie *BBC in Big Movie Gamble* (The Sun, 15 August 1981)

Chutkow, Paul *Louis Malle Diagnoses His 'Murmur of the Heart'* (New York Times, 19 March 1989)

Davis, Victor *All-Stars Versus The Nazis* (Daily Express, Summer 1980)

De Semlyen, Nick *DVD Review* (Empire, July 2006)

Dignam, Virginia *Morals Fought Out on Football Field* (Morning Star 4 September 1981)

French, Phillip *Third Reich v The Allies* (The Observer 6 September 1981)

Gimello-Mesplomb, Frédéric Bill *Conti Interview* (9 August 1999)

Gold, Jon *Farewell to The King: When Pele played his last game 40 years ago* (ESPN 29 September 2017)

Harrisworth, Madeleine *Review* (Sunday Mirror 4 September 1981)

Hinxman, Margaret *Review* (Daily Mail, 4 September 1981)

Hislop, Andrew *Aristotle and the Art of Football* (Times Literary Supplement Review, 11 September 1981)

Hitchens, Christopher *Review* (New Statesman 4 September 1981)

Jack, Ian *Can Pele's XI Beat Hitler's Handpicked Aces* (Sunday Times, 10 May 1980)

Katz, David *Evan Jones Obituary* (The Guardian 5 June 2023)

Lawrence, Will *DVD Review* (Empire, December 2005)

Malcolm, Derek *Huston's Whole New Ball Game* (The Guardian, 3 September 1981)

Mills, Bart *Goalmouth Action in Hungary* (The Guardian 26 July 1980)

Milne, Tom *Review* (Monthly Film Bulletin, September 1981)

Nathan, Ian *The Making of Escape to Victory – War Game – How Tinseltown met Ipswich Town to create the greatest footie flick ever made* (Empire, July 2002)

No Journalist Credited *Downton Abbey star Penelope Wilton on sister marrying ex-husband* (HELLO! 31 August 2021)

No Journalist Credited *Freddie Fields Obituary* (Sight and Sound, February 2008)

No Journalist Credited *Freddie Fields Obituary* (Daily Telegraph, 11 December 2007)

No Journalist Credited *Freddie Fields Obituary* (The Times 15 December 2007)

No Journalist Credited *Not Even Pelé Can Save This War Game* (Daily Express, 5 September 1981)

No Journalist Credited *Escape to Victory – The Allies Team in Full* (Empire, November 1994)

No Journalist Credited *When Bobby Moore went to manage Oxford City for £14,000* (MorrisOxford.co.uk)

No Journalist Credited *"Victory" Star Werner Roth on Playing Baumann and the Penalty Scene with Stallone* (Q&A) (Kicking and Screening, 30 July 2021)

Pearce, Garth *Bobby Tackles a New Job Among the Film Stars* (Daily Express, 3 September 1981)

Penman, Ian *Footer Phutter!* (NME, 1981)

Phipps, Keith, Murray, Noel, Grierson, Tim, Montgomery, James & Fear, David *30 Best Sports Movies of All Time*

From 'Rudy' to 'Rocky,' counting down the greatest films to play the game and get in the ring (Rolling Stone, 12 August 2020)

Plowright, Molly *Huston Scores with Soccer Thriller* (Glasgow Herald 4 September 1981)

Purnell, Tony *'Escape' Stars Snub Their Own Big Party* (Sunday People 6 September 1981)

Ramsden, John *England versus Germany, Soccer and War Memory – John Huston's Escape to Victory 1981* (Historical Journal of Film, Radio and Television, Volume 26 Number 4 – October 2006)

Robinson, David *Sure Attractions of Football Hold the Casting Vote* (The Times 4 September 1981)

Sarris, Andrew *Review* (The Voice 4 September 1981)

Schicker, Richard *Winning Points* (Time Magazine 3 August 1981)

Shorter, Eric *Review* (Daily Telegraph 4 September 1981)

Strachan, Graeme *Escape To Victory: Aberdeen FC's '80s heroes could have shared the stage with Stallone, Caine and Pelé* (The Press and Journal, 20 July 2021)

Turner, Adrian *Review* (Films and Filming, October 1981)

Upton, John *The 1980s Films of Michael Caine: Escape to Victory* (Football Stories, 27 March 2024)

Walker, Alexander, *Paying Pelé's Price* (New Standard, 23 July 1981)

Walker, Alexander *No Light at the End of the Tunnel* (New Standard 3 September 1981)

Waterman, Ivan *Pelé Plays a War Game* (News of the World 6 September 1981)

Welkos, Robert, W. *Hollywood super agent helped shape playing field* (Los Angeles Times, 13 December 2007)

PODCASTS

Escape to Victory: 40th Anniversary – Talksport – Johnny Owen and Mark Webster (2021)

The Armourer's Bench Fighting On Film Podcast: Escape To Victory – Robbie Maguire & Matthew Moss with Paul Woodage (2021)

Retrofiend Radio – Escape to Victory with Producer Tom Stern – Kristian Smock & Dustin Niño (2022)

The 80s Movie Podcast S5 E02 – Escape to Victory – Edward Havens (2023)

TELEVISION

Brass Tacks – A Whole New Ball Game (BBC, 1979)
Clapperboard (ITV, 1981)
Film '81 (BBC, 1981)
Newsnight (BBC, 1981)
Sneak Previews (PBS, 1981)
Soccer Bowl '80 (ABC, 1980)

About the Author

This is John Smith's fourth book and follows the trilogy about football autobiographies, *Booked!*, *Second Yellow* (with Dan Trelfer) and *Final Third!*. Alongside a day job in television, working mainly in comedy and sport, John has written about football for *The Blizzard*, *FourFourTwo*, *The Guardian* Online, *Late Tackle* and various West Ham-related publications. His writing for TV includes script-writing for football and snooker coverage and entertainment shows such as *Blankety Blank*.